A-Z LONDON
HANDY GUIDE AND ATLAS

CONTENTS

Geographers' A-Z Map Company Ltd.

Head Office :
Vestry Road, Sevenoaks, Kent, TN14 5EP
Telephone 0732- 451152

Showrooms :
44 Gray's Inn Road, London, WC1X 8LR
Telephone 071-242 9246

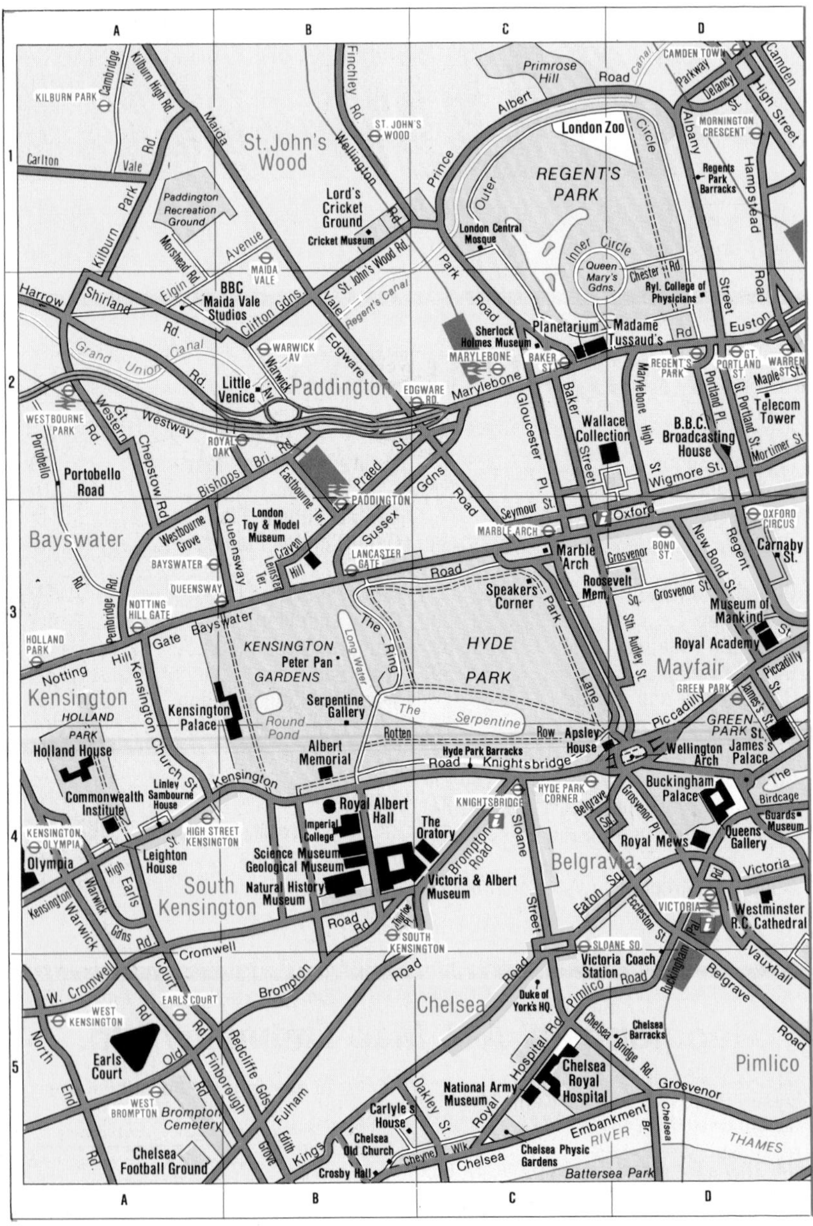

St. John's Wood
Lord's Cricket Ground
Cricket Museum
London Zoo
REGENT'S PARK
London Central Mosque
Queen Mary's Gdns.
Ryl. College of Physicians
Planetarium
Madame Tussaud's
Sherlock Holmes Museum
BBC Maida Vale Studios
Paddington Recreation Ground
Little Venice
Paddington
Wallace Collection
B.B.C. Broadcasting House
Telecom Tower
Portobello Road
London Toy & Model Museum
Bayswater
Marble Arch
Roosevelt Mem.
Speakers Corner
HYDE PARK
KENSINGTON GARDENS
Peter Pan
Serpentine Gallery
Round Pond
The Serpentine
Kensington Palace
Holland House
HOLLAND PARK
Kensington
Mayfair
Royal Academy
Museum of Mankind
Carnaby St.
Apsley House
Wellington Arch
Hyde Park Barracks
Albert Memorial
Royal Albert Hall
Imperial College
Science Museum
Geological Museum
Natural History Museum
The Oratory
Victoria & Albert Museum
Commonwealth Institute
Linley Sambourne House
Leighton House
Olympia
South Kensington
Buckingham Palace
St. James's Palace
Guards Museum
Queens Gallery
Royal Mews
Belgravia
Westminster R.C. Cathedral
Victoria Coach Station
Duke of York's HQ.
Chelsea
Chelsea Barracks
Chelsea Royal Hospital
National Army Museum
Carlyle's House
Chelsea Old Church
Crosby Hall
Chelsea Physic Gardens
Pimlico
RIVER THAMES
Earls Court
Brompton Cemetery
Chelsea Football Ground

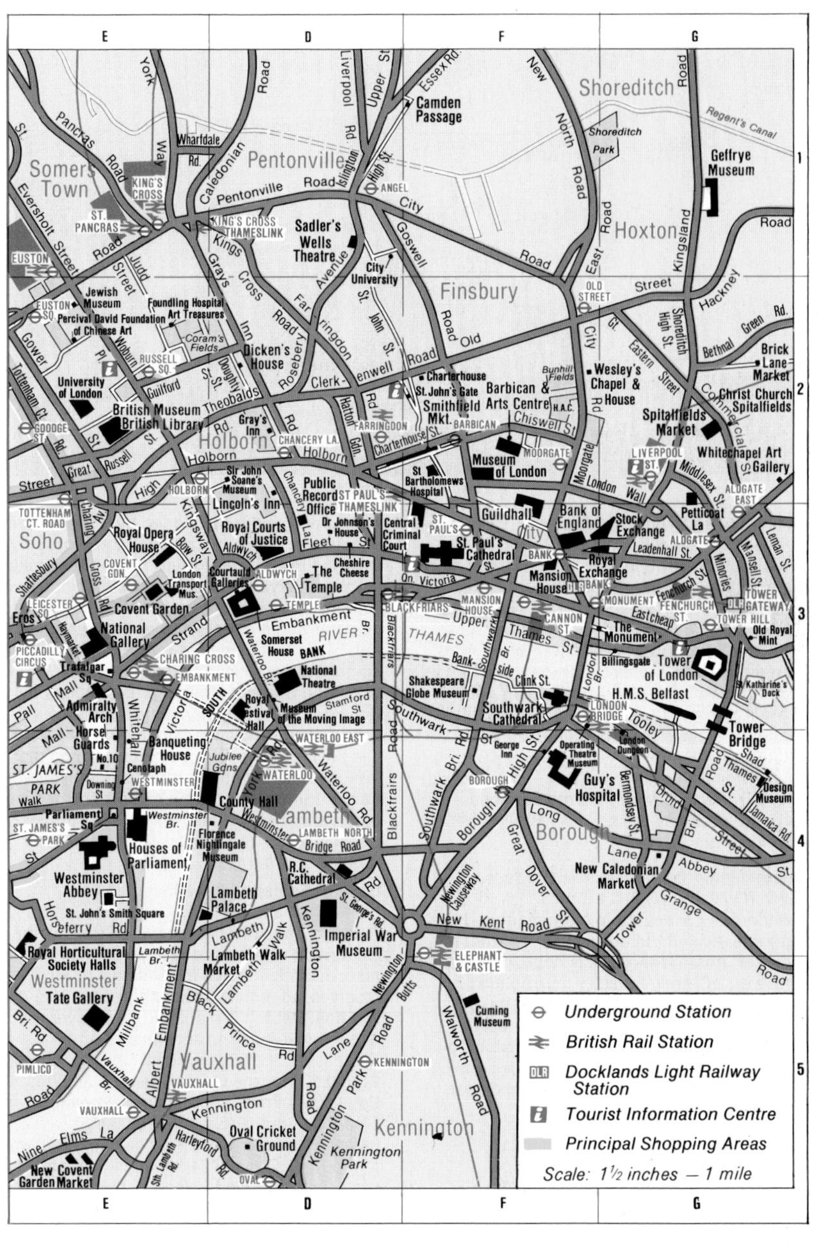
E
D
F
G
1
2
3
4
5
Shoreditch
Regent's Canal
Shoreditch Park
Geffrye Museum
Hoxton
Camden Passage
Pentonville
Somers Town
Wharfdale Rd.
KING'S CROSS
ST. PANCRAS
KING'S CROSS THAMESLINK
EUSTON
ANGEL
Sadler's Wells Theatre
City University
Finsbury
OLD STREET
Jewish Museum
EUSTON SQ.
Foundling Hospital Art Treasures
Percival David Foundation of Chinese Art
Coram's Fields
RUSSELL SQ.
Dicken's House
University of London
British Museum
British Library
Charterhouse
St. John's Gate
Smithfield Mkt.
Barbican & Arts Centre
Bunhill Fields
Wesley's Chapel & House
Brick Lane Market
Christ Church Spitalfields
Spitalfields Market
Whitechapel Art Gallery
GOODGE ST.
Gray's Inn
CHANCERY LA.
FARRINGDON
BARBICAN
MOORGATE
LIVERPOOL ST.
ALDGATE EAST
Holborn
HOLBORN
Sir John Soane's Museum
Lincoln's Inn
Public Record Office
ST PAUL'S THAMESLINK
St Bartholomews Hospital
Museum of London
Guildhall
Bank of England
Stock Exchange
Petticoat La
TOTTENHAM CT. ROAD
Soho
Royal Opera House
Royal Courts of Justice
Dr Johnson's House
Central Criminal Court
ST. PAUL'S
St. Paul's Cathedral
BANK
Royal Exchange
Mansion House
ALDGATE
COVENT GDN.
London Transport Mus.
Courtauld Galleries
ALDWYCH
The Temple
Cheshire Cheese
Covent Garden
TEMPLE
BLACKFRIARS
MANSION HOUSE
CANNON ST.
MONUMENT
FENCHURCH ST.
TOWER GATEWAY
TOWER HILL
LEICESTER SQ.
Eros
National Gallery
Somerset House
RIVER THAMES
The Monument
Old Royal Mint
PICCADILLY CIRCUS
Trafalgar Sq
CHARING CROSS
EMBANKMENT
National Theatre
Shakespeare Globe Museum
Billingsgate
Tower of London
H.M.S. Belfast
St Katharine's Dock
Admiralty Arch
Horse Guards
Royal Festival Hall
Museum of the Moving Image
Southwark Cathedral
LONDON BRIDGE
Tower Bridge
Banqueting House
WATERLOO EAST
George Inn
Operating Theatre Museum
London Dungeon
No.10
Cenotaph
Jubilee Gdns
WATERLOO
ST. JAMES'S PARK
WESTMINSTER
County Hall
BOROUGH
Guy's Hospital
Design Museum
Parliament Sq
Westminster Br.
Lambeth
LAMBETH NORTH
Borough
ST. JAMES'S PARK
Houses of Parliament
Florence Nightingale Museum
New Caledonian Market
Westminster Abbey
R.C. Cathedral
Lambeth Palace
St. John's Smith Square
Imperial War Museum
Royal Horticultural Society Halls
Lambeth Walk Market
ELEPHANT & CASTLE
Westminster
Tate Gallery
Cuming Museum
Vauxhall
KENNINGTON
PIMLICO
VAUXHALL
Oval Cricket Ground
Kennington
Kennington Park
New Covent Garden Market
OVAL
Underground Station
British Rail Station
Docklands Light Railway Station
Tourist Information Centre
Principal Shopping Areas
Scale: 1½ inches — 1 mile

ADMIRALTY ARCH

Admiralty and Admiralty Arch, Whitehall, The Mall, SW1. 4B 92 and 3E 3
This complex of buildings includes the austere Citadel, the operational centre for Churchill and chiefs of staff in World War II; 18th-century buildings 'Old Admiralty' approached via Whitehall through a handsome Robert Adam screen of 1760; and also 19th-century additions which link to ADMIRALTY ARCH. This imposing structure of 1910 was built as part of the national memorial to Queen Victoria, its central gateway is opened only for royal processions; see the long view through from *Trafalgar Square,* the red surfaced processional way of The Mall leading direct to *Buckingham Palace.*

Albert Memorial, Kensington Gardens, SW7 7G 89 and 4B 2.
London's most eccentric monument and the epitome of High Victorian taste. The 180 ft. spire of ornate stonework is encrusted with mosaics, gilt and pinnacles, surrounded by allegorical statues and relief portraits of famous artists; within sits Prince Albert, holding a copy of the 1851 Great Exhibition catalogue. It was built 1863-72 to designs by George Gilbert Scott, in memory of Queen Victoria's Consort.

Apsley House, Hyde Park Corner, W1. 071-499 5676 6E 90 and 4C 2
From 1817-52 the home of the 1st Duke of Wellington and known as Number One London, it was presented to the Nation by the 7th Duke in 1947 and now contains the WELLINGTON MUSEUM. Of the original 18th century house designed by Robert Adam only two fine interiors remain : the Piccadilly Drawing Room and Portico Room. The Duke employed Wyatt to add the classical front, new sections including the Waterloo Gallery and to clad the whole in Bath stone. The interior is rich in opulent 19th century furniture and all manner of personal artifacts, trophies, decorations and uniforms; presentations by Royalty—especially porcelain ; a nude statue of Napoleon, and an outstanding collection of Old Masters. The 'Iron Duke' celebrated his famous victory with an annual officers reunion held in the Waterloo Gallery, here the original banqueting table is laid with his Portuguese Service. *Open 11.00-17.00 Tues to Sun. Admission Charge*

Bank of England, Threadneedle Street, EC2. 1D 94 and 3G 3
The 'Old Lady of Threadneedle Street' is the Government's Bank ; acting as the central reserve bank, it holds the Nation's gold reserves, administers exchange control and National Debt. It is managed by a governor, deputy governor and sixteen directors. Established in 1694 by Royal Charter to find £1,200,000 for the Government's war with Louis XIV's France, it remained a private company until 1946 when it became nationalized. Land in Threadneedle Street was first purchased in 1724, the bank having previously operated in Grocers Hall ; by the end of the 18th century the whole of the present island site had been acquired. Soanes' designs of 1788-1833 for the bank were strikingly original, although they are only

preserved in drawings to be seen at *Sir John Soane's Museum,* his massive fortress-like perimeter wall alone being retained in the 1925-39 rebuilding designed by Sir H. Baker. Liveried messengers and gate keepers can be seen in the entrance hall which leads to Garden Court, once the churchyard of St Christopher-le-Stocks (a Wren church demolished 1781) and a restored Roman mosaic. Until the 1970's a military guard protected the bank at night, a measure instigated during the Gordon Riots 1780 and origin of the saying, 'Safe as the Bank of England'

Bank of England Museum, Bartholomew Lane, EC2. 071-601 5545 1E 94
History of the Bank, exhibits include items from the Bank treasury collection, gold bars and an interactive video to show the working of the Bank today. *Open 10.00-18.00 Mon. to Fri. (and Sat. 10.00-18.00. Sun 14.00-18.00 Summer months only).*

Banqueting House, Whitehall, SW1. 071-930 4179 5C 92 and 4E 3
A jewel of a building set amongst ranks of government office blocks. Completed in 1622 this is the only surviving building of Whitehall Palace destroyed by fire in 1678. Commissioned by James 1st it represents, along with the Queen's House *Greenwich,* designed three years earlier, the introduction of the Italian classical Palladian style into English architecture. Inigo Jones's design is a hall of double cube proportions incorporating a beautiful ceiling added by Rubens in 1630-36 (representing the Apotheosis of James 1st) and for which he received £3,000 and a knighthood from Charles 1st. Jones was not only the King's surveyor but also a famous masque designer, the hall being frequently the scene of courtly entertainments with Jones's scenery and costumes. From a window here, Charles 1st. walked to the scaffold and his execution in 1649; at the restoration in 1660, Charles II received the Lords and Commons ; and here also in 1689, William and Mary received their formal offer of the throne. *Open 10.00-17.00 Tues to Sat. 14.00-17.00 Sun. Admission charge.*

Barbican, Silk Street, EC2. 5C 86 and 2G 3
Following the destruction of a large area to the north of *St. Paul's Cathedral* by World War II bombing, the City Corporation has built a modern precinct designed to reintroduce a balanced residential and cultural life into the *City of London.* Pedestrians are segregated from traffic on elevated levels; accommodation (in three tower blocks and groups of terraces) is sited about landscaped quadrangles with trees, lakes and fountains ; incorporated are the City of London School for Girls, Guildhall School of Music and Drama, *Museum of London* and the Barbican Centre for Arts and Conferences. The Barbican Arts Centre is the London equivalent of the Lincoln Center New York or the Centre Pompidou Paris; its wide range of facilities including ; Barbican Hall, Barbican Theatre, The Pit studio theatre, Barbican Library (the City Lending Library), art gallery, sculpture court, cinemas, conference and trade exhibition areas, roof-top conservatory, restaurants, bars and car park. 'Barbican' is derived from a former Medieval defence tower that existed outside the city wall ; historical elements incorporated into the precinct are fine sections of the Roman and Medieval City Wall and the ancient church of St Giles, Cripplegate, here Oliver Cromwell married in 1620; Frobisher d.1594, Speed d. 1629, and Milton d. 1674. are among those buried here.

Arts Centre. *Open 09.00-23.00 Mon. to Sat: 12.00-23.00 Sun. Telephone 071-638 4141 (Information). 071-638 8891 (Bookings).*

B.B.C. Broadcasting House, Portland Place, W1. 6G 83 and 2D 2
The Marconi Wireless and Telegraphy

HMS BELFAST

Company established the first ever public broadcasting station at Marconi House, Strand in 1922; and in 1923 were taken over by the British Broadcasting Company who moved to Savoy Hill. 1927 was the year of the incorporation of the British Broadcasting Corporation which has since grown into one of the world's most professional and respected broadcasting services. B.B.C. Headquarters and Sound Division are now at Broadcasting House, completed in 1932; and features a sculpture by Eric Gill 'Prospero and Ariel'. B.B.C. Television Centre is at Wood Lane, W12, and B.B.C. external services are at Bush House, Strand. 2E 93

Belfast H M S, Morgan's Lane, SE1. 071-407 6434 4G 95 and 3H 3
London's floating naval museum, this 11, 500 ton World War II cruiser is now part of the *Imperial War Museum.* Launched in 1938, her main armament of twelve 6 inch guns and eight 4 inch guns made her one of the most powerful cruisers afloat. Her battle honours include Artic Convoys 1943, Battle of North Cape 1943, D-Day landings 1944 and Korea 1950-52. Best seen from the *Tower of London* on the opposite bank, from where a ferry service operates in summer months.
Open 10.00-17.50, to 16.30 winter. Admission charge.

Bethnal Green Museum of Childhood, Cambridge Heath Road, E1. 081-980 2415
The Victoria and Albert Museum collection of toys, games, doll's etc; also Spitalfields silks.
Open 10.00-17.50, 14.30-17.50 Sun. Closed Fridays.

Billingsgate, EC3. 3E 95 and 3H 3
Billingsgate Market, one of the City's ancient markets moved to modern premises in West India Docks, E14 in 1982. The historical market site in Lower Thames Street dated back to pre-Norman times and although corn and coal trades flourished there until 1699, thereafter Billingsgate dealt exclusively in fish. Tradesmen acquired a great reputation for vituperative language and 'bobbing hats', the flat topped hats made of wood and leather (often passed down from father to son) on which men were capable of carrying up to 50 kilos of fish. The building of 1874, with its fish weathervanes, carved Britannia and dolphins is now used as offices.

Bloomsbury, WC1. 5C 84 and 2E 3
An area famous for national institutions, educational establishments and Georgian domestic architecture set around peaceful squares—Bloomsbury, Bedford, Tavistock and Fitzroy. There are many places to visit—the *British Museum, British Library, Jewish Museum* and the *Percival David Foundation of Chinese* Art. Also usually open to the public are the *Foundling Hospital Art Treasures,* including works by Hogarth and Gainsborough donated to raise funds for the hospital for destitute children founded in 1734 by Thomas Coram; Corams Fields—playing fields with no admittance for adults unaccompanied by children!—now occupy the site. Bloomsbury was once a highly fashionable residential area, especially in the early 1900's with the intellectual and artistic Bloomsbury Group; the area is now visually dominated by the colossal University of London Senate House. Founded by Royal Charter in 1836 as an examination organisation, the UNIVERSITY OF LONDON was in 1878 the first British University to admit women for degrees on equal terms with men-and it became a teaching university in 1900.

British Library, Gt Russell Street; WC2. 071-636 1544 6C 84 and 2E 3
To commence moving to its purpose built home at Euston Road, St. Pancras 1B 84 1993 onwards.
The British Library was established in 1973, its Reference Division (housed within the *British Museum* building), acquired the many book and manuscript collections amassed since the Museum's foundation in 1753. The three departments: Printed Books (including maps, music and stamps); Manuscripts; and Oriental Manuscripts and Printed Books, each have their own reading room open for research and reference which cannot be carried out elsewhere, (admission for reading rooms is by ticket only and prior application is necessary). The main circular reading room with its 40ft wide domed roof and 25 miles of shelving seats 390, and can usually be seen by interested visitors.
The departments all have exhibitions in the Library's galleries. Among the many invaluable objects on view are: Lindisfarne Gospels 698; Articles of the Barons complete with the seal of King John 1215, and subsequent charters including 'Magna Carta' 1225; Anglo-Saxon Chronical; Gutenberg Bible; block printed 'Diamond Sutra'; printed books of Caxton and Wyken de Worde; First Folio editions of Shakespeare's works; selections of letters and documents including those of Kings and Queens of England; Scott's Antarctic Journals; Nelson's HMS Victory log-books.
Galleries Open 10.00-17.00 Mon. to Sat. 14.30-18.00 Sun.

British Museum, Gt. Russell Street, WC2 071-636 1555 6C 84 and 2E 3
Storehouse of unrivalled treasures, the British Museum collection is one of the world's most

comprehensive records of man's achievements. It was founded in 1753 following the bequest to the Nation of Sir Hans Sloane's collection of books and antiquities; many other collections followed and the original building Montague House soon became too small. Designs for the present imposing building were prepared by Robert Smirke in 1824, the famous Reading Room, now part of the *British Library* being added by Sidney Smirke 1853-7. (Its Natural History Collection moved to South Kensington 1880-3 and since 1963 has been a completely separate institution. The Ethnography Department. is now at the *Museum of Mankind).*
PRINCIPAL DEPARTMENTS
Eygptian Antiquities: include the 'Rosetta Stone' sculptures, mummies, wall paintings, funerary furniture, papyri, jewellery and scarabs. Western Asiatic Antiquities: include the colossal Assyrian sculptures, Hittite, Babylonian and Sumerian antiquities and the Room of Writing with cylinders inscribed in reverse for imprinting on seals. Greek and Roman Antiquities : include the 'Chatsworth' Head of Apollo, the Elgin Marbles-sculptures from the Parthenon Frieze and pediments, the Portland Vase. Medieval and Later Antiquities: include the Anglo-Saxon Royal burial ship treasure from Sutton Hoo, the Lewis Chessman, the 14th century Royal Gold Cup, the Lyte Jewel; Horological and Coins and Medals galleries etc., Prehistoric and Romano-British Antiquities: including the 4th century silver tableware Mildenhall Treasure. Oriental Antiquities: finds from the civilizations of the Far East from the neolithic period onwards. Prints and Drawings: one of the great collections of European prints and drawings, including the Turner collection of watercolours, variously displayed in exhibitions of selected works.
Open 10.00-17.00 Mon to Sat. 14.30-18.00 Sun.

Buckingham Palace, The Mall, SW1.
7G 91 and 4D 2
This, the London Palace of Her Majesty Queen Elizabeth II is one of the Capital's magnetic focal points for visitors where at 11.30 daily (alternate days in winter months) the ceremony of *Changing the Guard* draws large and enthusiastic crowds. When the Sovereign is in residence the Royal Standard is flown from the central flagpole. From the balcony beneath, the Royal Family appear on great public occasions. 'Buckingham House', built 1703 for the Duke of Buckingham on the site of a mulberry garden planted by James 1st, was bought in 1762 by George III as a retreat from court life at St. James's. George IV commissioned John Nash in 1824 to build a palace of grandiose proportions to his taste, a scheme not completed during his reign or that of his brother William IV. Queen Victoria took up residence soon after her accession in 1837. In 1847 an east wing was added creating the

BUCKINGHAM PALACE

quadrangle layout of to-day and the original ceremonial entrance *Marble Arch* was moved to *Hyde Park.* The classical Portland stone facade was added 1912-13 as part of the National Memorial to Queen Victoria together with the construction of Queen Victoria Memorial and *Admiralty Arch.* The State Apartments, including the Throne Room, State Ballroom and Picture Gallery remain much in the grand style created for George IV, complete with magnificent decorations, furniture and works of art. Investitures and State Banquets are held in the Ballroom. The Bow Room is used in summer months by those invited to attend Royal Garden Parties in the 40 acre garden. Only the *Queen's Gallery* and *Royal Mews* are open to the public.

Cabinet War Rooms, Clive Steps, King Charles St., SW1. 071-930 6961 6B 92
One of the Second World War bunkers used by Winston Churchill and his staffs. All rooms now restored to their authentic war time appearance. *Open 10.00-18.00 daily. Admission charge.*

Cenotaph, Whitehall, SW1. 6C 92 and 4E 3
'To the Glorious Dead'; this simple white stone monument, decorated with flags of the three armed services and mercantile marine commemorates the dead of both World Wars. Designed by Edwin Lutyens and initially erected in plaster for the Allied Victory March 1919, and then rebuilt in stone and unveiled on Armistice Day 1920, the later inscription being added in 1946. Here on Remembrance Sunday (the second in November) a service is held attended by the Sovereign, political and armed forces leaders and the British Legion; two minutes silence is observed at 11.00 in memory of the fallen.

Central Criminal Court, Old Bailey, EC4. 071-248 3277 7A 86 and 3G 3
The 'Old Bailey'; London's principal criminal court makes its mark on the skyline with the famous gold 'Figure of Justice', her hands outstretched, scales in one, sword in the other. Each court has a public gallery, (*normally open 10.30-13.00; 14.00-16.00*), Court no 1 deals with the most important trials. The building dating from 1902-7, occupies the site of the former notorious Newgate Prison some stones from which were used in the construction. Public executions took place at the prison between 1783-1867—outside the debtors' door, and near the present Court's entrance. Prior to 1783 condemned prisoners were taken by cart to Tyburn (*Marble Arch*), to the tolling of St Sepulchre's bell. Standing opposite, this church also once followed the custom of presenting prisoners with a nosegay each as they passed; inside may be seen the handbell of 1605 rung outside the condemned cell at midnight on the eve of execution. Judges still carry posies when the Lord Mayor in State sits in attendance-usually for the first two days of the new session each September—a custom designed to counteract the noxious smells emanating from Newgate Prison to which the courts formerly abutted. The impressive main hall has a statue of Elizabeth Fry the great Quaker reformer of prison conditions.

Changing the Guard
One of the Capital's great traditions with impeccable displays of pageantry, military precision, colour and music. The Changing of the Queen's Guard takes place at *Buckingham Palace* every morning at 11.30 during the summer, on alternate days in winter months. The ceremony is carried out by one of the five regiments of Foot Guards marching to a military band (no band in wet weather). Scarlet tunics and bearskin caps are the ceremonial dress of all five regiments, each of which is distinguished by the type of plume; Grenadiers-white, Coldstream-red, Irish-blue, Welsh-green and white and Scots Guards without a plume; and also by button settings and hatbands. Together they comprise the Guards Division. Besides taking part in this and other ceremonies ie Trooping the Colour (see *Horse Guards),* the Guards can be seen on guard duty outside *Buckingham Palace, St James's Palace,* Clarence House 6J 91 and *Windsor Castle* which also has a guard changing ceremony daily at 11.00. The Changing of the Queen's Life Guard takes place in the small courtyard of *Horse Guards* daily at 11.00 (Sundays 10.00), carried out by the Household Cavalry comprising two regiments, the Life Guards in scarlet tunics with white helmet plumes and the Blues and Royals in blue tunics and red plumes. Both regiments provide a mounted personal bodyguard for the Sovereign on all State occasions. The Foot Guards and Household Cavalry together comprise the seven regiments of the Household Division of which Her Majesty the Queen is Colonel-in-Chief. It is to be remembered that these men are members of operational units and available at short notice for active service with the British Army.

Chelsea, SW3. 5J 97, 6D 98 and 5C 2
Once a country village but from the 16th century increasingly adopted as home by the eminent; Sir Thomas More, Sir Isaac Newton, Johnathan Swift, Henry Fielding, J M W Turner, Thomas Carlyle, Elizabeth Fry, the Brunels; and during the 19th century a great many well known authors and artists including

the Pre Raphaelites. Many buildings carry commemorative plaques. In the 1960's it became the turn of a whole generation of young people to find Chelsea a desirable place, when Kings Road became a centre for trendy fashion shops. In 1537 Henry VII built his Chelsea Palace fronting the river at Cheyne Walk, owned in the 17th century by the Cheyne family, and by Sir Hans Sloane in the 18th, upon whose death it was demolished. (his collection of books and antiquities helped to found the British Museum).

CHELSEA PHYSIC GARDENS: 66 Royal Hospital Rd., SW3. 071-352 5646 7C 99 & 5C 2 were established by the Worshipful Society of Apothecaries in 1673 for the propagation and study of new plant species. Industries derived therefrom in former British Colonies include tea from China in India; cotton from the South Seas in Georgia; rubber from S. America in Malaysia. *Open 14.00-17.00 Sun & Wed only, Easter to Oct. Admission charge.*

ROYAL HOSPITAL: Royal Hospital Rd, SW3. 071-730 0161 6D 98 and 5C 2
The home for old or invalid soldiers—the Chelsea Pensioners, who may be seen wearing a scarlet frock-coat in the summer and a blue tunic in winter. This was founded by Charles II in 1682 at the instigation of Nell Gwyn according to popular belief; certainly at the inspiration of the Hotel des Invalides, Paris, founded 1670 by Louis XIV. The principal buildings including the impressive portico, Great Hall and Chapel are designed by Wren; there is also work by Robert Adam and additions by John Soane—the stable block and a wing housing the Royal Hospital Museum. A Statue of Charles II by Grinling Gibbons is decorated with oak branches on 29th May the annual 'Oak Apple Day' when the pensioners also wear tricorn hats. Another more famous spring event the 'Chelsea Flower Show' takes place in the extensive grounds which encompass Ranelagh Gardens the fashionable 18th century pleasure gardens. *Open 10.00-12.00; 14.00-16.00, 14.00-16.00 Sun.*

NATIONAL ARMY MUSEUM: Royal Hospital Rd., SW3. 071-730 0717 7C 98 & 5C 2
Housed in a modern purpose built building, it covers the history of the army from Henry VIII's founding the Yeomen of the Guard at the battle of Bosworth Field 1485 up to Falklands War. There are displays of uniforms, weaponry, insignia, and paintings including works by Reynolds, Gainsborough and Romney.
Open 10.00-17.30, 14.00-17.30 Sun.

CHANGING THE GUARD: at Buckingham Palace

CROSBY HALL: Cheyne Walk, SW3. 071-352 9663 5B 2
The 15th century Great Hall from the former mansion of John Crosby was moved here in 1910 from its original site in Bishopsgate, its features include a massive hammerbeam roof and three tier oriel window. *Open 10.15-12.15; 14.15-17.00. 14.15-17.15 Sun.*
CARLYLES HOUSE: 24 Cheyne Row, SW3. 071-352 7087 7J 97 & 5B 2
Now a National Trust property, this was the town house of Thomas Carlyle from 1834 until his death, in it may be seen his furniture, books, manuscripts, personal relics and portraits. *Open 11.00-17.00 Wed. to Sun. April to end Oct. Admission charge.*
CHELSEA OLD CHURCH: Cheyne Walk, SW3. 5B 2
Of Medieval origins but mostly rebuilt after World War II bombing, the More Chapel is however an original 14th century feature; the Chained Books presented by Hans Sloane and a great many monuments record important and historical people connected with Chelsea.

Cheshire Cheese, Ye Olde, 145 Fleet Street., EC4. 071-353 6170 1H 93 and 3F 3
One of the City's many historic Inns, wherein, the low beamed ceilings and smoke tarnished atmosphere exude something of the past which museum set-pieces are unable to do. Built in 1667 over cellars dating back to 1538, the Cheshire Cheese is a journalists' 'local' and traditionally also was one of Dr. Johnson's (although Boswell does not mention it in his biography). Lunch here can include the famous Pudding served between October and April.

Churches See also page 61
Churches of almost every denomination are to be found in London, and those of historical interest are numerous. Ancient churches of Medieval and Saxon origin are to be found in 97 medieval 'City' parishes and outlying villages. Among those to survive both the Great Fire of London 1666 and World War II bombing are St. Bartholomew the Great 1A 11, St. Ethelburga 2D 11 and St. Helen Bishopsgate 2C 11, and upstream adjacent to *Westminster Abbey,* St. Margaret's Westminster 3C 38, (the parish church of Westminster and the House of Commons), rich in 15th and 16th century architecture and historical associations. Christopher Wren was responsible for the rebuilding of 51 of the 81 'City' churches destroyed in the Great Fire, besides the new *St. Paul's Cathedral.* Wren churches on ancient foundations and undamaged by bombs include St. Margaret Lothbury, 2C 11, St. Peter Cornhill 3C 11 and among those many faithfully restored after the war are St. Bride Fleet Street 3D 14, St. Mary le Bow 3B 11, St. Stephen Walbrook 3B 11, St. Clement Danes 3C 14 and St. James's Piccadilly, 1B 38, the latter having been a new foundation for the fashionable Restoration developments at St. James's. Many are the impressive designs born of the peculiarly English fusion of Palladian and Baroque styles built during the relentless growth of 18th and 19th century suburbs. The most famous, *St. Martin-in-the Fields* 1C 38 built 1721-6 by James Gibbs with its Corinthian portico, layered tower and spire commands equal attention alongside the *National Gallery* and Nelsons Column. Elswhere are: All Soul's Langham Place 2C 37, Christ Church Spitalfields 2H 3, St. George Hanover Square 3C 37, St. John Smith Square (now a concert hall) 4E 3, St. Mary-le-Strand 3B 14. Other places of worship of great interest and with long historical associations include, St. Peter-ad-Vincular, Chapel of St. John (both within the *Tower of London);* Chapel Royal and Queen's Chapel *St. James's Palace,* Queen's Chapel of the Savoy 3A 14, the Spanish and Portuguese Synagogue Bevis Marks 2D 11, Englands oldest synagogue; Guards Chapel 3B 38, the Royal Military Chapel; Grosvenor Chapel 3B 37, adopted by U S forces in World War II, and so on.

City of London, 3G 3 and see page 11
The City of London is that 'square mile' devoted to international banking, insurance and commerce, packed by day with a multitude of office workers and largely deserted at night and weekends (see also *Barbican*). At its heart are the *Bank of England, Royal Exchange* and *Mansion House.* Lombard Street 3C 11, named after the Lombard goldsmiths and money-lenders established here in the Middle Ages, is now the centre of British banking, a very distinguished environment enhanced by numerous bank signs hung medieval fashion over the pavements. The City's fascinating history from Roman times through to the 20th century is presented chronologically in the *Museum of London.* The City's corporate municipal government was born c.1192 with the election of the first Lord Mayor, Henry Fitz Alwyn—a post still elected annually by the historic Livery Companies in the medieval *Guildhall.* It is here that the Court of Common Council, the City's principal administrative body sits under the Lord Mayor; meetings are in public. The modern City retains much of its historical independance having its own Police Force and Law Courts. Ancient customs are still observed—on State occasions the Lord Mayor and Aldermen precede the Sovereign into the City following formal surrender of the Pearl Sword at Temple Bar, 2C 14, thus symbolising

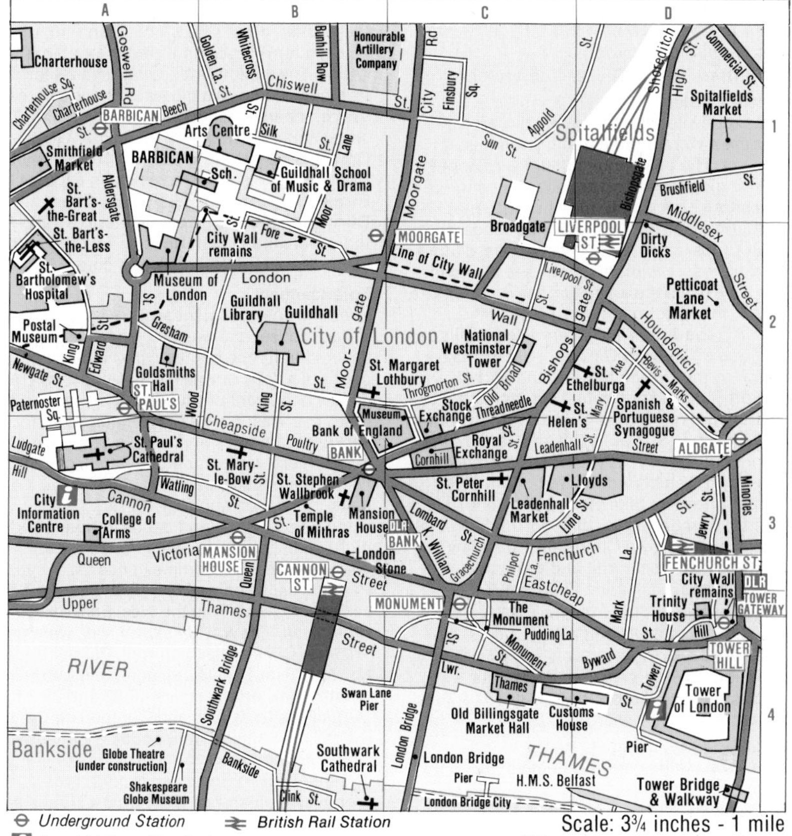

THE CITY OF LONDON

the over-lordship of the Sovereign. The City Information centre 3A 11, provides useful details of all aspects of City Life, daily events, lunchtime concerts at City churches, Livery Hall open days, Ceremonial events like the Lord Mayors Show (November).

College of Arms, Queen Victoria Street, EC4. 071-248 2762 3A 11
The official authority in all matters relating to armorial bearings and pedigrees has occupied this site since 1554, the present charter having been presented by Elizabeth I in 1555. This great brick town house is one of the few surviving secular buildings erected in the City immediately after the Great Fire. The Corporation comprises three Kings of Arms, six Heralds and four Pursuivants all members of the Royal Household and appointed by the Crown on the Earl Marshall's advice (Dukes of Norfolk by hereditary right and one of whose tasks is the arrangement of State Ceremonies). Open for personal heraldic and genealogical enquires. The history and development of heraldry is explained in the Colleges museum at the *Tower of London.*

Commonwealth Institute see Kensington

Courtauld Institute Galleries,
Fine Rooms, Somerset House, Strand, WC2. 071-873 2777 2E 93 and 3F 3
This famous art collection is housed in the north wing of the imposing neo-classical Somerset House and includes: the Courtauld Collection of Impressionist and Post-Impressionist painting, the Lord Fareham Collection (14th-18th century art); the Roger Fry Collection (Bloomsbury Group and Impressionists); the Witt Collection of Old Master Drawings. The Courtauld Collection is Britain's most important group of Impressionist and Post Impressionist paintings: Bonnard, Cezanne, Degas, Gauguin, Manet, Monet, Renoir, Seurat,

Sisley, Toulouse-Lautrec, Van Gogh. *Open 10.00-18.00 Mon. to Sat. 14.00-18.00 Sun. Admission charge.*

Court Dress Collection see Kensington

Covent Garden, WC2. 2D 92 and 3E 3
Since redevelopment, Covent Garden has become a vibrant retail trading and leisure precinct. The old market buildings restored to their original condition are now the centre of a pedestrian area which, together with the surrounding streets offers a wide range of small shops, crafts, gifts, food, books, clothes, art galleries, restaurants, pubs see also pages 72, 73. Here are the world famous *Royal Opera House,* the historic *London Transport Museum and Theatre Museum.* Historically the area was a 'Convent Garden', sold in 1552—following the Dissolution—to the Earl of Bedford, and laid out in the 17th century for the 4th Earl as a residential piazza by Inigo Jones. Also by him is St. Paul's Covent Garden, the 'actors church', occupying the eastern side, who's portal sheltered the first of Punch's Puppet Shows to take place in England, a fact noted in Samuel Pepy's diary for 1662. A small market, given Royal Charter in 1671 grew into London's wholesale fruit and vegetable market, removed to Nine Elms in 1974.

Design Museum, Shad Thames, SE1.
071-403 6933 6J 95 and 4H 3
Covers the history, practice, theory and future of design in mass-produced consumer products and services. *Open 11.30-18.30 Tues. to Sun. Admission charge.*

Dickens House, Doughty Street,
WC1. 071-405 2127 4F 85 and 2F 3
The home of Charles Dickens between March 1837 and the end of 1839; it was here that he completed Pickwick Papers, wrote Oliver Twist, Nicholas Nickleby and planned Barnaby Rudge. Bought by the Dickens Fellowship, the house is open to the public and has a collection of personal relics—desk, letters, portraits; also an important library collection of manuscripts and first editions. Dickens drawing room has been reinstated following meticulous research into wallpaper, paints, furniture and furnishings.
Open 10.00-17.00 Closed Sun.

Dr. Johnson's House, 17 Gough Square, EC4
071-353 3745 7H 85
Where he lived 1748-59 during the compilation of his Dictionary, fine collection of memorabila. *Open 11.00-17.30 Mon to Sat: 11.00-17.00 Oct. to April. Closed Sun. Admission charge.*

Downing Street, Whitehall, SW1. 6C 92 and 4E 3
Here, behind the hubbub of sightseers, diplomatic cars and police, are numbers 10 and 11 Downing Street, the Official residences of the Prime Minister and Chancellor of the Exchequer; other senior politicians can often be seen hurrying to and from the Cabinet Office. The mellow brick, small scale Georgian frontages come as a pleasant change to the grand,impersonal buildings on *Whitehall.* The street name derives from its builder George Downing-notorious for his opportunist switch from Cromwell backer to a post in Charles II's Exchequer, as derided in Pepy's diaries. During the rebuilding of the interiors 1960-64, there were many historic finds relating to the Tudor Palace of Whitehall and before.

Entertainment
Londons entertainment scene is so rich and varied that several weekly magazines are devoted to it; one of these, or the relevant pages of a daily or weekly newspaper will give details of current productions and events of note. The *West End* is rightly famous as the centre of London's night-life: a great conglomeration including theatres, cinemas, two opera houses, dance facilities, restaurants, jazz and rock music, discotheques, dine and dance in hotels and night clubs, public house entertainment, music hall, and lunch time concerts. Paradoxically some of the most important venues are away from the West End: the *Royal Albert Hall.* The *Royal Festival Hall,* National Theatre, Queen Elizabeth Hall, Purcell Room, National Film Theatre, all comprising the 'South Bank' arts complex 4E 93 and 3F 3 the *Barbican* with its Arts and Conference Centre is both the home of the London Symphony Orchestra and Royal Shakespeare company; Sadlers Wells in Rosebery Avenue 1F 3, Wembley Conference Centre 1B 42 Open air attractions, brass bands, concerts and theatre productions, are a feature of the summer months for those willing to trust to the vagaries of English climate.

Florence Nightingale Museum, St. Thomas' Hospital, 2 Lambeth Palace Rd.,
SE1 071-620 0374 7E 93
Illustrates the life and work of this famous woman, including a life size recreated ward at the Crimea. *Open 10.00-16.00 Tues. to Sun. Admission charge.*

Fleet Street, EC4, 1G 93 and 3F 3
The 'Street of Ink'. A prestigious address long associated with newspapers, periodicals and news agencies; a trend begun in the 16th century when Wynkyn de Worde, assistant and successor of Caxton moved his master's press here from Westminster and ended, with the introduction of modern technologies and the move to more suitable premises including redeveloped docklands. The St. Bride Institute Printing Library—near the famous Wren

Church of St. Brides with its 'Wedding Cake' spire and Crypt Museum—is an important information source on printing techniques and type design, and has a collection of early presses and type. Samuel Pepys and Dr Johnson are among the many historical figures associated with the street. Its name derives from the Fleet River, (one of London's now lost rivers), which still runs into the River Thames near Blackfriars Bridge, following the line of Farringdon Street which was also the site of Fleet Prison for debtors, so vividly described by Dickens in Pickwick Papers.

Foundling Hospital Art Treasures, Thomas Coram Foundation, 40 Brunswick Sq. WC1. 071-278 2424 3D 84 & 2E 3 Includes works by Hogarth and Gainsborough; see also *Bloomsbury Open 10.00-16.00 Mon. to Fri. Admission charge.*

Geffrye Museum, Kingsland Road, E2. 071-739 9893 1H 3
Housed in Almshouses erected in 1715 by the Ironmongers' Company, the museum has a unique display 5 centuries of the English front room—furniture and domestic equipment from Tudor times to the 1930's. *Open 10.00-17.00 Tues. to Sat. 14.00-17.00 Sun.*

Geological Museum, Exhibition Road, SW7. 071-938 8765 2H 97 and 4B 2
The National Museum of Earth Science and part of the Institute of Geological Sciences; is an important research centre with specialist library, study room, demonstration laboratory and lecture hall. The museum besides its huge collection of rocks (including moon rock), minerals and fossils, features several modern theme exhibitions of great interest: The Story of the Earth, Britain before Man, British Fossils, and Treasures of the Earth. *Open 10.00-18.00 Mon. to Sat. 13.00-18.00 Sun. Admission charge.*

Gray's Inn, Holborn, WC1. 5F 85 and 2F 3
One of the four great Inns of Court that perform the function of University to the legal profession. Each has its own peculiar maze of courts, alleys and gardens preserving the tranquil atmosphere of earlier times. Among the blocks of chambers are several historic buildings although heavily restored following World War II bombing; the 16th century hall where Shakespeare's 'Comedy of Errors' received its first performance; 17th century Chapel and Gateways; the Library established c.1555. The 16th century philosopher Francis Bacon resided here, and is thought responsible for creating Gray's Inn Gardens—his statue can be seen in South Square.

Green Park, SW1. 5G 91 and 3D 2
Laid out by Charles II in 1667 as an extension to St James's Park. Great wrought iron gates stand at each end of Broad Walk: Dominion Gate facing The Mall and gates from old Devonshire House towards Piccadilly. Queen's Walk on the eastern edge is overlooked by the Ritz Hotel and many former mansions.

Greenwich see Outer London

Guards Museum & Chapel, Wellington Barracks, Birdcage Walk SW1. 071-930 4466 7J 91 and 4D 2
Illustrates the 300 year history of the Brigade of Guards. *Open 10.00-16.00 Closed Fridays. Admission charge.* Adjacent is GUARD'S CHAPEL, rebuilt 1963 incorporating the surviving apse of the earlier chapel devasted in 1944 by a flying bomb during morning service with the loss of 121 lives.

Guildhall, Gresham Street, EC2. 7C 86 and 3G 3 071-606 3030
'O Lord direct us', reads the motto high above the doorway to this centre of the *City of London's* civic government for more than 1000 years. Stonework of the Great Hall and porch date from the 15th century, the crypt has one of the few medieval secular vaults surviving both the Great Fire 1666 and 1940 bombs. Restoration was completed in 1954, the oak roof being the fifth to span the ancient hall. Interesting features include the banners and wall frieze depicting the Arms of the 12 principal Livery Companies, the Arms of England and the City; shields of 84 Livery Companies incorporated in the roof design; the 9ft 3inch Gog and Magog statues and many monuments.
The City's municipal meetings are held here, as are presentations of the Freedom of the City, important civic and state functions including the annual Lord Mayor's Banquet. *Open 10.00-17.00 Mon. to Sat. (Sundays Summer only).* A modern extension adjoining contains the important Guildhall Library (Reference only) and the Corporation of London Record Office—regarded as the most complete collection of ancient municipal records in existence. *Open 09.30-17.00 Mon. to Sat. Closed Sun.* The library also houses the Clockmaker's Company Museum-illustrating 500 years of timekeeping

Hampstead see Outer London

Hampton Court Palace see Outer London

Holborn—Strand 2F-3F 3 and see page 14
This historic area linking its more famous neighbours *City of London/West End/ Westminster,* has an identity bound up with many aspects of Law. The four great Inns of Court—*Grays Inn, Lincoln's Inn,* Middle and Inner *Temple* form a north to south backbone; the principal courts are here, the *Royal Courts*

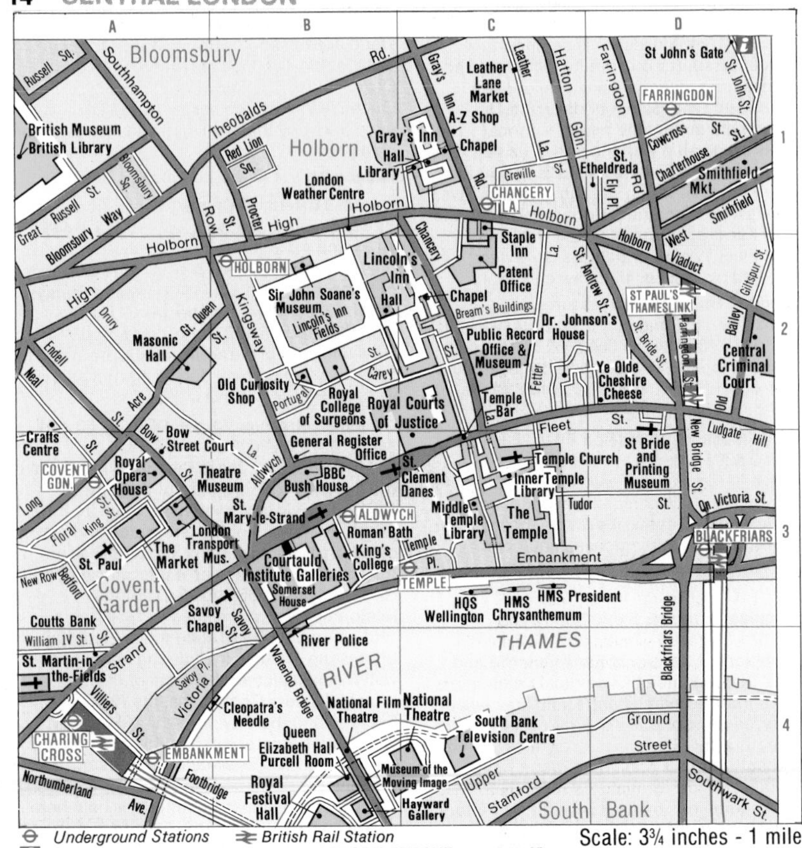

HOLBORN-STRAND: see page 13

of Justice and *Central Criminal Court* while in *Covent Garden,* Bow Street Magistrates Court 3A 14, has links with the origins of the police via the 'Bow Street Runners' established by Robert Peel 1829; here also are the main depositories of records, the Office of Population Censuses and Surveys and General Register Office, 10 Kingsway, WC2. 3B 14, and the *Public Record Office.* There are many other interesting places tucked away awaiting discovery— *Sir John Soane's Museum, Old Curiosity Shop, Staple Inn;* the very special atmosphere of *Fleet Street;* the old pub *Cheshire Cheese* and *Dr Johnson's House;* and the famous Strand 4A 14, originally a riverside walk, once lined with mansions of nobility see *Somerset House,* in Edwardian times with palatial hotels like the Savoy, where the ancient churches of St Clement Danes and St Mary-le-Strand are now marooned on islands, like old sailing ships in a sea of endless traffic.

Horse Guards, Whitehall, SW1. 5C 92 and 4E 3
The focal point in *Whitehall.* Throngs of people buzz around the twin mounted sentries, growing to a crush at 11.00 (10.00 Sundays) when *'Changing the Guard'* is performed here by the two regiments of the Household Cavalry—Life Guards in scarlet tunics and Royal Horse Guards in blue. There is public access through the towering baroque pile of the Horse Guards building erected 1750-60 to designs by William Kent, to Horse Guards Parade; this wide, flat, grey expanse, site of the Tudor Whitehall Palace tiltyard, annually in June turns chameleon-like into a whirling mass of colour and music on the occasion of 'Trooping the Colour', celebrating the official birthday of our Sovereign.

Houses of Parliament, Parliament Square, SW1. 071-219 3000 1D 100 and 4E 3
This enormous Victorian Gothic building stands throughout the world as a symbol of

LIFEGUARDS

democratic government; its great agglomeration of fairy-tale towers and pinnacles add up to a memorable skyline, and its Clock Tower has become an unofficial symbol of London (although 'Big Ben' is in fact not the name of the tower or clock but of the hour bell). Erected between 1840-68 to designs of Charles Barry, with a lavish wealth of detail and splendiferous fittings and furnishings by his assistant, Augustus Pugin.

The building occupies the site of the old Palace of Westminster, the chief Royal residence from Edward the Confessor's time to that of Henry VIII (who preferred the more modern apartments of his newly acquired palace in *Whitehall).* Parliament grew from the ancient Great Council (see *Westminster Hall),* the Lords and Commons separating during the reign of Edward 1st. While the Lords continued to meet in the palace, the Commons sat in the

HOUSES OF PARLIAMENT: from the Albert Embankment

Chapter House of *Westminster Abbey* until 1547, when they transferred to St. Stephens Chapel. In 1834 however, the old palace buildings, with the exception of Westminster Hall, St. Stephens Chapel crypt and the Jewel Tower, were destroyed in a great fire—for which we have to thank our now famous Victorian landmark.
Sittings of Parliament are indicated by a Union Jack flying from Victoria Tower and, by night, a light towards the top of the Clock Tower. For admission to hear debates apply in advance to an M.P. or join the queue outside St Stephen's Entrance for the Strangers Gallery only when Parliament is in session, normally from mid Oct. to end July, except week following Christmas and Easter; Mon. to Thurs. from approx 14.30 (Fri. from approx 09.30)

Hyde Park and **Kensington Gardens,** W2. 4A 90 & 3C 2—5E 89 & 3B 2
An oasis in the heart of London of over 600 acres to explore; the two Royal Parks share the same lake as a centre piece, although known as 'The Serpentine' in Hyde Park and 'The Long Water' in Kensington Gardens. This is a place of relaxation; you can hire a rowing boat or yacht on the Serpentine, or sail a model boat on Round Pond; join in an impromptu debate at Speakers Corner (Tub-Thumping and heckling are most vociferous on Sundays); listen to a brass-band concert; visit the Serpentine Art Gallery, *Kensington Palace* or *Apsley House;* there are dozens of sculptures and monuments, no lack of refreshments. Failing all else, you can sit, not more than 20 minutes walk from *Piccadilly Circus,* and wonder at the tranquillity.

Imperial War Museum, Lambeth Road, SE1. 071-735 8922 2H 101 and 4F 3
In the words of Burns—'Man's inhumanity to man, makes countless thousands mourn'—and here are just a few of the instruments. The collection encompasses all aspects of warfare in which British and Commonwealth Forces have been involved since 1914. Most of the large exhibits date from the two World Wars and include the following: a pair of 15 inch naval guns (entrance courtyard), mark V tank, howitzers, 'Ole Bill' the famous B type bus used to carry troops to the 1914 front line, Sopwith Camel aircraft, Fairey Swordfish torpedo bomber, Spitfire Mk 1, Focke-Wolf 190 (most of museum's aircraft are however at its Duxford site). There are torpedos, a German one-man submarine, and many models of ships; both the V1 flying bomb and the V2 rocket can be inspected. Dramatic recreations with sounds, smells and special effects include WW1 "Trench Experience" and WW11 "Blitz experience" Art galleries show works by war artists including William Coldstream, Jacob Epstein, Anthony Gross, Henry Moore, Paul Nash, John Piper. The museum, founded in 1917, occupies a building designed in 1812 as Bethlem Hospital for the Insane— whence 'Bedlam'. *Open 10.00-18.00 daily. Admission charge, free on Fridays.*

Jewel Tower, Old Palace Yard, SW1. 1C 100 and 4C 38
14th century corner tower of the old Palace of Westminster. *Open 10.00-18.00, (to 16.00 winter); Closed Sun.*

Jewish Museum, Tavistock Square, W1. 071-388 4525 3B 84 and 2E 3
Open Sun, Tues. to Fri. 10.00-16.00 April to Sept. Oct. to Mar. Fridays only 10.00-12.45. Closed Mon. Admission charge.

Keats House see Hampstead

Kensington, W2. 7B 88 and 3A—4A 2
This Royal Borough with its diverse mix of places to visit, centres on its busy High Street shopping centre. KENSINGTON PALACE, 5D 88 & 3A 2 at one end of the High Street, is largely the work of Christopher Wren for William III who bought what was then Nottingham House in 1689; later additions being made for George I by William Kent. Queen Victoria was born here in 1819 and her statue by daughter Princess Louise stands outside in the beautiful Kensington Gardens, once the Palace's private parkland; STATE APARTMENTS & COURT DRESS COLLECTION: Kensington Palace, 071-937 9561 5D 88 *Open 09.00-17.00. 13.00-17.00 Sun. Admission charge.* Towards the opposite end of High Street is LEIGHTON HOUSE, 12 Holland Pk. Rd., W14 071-602 3316 4A 2 home of Lord Leighton 1866-96, containing an amazing Arab Hall decorated with 13th-17th century middle eastern tiles; collections of High Victorian art with works by Burne-Jones, Millais etc, displayed alongside period interior decoration and furniture, William de Morgan pottery and tiles. *Open 11.00-17.00 Closed Suns.* In between are the COMMONWEALTH INSTITUTE, 071-603 4535 1A 96 and 4A 2 with its exhibition galleries devoted to over forty countries, arts centre, library and coffee shop; *Open 10.00-17.00 (Sun. 14.00-17.00).* LINLEY SAMBOURNE HOUSE, 18 Stafford Terrace, W8. 081-994 1019 1A 96 & 4A 2 home of 'Punch' cartoonist Linley Sambourne 1870-1910 with its interiors recreated by the Victorian Society; *Open 10.00-16.00 Wed. 14.00-17.00 Sun. March to Oct. only. Admission charge.* HOLLAND HOUSE, stands in the extensive HOLLAND PARK. Remnants of this Jacobean mansion—largely destroyed by 1941 bombing—are utilised as a backcloth

for the open air Court Theatre; while the restored east wing c. 1640, is now part of the King George VI Memorial Youth Hostel. In SOUTH KENSINGTON 4B 2, the emphasis (started by Prince Albert following the success of his Great Exhibition 1851), is on education and the arts. Here are the Imperial College; Royal Colleges of Music and Art; Royal Geographical Society; the impressive Italian Baroque Brompton Oratory completed 1884; the *Royal Albert Hall, Victoria and Albert Museum, Natural History Museum, Science Museum and Geological Museum.*

Kew see Outer London

Lincoln's Inn and **Fields,** WC2. 7F 85 and 2F 3
One of the four great Inns of Court wherein charming brick courts encapsulate a stunning peace. Its origins are closely associated with Edward I's legal advisor, the Earl of Lincoln (d.1311), however not with this site until c.1415-22, when this legal college acquired the palace of the Bishops of Chichester. See the Old Hall 1489-91; Chancery Lane Gateway carved with arms of the Earl, also Henry VIII and date '1518', the Chapel of 1623 with its unique open undercroft created so that, protected from the worst of English weather, barristers their students and clients, could meet 'for a chat'; also the Great Hall and Library added 1845-9.
LINCOLN'S INN FIELDS, London's largest square is a place of resort for large numbers of office workers who, in summer months, relax under the plane trees and listen to brass band concerts along with the many visitors. Here are the Royal College of Surgeons, and the Land Registry building; No 58 was the home of Dickens' biographer J Forster, and was adopted as Mr Tulkinghorn's residence in 'Bleak House' (the Old Hall *see above* is the setting for the interminable case Jarndyce V Jarndyce). No's 59 & 60 Lindsey House—believed to be one of the original buildings by Inigo Jones, designer of the Squares' initial lay-out (first half of the 17th century)—is of fine classical proportions. Prior to this development the area was one of ill-repute, a notorious duelling ground and occasionally of executions. On the north side is the remarkable *Sir John Soanes Museum.*

Lloyds, Lime Street, EC3. 071-623 7100 1F 95
Lloyds, one of the famous City institutions, is a world renowned insurance market and centre of shipping intelligence. 'A1' at Lloyds is accepted as a guarantee of good faith. In the Underwriting Room hangs the famous Lutine Bell, rung once for bad news and twice for an arrival when information about a vessel posted 'overdue' is received. The exciting modern building has external observation lifts giving access for the public to the Underwriting Room Viewing Gallery and exhibition of Lloyds history. *(Open 10.00-14.30 Mon. to Fri.)*
The origins of marine insurance go back to the middle ages and were first practised in this country during the 16th century. Bankers and merchants who undertook such risks became known as 'underwriters' from the style of inscribing their name to documents one under the other in order of responsibility for their proportion of the insurance risk. Following the destruction of the Royal Exchange in the Great Fire 1666, Coffee Houses were used as alternative meeting places—that of Edward Lloyd being frequented by those involved in shipping and marine insurance. In 1771, Lloyds became a formal organisation and one hundred years later became the Corporation of Lloyds by act of Parliament. In 1986, the market moved to its present headquarters, incorporating the latest in electronic communications technology, its flexible design will enable the market to expand as business dictates well into the next century.

London Bridge, EC4. 4E 94 and 3G 3
One of London's most historical landmarks and perhaps the *raison d'être* for the City's location. Being the lowest feasible point for the Romans to construct their timber bridge, it was natural for Londinium to grow here at the meeting point of trade routes. It was not until 1176 that a stone bridge was begun (to the west of the wooden one), by Peter of Colechurch; on its completion it was 905 ft long, houses, shops and a chapel dedicated to St Thomas a Becket (murdered 1170) were built on it; and later heads of traitors were impaled on spikes over the two fortified gates. The piers of its 19 pointed arches slowed down the current upstream to the extent that the river froze over in severe weather—hence the tradition of 'Frost Fairs', held on the ice—and of disturbing the flow of water between the piers to the extent that a skilled boatman became necessary for its safe navigation. Frequently the victim of damage by fire, boats, ice etc. the bridge acquired the ignoble reputation of 'London Bridge is falling down', and yet was still one of the'sights' of Europe. It remained the only river bridge until the construction of Westminster Bridge 7D 92 in the mid 18th century. The Medieval London Bridge itself survived until well into the 19th century, its granite replacement (again sited to the west) being designed by J. Rennie, is now however in Arizona. The present bridge is a three-arched, 100ft wide, concrete structure, built 1967-73. See also *River Thames.*

London Planetarium, Marylebone Road, NW1. 071-486 1121 4D 82 and 2C 2
You are invited herein on an exploration of cosmic vastness, perhaps as an antidote to the

LONDON ZOO

human frailties of *Madame Tussauds* next door. The beauty of the night sky is projected over the dome interior by a two ton Zeiss instrument showing how the sun, planets and stars rotate, their relative positions from various locations on earth, from outer space, at different points in time, past or future. All sorts of special effects can be created: a solar eclipse, close-up views of planets, the passage of satellites and spacecraft, panoramic views of London, Medieval Europe and the moon. LASERIUM entertainments are presented evenings. *For details 071-486 2242. Performances regularly 11.00-18.00 daily. Admission charge.*

London Toy and Model Museum, 23 Craven Hill, W2. 071-262 7905 2F 89
Superb collections of trains, cars, boats, 'planes, dolls, also shop displays, garden train rides and playground. *Open 10.00-17.30 Tues. to Sat. 11.00-17.30 Sun.*

London Transport Museum,
Covent Garden, WC2. 071-379 6344
2D 92 and 3E 3
An evocative collection of buses, trams, trolleybuses and railway rolling stock together with maps, models, working displays, documentation and posters, it tells the story of nearly two centuries of public transport and its impact on the growth of the Capital. Vehicles include a knifeboard horse bus, the 'B' type motor bus, London's first trolley bus and an 'Underground' steam locomotive. *Open 10.00-18.00 daily. Admission charge.*

London Zoo, Regents Park, NW1.
071-722 3333 off 1E 82 and 1C 2
The 'lure of the wild' in the heart of London; a day among the thousands of animals here is a day with a difference. Special attractions include the aquarium, the walk-through Snowdon Aviary, the Nocturnal Hall where day and night are reversed, the Penguin Pool—an essay in delicate curves, the Elephant House—a great concrete fortress. There's a Childrens Zoo and Farm; various rides and animal feedings take place at certain times. *Open March to Oct. 09.00-18.00, (19.00 Sun. & Bank Hols.); Nov. to Feb. 10.00-Dusk. Admission charge.*

Madame Tussauds, Marylebone Road, NW1. 071-935 6861 4D 82 and 2D 2
One of the entertainments of London since 1835, an experience that can be taken as pure fun or considered as an art form. Madame Tussaud came to England in 1802 with life size wax portraits, including death masks of French Revolution victims; her collection soon grew and attained great popularity assuming the stature of an institution. Royalty are well represented—this is as close to the Royal Family as many can hope to get—while the Chambers of Horrors may well be too close to notorious murderers, 'la guillotine' and the gallows. Both historical and contemporary world leaders are represented, royalty, politicians, sportsmen, famous personalities from all walks of life; The 'Battle of Trafalgar' is a set-piece including the lower gun deck of the Victory in action and the dying Nelson. Other set piece exhibitions include a celebrities "Garden Party" and "200 Years" the history of Madame Tussauds. *Open 10.00-17.30 daily, (from 09.00 summer months, from 09.30 winter weekends). Admission charge.*

Mansion House, Bank, EC4. 1D 94 and 3G 3
The official residence of the Lord Mayor of London. A grand classical pile built 1739-53, it contains residential quarters and ceremonial apartments including the renowned Egyptian Hall used for banquets and receptions and also the only Justice Room in a private house. With the *Bank of England* and *Royal Exchange,* it contributes to a trio of porticos around the

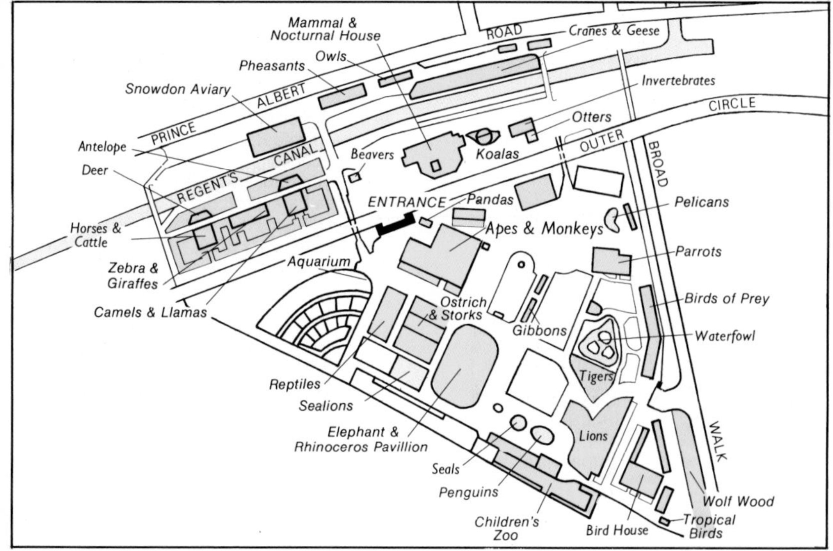

Plan of LONDON ZOO

City's focal point; the business sector 'Piccadilly Circus'.

Marble Arch, W1. 2C 90 and 3C 2
The original gateway to Nash's *Buckingham Palace* for George IV; said to have been modelled on Rome's Arch of Constantinople. Popularly said to have been too narrow for the State Coach, its function was anyway superseded after the 1847 addition of an east wing to the Palace. Subsequently in 1851 re-erected as a gateway to *Hyde Park,* an entrace to nowhere since 1908 when traffic islands were created. A stone on the second island marks TYBURN, where public executions took place for 600 years up to 1783; the condemned travelled in carts through great crowds, along the line of Oxford Street from Newgate Prison, see also *Central Criminal Court.*

Markets
It is at the traditional street market that the Cockney spirit is most accessible, intermingled as it must be in a cosmopolitan city, with a diverse mix of ethnic minorities and tourists. Petticoat Lane 7H 87 and Portobello Rd., 3A 88 are the best known street markets, although the numerous smaller ones serving local communities are equally atmospheric. Central ones include: Berwick Street 3C 37, Leather Lane 1C 14, Brick Lane (including Club Row & Sclater St.) 3J 87, Lambeth Walk 3F 101. Antiques have their own special venues, New Caledonian Market 4H 3, Portobello Rd. 3H 88 and Camden Passage 1G 3 included; Kings Rd. 6A 98, and Kensington High St. 7C 88 have covered antiques 'Supermarkets'. Details of specialities and the best time to visit available from the London Tourist Board. For wholesale markets see *Billingsgate, Covent Garden, Smithfield.*

Mayfair, W1. 3F 91 and 3D 2
'May Fair', once a popular annual event, became so notorious as to merit official closure in 1706; the area so named is now a synonym for High Class—hotels especially on Park Lane 3A 37, and Piccadilly 4B 37, shops on Bond Streets Old and New 3C 37, Audley Streets North and South 3A 37, Mount Street, 3A 37, Burlington Arcade 3C 37, South Molton Street 2B 37. SHEPHERD MARKET 4B 37, a nucleus of narrow alleys crowded with small shops and pavement cafes, retains the character of a bygone age. The wealthy of the 18th century built mansions here among the fields, away from 'City' life, including Burlington House see *Royal Academy,* Crewe House 4B 37, and Bourdon House 3B 37, while many others exist only in name. The Royal Institution, founded 1799 with its FARADAY MUSEUM 071-409 2992 1A 38 can be visited. The embassies and legations of many nationalities are to be found here but the particularly strong ties for Americans via the embassy are ROOSEVELT MEMORIAL 3A 37 and the colonial style GROSVENOR CHAPEL 3B 37 of 1730, adopted by U.S. armed forces during World War II.

SIR WINSTON CHURCHILL:
Parliament Square

Monuments and Statues
As in any Capital city there are a great many statues and monuments in the principal streets, squares and parks. Among the most famous must be listed the *Cenotaph 6C 92;* Eros in *Piccadilly Circus 3A 92* ,Peter Pan in Kensington Gardens 4G 89; Queen Victoria Memorial strategically sited in front of *Buckingham Palace 7H 91;* the *Albert Memorial 7G 89;* Sir Winston Churchill in *Parliament Square 7C 92;* Franklin. D. Roosevelt see *Mayfair 2E 90;* Cleopatras Needle 4E 92, 3500 years old from Heliopolis, set up here in 1878—its twin is in Central Park New York; Nelsons Column see *Trafalgar Square 4B 92 ;* and also aloft on column, the Duke of York 5A 92, whose only command now is a flight of steps linking The Mall and Pall Mall. Perhaps the most monumental is THE MONUMENT 3E 95, designed by Christopher Wren to commemorate the Great Fire of London 1666, being 202 ft. high and 202 ft.from the origin of the fire in Pudding Lane; the stone column contains 311 steps to its eyrie like viewing platform. *Open 09.00-18.00 Mon. to Fri. (14.00-18.00 Sat. & Sun.) Winter months 09.00-16.00 (Closed Sun.). Last admission 20 mins. before close. Admission charge.*
Art sculptures are rare compared with purely representational statues and busts; among the more notable works may be seen-Achilles, Londons first nude statue at Hyde Park Corner 5E 90; in impressive simplicity Nurse Cavell, outside the National Portrait Gallery 3C 92; Charles I at Charing Cross 2C 38; London's oldest (1633) and finest equestrian piece; James II in Roman dress outside the *National Gallery 3B 92;* Abraham Lincoln and Field Marshal Smuts in *Parliament Square 7C 92;* 'Burghers of Calais' by Rodin, Victoria Tower Gardens 2D 100; Prospero and Ariel by Eric Gill, BBC Broadcasting House 6G 83; Jacob Epsteins: 'Rima' and 'Pan' group in Hyde Park 4A 90, 'Madonna' Cavendish Sq. 7G 83; Henry Moores: 'Knife Edge near the Jewel Tower 1C 100, 'Locking Piece' Millbank 5C 100, 'The Arch' Hyde Park 3C 2, 'Draped Figures' Battersea Park 5C 2; Barbara Hepworths: 'Maridian' State House, Holborn 6F 85, 'Family of Man' Hyde Park 3C 2, 'Winged Figure' John Lewis Store, Oxford Street 1G 91.

EROS:
Piccadilly Circus

Museum of Garden History,
St. Mary-at-Lambeth, 071-261 1891 2E 100
A centre for gardeners in honour of the Tradescants, gardeners to the Stuart Kings, and responsible for the introduction of many exotic plants. *Open 11.00-15.00 Mon.-Fri. 10.30-17.00 Sun. March to December. Closed Sat. Admission charge.*

Museum of London, London Wall, EC2. 071-600 3699 6B 86 and 2G 3
One of London's modern purpose-built museums; constructed as part of the *Barbican* it is designed to lead visitors through the chronological development of London and environs from prehistoric times to the present day. The imaginative display and excellence of facilities earned it the Museum of the Year award 1978. Artifacts on display include: Prehistoric weapons and tools; Roman mosaic, sculptures and artifacts of everyday life; Elizabethan jewellery from the Cheapside Hoard; Great Fire of London Room; lock-up doors from Newgate Prison; Lord Mayors State Coach 1757; horse-drawn fire engine 1862; 19th century shop interiors—barber,

chemist, draper, grocer, public house, tobacconist; Selfridges 1928 art deco lifts; Ford's 1936 model Y; a World War II Anderson shelter, and model of the Festival of Britain (1951). *Open 10.00-18.00 Tues. to Sat. 14.00-18.00 Sun. Closed Mondays.*

Museum of Mankind, Burlington Gardens, W1. 071-437 2224 3H 91 and 3D 2
The Museum of Mankind is the gallery of the Ethnography department of the *British Museum;* its displays illustrate aspects of life and origins of the worlds cultures. As only a small amount of the enormous collection can be shown at once, the thematic exhibitions and displays are periodically changed. Certain treasures on permanent show include: Aztec turquoise mosaic work, crystal skull; Javanese shadow puppets; wooden spirit carvings from the Solomon Islands; a Benin bronze figure; a Gabonese dance mask. *Open 10.00-17.00 Mon. to Sat. 14.30-18.00 Sun.*

Museum of the Moving Image, South Bank Arts Centre, SE1. 071-928 3232 4F 93
Devoted to the history and development of cinema, television and video; included displays on pre cinema and future technologies. *Open 10.00-20.00 Tues. to Sat. 10.00-18.00 Sun. Closed Mondays. Admission charge.*

National Army Museum see Chelsea

National Gallery, Trafalgar Square, WC2. 071-839 3321 3B 92 and 3E 3
To experience some of man's finest artistic achievements is but a step from the fountains of *Trafalgar Square.* The gallery covers all the major European artists and movements (arranged under schools), between the 13th and 19th centuries. Having first rubbed out the street grime, your eyes are free to feast on such works as: Leonardo 'Virgin of the Rocks'; the 'Wilton Diptych'; Uccello 'Rout of San Romano'; Piero della Francesca 'Baptism of Christ'; Michelangelo 'The Entombment'; Titian 'Bacchus and Ariadne'; Bellini 'The Doge'; self portraits of Rembrandt; Rubens 'Rape of the Sabines'; Van Dyck 'Charles I'; Canaletto 'Grand Canal'; Van Eyck 'Arnolfini Marriage', Vermeer 'Lady at the Virginals'; Valazquez 'Rokeby Venus'; Turner 'Fighting Temeraire'; Constable 'Salisbury Cathedral'; Van Gogh 'Sunflowers'; Degas 'La Toilette', Monet 'Water-lilies'.
Founded in 1824, the gallery moved here in 1838 into buildings designed by William Wilkins. The portico incorporates columns from Prince Regents Carlton House, demolished 1826 (see *Regent Street).* For modern painting, sculpture and the National Gallery of English Art see *Tate Gallery. Open to 10.00-18.00; 14.00-18.00 Sundays.*

National Maritime Museum see Greenwich

National Portrait Gallery, St. Martins Place, WC2. 071-930 1552 3B 92
The purpose of this gallery being to illustrate British history by focussing on historically significant characters, its paintings—though many are 'great works of art'—are not selected for that reason. The portraits are in chronological order; coins and early copies represent the pre-Tudor monarchs, leading up to the unrivalled collection of 16th century works commissioned by Tudor and Elizabethan sovereigns, their advisors and courtiers. When the 18th century is reached the display divides into two parallel series: one shows rulers, statesmen and men of action; the other great names in art and science. As a general rule—with the exception of Royalty—portraits are not hung within the sitters' life-time. The portraits of Elizabeth II, the Prince and Princess of Wales are particularly subject to intense public scrutiny. *Open 10.00-17.00 Mon. to Fri. 10.00-18.00 Sat. 14.00-18.00 Sun.*

National Postal Museum, King Edward Street, EC1. 071-239 5420 7A 86
Of great interest to philatelic enthusiasts and specialists, are its valuable collections of British and World stamps, special exhibitions, displays covering the stamp printing process and career of Rowland Hill; the archives of Thos De La Rue & Co. who printed stamps for 200 countries between 1855-1965.
Open 09.30-16.30 Mon. to Thurs. 09.30-16.00 Friday. Closed Sat. & Sun.

Natural History Museum, Cromwell Road, SW7. 071-589 6323 2G 97 and 4B 2
One of London's most exciting museums and a far cry from the endless lines of dusty cases image. Display cases and stuffed animals there still are, covering all aspects of natural history, but, interspersed are a series of modern theme displays that invite the visitor to discover the world with recorded sound, slides and diagrammatic explanations; themes include: Dinosaurs and Their Living Relatives, Hall of Human Biology, Man's Place in Evolution, Introducing Ecology, Origin of Species, British Natural History. The traditional displays include a range of exhibits from huge Dinosaurs, Whales and Elephants to tiny birds and insects; also living and fossil plants, minerals, rocks and meteorites. The Children's Centre can provide trail sheets for an indoor nature trail. *Open 10.00-18.00 Mon. to Sat. 11.00-18.00 Sun. Admission charge.*

Old Curiosity Shop, Portsmouth Street, WC2. 1E 93 and 2B 14
A Tudor house, now an antique and souvenir shop, which claims to be the original Dickens

'Old Curiosity Shop'. Dickens certainly drew a lot of inspiration from the vicinity: the *Temple* in 'Martin Chuzzlewit', *Lincolns Inn* in 'Bleak House', Temple Bar as a rendezvous for characters in a number of novels, and here was Telson's Bank in 'Tale of Two Cities' (Child's Bank in real-life, one of the oldest, founded 1671, with Oliver Cromwell, Samuel Pepys, Nell Gwynn and John Dryden among its famous clients). See also *Dickens House.*

Old Royal Observatory see Greenwich

Operating Theatre, Museum and Herb Garrett, 9a St. Thomas' Street, SE1. 071-955 4791 5E 94
An original Victorian operating theatre dating from 1822, together with displays of surgical instruments and medical apparatus. *Open 12.30-16.00 Mon, Wed. and Fri. only. Admission charge.*

Oratory, The, Brompton Road, SW7. 071-589 4811 2J 97 and 4C 2
Also known as Brompton Oratory; a Roman Catholic church served by secular priests of the Institute of the Oratory founded in 16th Century Rome. The church, completed 1884 to designs by Herbert Gribble, is in monumental Italian Baroque style, its dome rising to 200ft. The interior of lavish marble floors, columns and statuary, contains 17th century carvings, an alterpiece from Italy; in the forecourt stands a statue of Cardinal Newman, who introduced the order to England in 1847.

Pageantry.
London's famous daily spectacle is '*Changing the Guard',* a ceremony is performed by the Foot Guards at *Buckingham Palace* daily 11.30 (alternate days in winter); at *Windsor Castle* daily 11.00; and by the Household Cavalry at *Horse Guards* daily 11.00 (Sundays 10.00). Another daily historic event is the 'Ceremony of the Keys' at the *Tower of London.* To see this it is necessary to apply for tickets to the Resident Governor, H. M. Tower of London, EC3. Glimpses of great annual events can be seen in JUNE—'Trooping the Colour' takes place at *Horse Guards;* JUNE/JULY—'Royal Tournament' at Earls Court; OCTOBER—Opening of the *Royal Courts of Justice;* NOVEMBER—Lord Mayors Show, Remembrance Sunday and State Opening of Parliament.
Royal Salutes are fired for Royal births and birthdays, and the accession of Sovereigns; salutes are also fired for important events and the visits of foreign Royalty—fired in Hyde Park by The Kings Troop, Royal Horse Artillery; at the Tower of London by the Honourable Artillery Company.

Parliament Square, SW1. 7C 92 and 4E 3
The Heart of *Westminster;*as with *Downing Street* there is often a feeling of expectancy here with crowds peering for official cars that swish to and from *Whitehall.* Around the Square are the *Houses of Parliament, Westminster Abbey,* St. Margarets Church, the old Middlesex Guildhall and blocks of government offices. Within the square, laid out c1868 on completion of the Houses of Parliament and re-laid for the 1951 Festival of Britain, can be seen a good range of statues among them—Winston Churchill, Abraham Lincoln, Field Marshall Smuts, Benjamin Disraeli, Robert Peel, Viscount Palmerston and the Earl of Derby.

Percival David Foundation of Chinese Art, University of London, 53 Gordon Sq. WC1. 071-387 3909 3D 84 & 2E 3
Open 10.00-17.00 Mon. to Fri.

Piccadilly and Piccadilly Circus, W1. 4H 91 & 4A 92
Piccadilly links two important junctions. At the western extremity is HYDE PARK CORNER 6E 91 with its sometimes alarming confusion of traffic and imposing architecture, including *Apsley House,* Decimus Burtons' great screen of columns, both c. 1828, and Wellington Arch, the latter surmounted by the Quadriga group by A. Jones, 1912 in memory of Edward VII. At the eastern end is PICCADILLY CIRCUS 4A 92 a swirl of people, traffic and coloured lights; this the focal point of London is emerging from a much needed modernisation, including the creation of a pedestrian piazza linking the famous EROS (memorial to Earl of Shaftesbury, 1893), to the Criterion side. Linking the two nodes, PICCADILLY itself forms the elite address for a procession of names that speak for themselves—hotels like The Ritz and Park Lane; clubs like Royal Air Force and American; stores like Fortnum & Mason and Simpsons. The Green Park railings are often utilized as an open-air art market.

Planetarium: See London Planetarium

Public Record Office and Museum, Chancery Lane, WC2. 081-876 3444 ext. 2258 1G 93 and 2F 3
Established in 1838 to provide both accommodation for, and management of, the National Archives accumulated since the Norman Conquest; and providing facilities for their use by members of the public; (Modern records are at Ruskin Av. Kew 081-876 3444 ext. 2350). Readers tickets on application to the secretary; reading rooms *open 9.30-17.00 Mon. to Fri. last call for documents 15.30.*
You can't get much closer to the nub of English

PICCADILLY CIRCUS

history than in a visit to the MUSEUM here, where the best known exhibit—Doomsday Book, is a tempting hors d'oeuvre for other fascinating exhibits; versions of Magna Carta dated 1225 and 1297; the earliest surviving Exchequer Pipe Roll (revenue accounts) dated 1129-30; Chancery Rolls from 1199 onwards; records of Parliament; Royal seals and charters; naval and military documents and treaties; letters by the famous and infamous from Medieval times to the 19th century; autographs of Sovereigns from Richard II to Elizabeth II. MUSEUM *Open 10.00-17.00 Mon. to Fri.*

Queens Gallery, Buckingham Palace Road, SW1. 071-799 2331 7G 91 and 4D 2
Built on the site of Royal Chapel destroyed by a World War II bomb, this tiny gallery is devoted to one of the largest and most valuable art collections—the Royal Collection. Works pooled from the various palaces and castles form thematic exhibitions of great interest, with custodians in Royal livery adding to the lustre. *Open (except during changes of exhibition) 10.30-17.00 Tues. to Sat. 14.00-17.00 Sun. Admission charge.*

Queen's House see Greenwich

Regents Park, NW1. 1C 82 and 1C 2
Some 40 acres of fine parkland containing tree-lined walks and flower displays; a large lake for yachting and rowing; Queen Mary's Gardens, famous for its rose and rockery layouts; an open-air theatre (summer performances of Shakespeare); children's boating pond and playground; refreshment pavilions, and *London Zoo.* Along its northern boundary, interesting boat trips and towpath walks are provided by Regents Canal; Primrose Hill gives the only natural vantage point for a close-up panoramic view of the Capital. This Royal Park was laid out in Regency times to the designs of John Nash (as part of his grand *Regent Street* development scheme) with its surround of elegant terraces and villas-some of his finest architectural work to survive. In keeping with them, are two interesting modern buildings, the Royal College of Physicians and the London Central Mosque.

Regent Street, W1 and SW1. 1C 91 and 3D 2
Planned and constructed from 1811 onwards by John Nash, under the commission of Prince Regent to create a grand and fashionable route between Carlton House and the new *Regents Park;* its high standard of grace and refinement are now reflected in its many quality stores, china, jewellery and fashion retailers. Nash's genius for grandiose layout and bold application of the clasical motif remain at their best in The Quadrant; All Souls Church; Regents Park terraces and crescent; Carlton House Terrace. The latter was constructed following the demolition of Carlton House 1826, leading to Nash redesigning *Buckingham Palace* (for the Regent by now George IV); creating the informal *St James's Park,* and as a by-product, one of London's most ethereal views: down Lower Regent

from *Piccadilly Circus* over the tree tops to the towers and pinnacles of *Westminster.*

Restaurants
There are restaurants in London offering most of the world's national cuisines; and the areas most densely served are *Mayfair, Soho, Covent Garden, Chelsea* and Fulham. Weekly entertainment guides can be a help to the uninitiated. There are traditional English restaurants where meat is carved at the table; many serve classic foreign menus with national costume and ambience to match; others specialise in types of food—seafood, health food; or are housed in historic buildings; you can eat at a Medieval banquet, Victorian Music Hall, theatre / restaurant with sophisticated entertainment, in a renowned hotel or in a boat on the *River Thames.* 'Quick-food' restaurants can be found on most principal shopping streets.

River Thames, River Boat Information Service 071-730-4812.
The River Thames is London's principal natural feature giving fine visual settings for many of the Capital's great buildings, and provides an ideal tree-lined promenade for walks or boating trips. *Tower Bridge Walkway* has perhaps the most dramatic river views; the historic *H.M.S. Belfast* may be visited; there are restaurant ships like the T.S. Queen Mary nr. Waterloo Bridge 3E 93, some river cruises include meals, others ply beyond Greenwich to the THAMES BARRIER 2D 43, a unique structure with enormous, movable steel gates, constructed to prevent the flooding of central London during abnormal weather and tidal conditions; on the south bank the Thames Barrier Centre has an exhibition and viewing platform. 081-854 1373 *Open 10.35-17.00 daily. Admission charge.* Historically the Thames was London's 'main road' used as a means of easy local transportation when roads were poor, dangerous, or non-existent; and at the same time linking the City directly with the world's other ports. The introduction of the 16th century coach marked the beginning of the end for the Watermen and their wherries; and the size of modern ships and container systems has removed the Port of London Authority's activities to Tilbury. See also Docklands.

Royal Academy of Arts, Burlington House, Piccadilly, W1. 071-439 7438 3H 91 and 3D 2
This, our leading independent art institution, is famous for its Summer Exhibition held annually May to August, of works by living artists. Throughout the rest of the year special exhibitions are mounted of artistic and historical significance. The academy, founded in 1768 under the patronage of George III, did not move here until 1869; Sir Joshua Reynolds—whose statue is in the forecourt—was its first president. Many other famous artists have passed through the Royal Academy Schools including Turner, Constable and Millais. Old Burlington House was the town house of the Earls of Burlington (see also *Chiswick House).* the 3rd Earl being responsible for the present building constructed 1715. The massive chunk of 19th century wings and Piccadilly frontage house several learned institutes and societies and create a tranquil courtyard at the centre of *West End* bustle. *Open 10.00-18.00 daily. Admission charge.*

Royal Albert Hall, Kensington Gore, SW7. 071-589 8212 7G 89 and 4B 2
A huge concert hall capable of holding 8000 people and the venue for the famous Promenade Concerts founded in 1895 by Henry Wood. Built 1867-71 at the inspiration of Prince Albert, its design in the form of a glass-domed amphitheatre, decorated externally by a terracotta frieze illustrating the Arts and Sciences, is of a simplicity in striking contrast to the ornate *Albert Memorial* opposite. The 'Proms' are held annually July to September; throughout the rest of the year, a wide variety of concerts, sporting events, and conferences take place here.

Royal Courts of Justice, Strand, WC2. 071-936 6000 1F 93 and 3F 3
A colossal Victorian-Gothic building, bristling with towers, pinnacles and pointed arches constructed 1874-82 to house the Supreme Court of Judicature. Its main feature is a central hall of cathedral-like proportions where display cases hold Daily Cause Lists—details of cases, courts and judges; there is free access to public galleries. Courts usually sit 10.30-16.30 on Weekdays. Prior to the 19th century, Courts of Justice sat in *Westminster Hall* having done so since the 12th century. There are a number of interesting ceremonies at the beginning of Michaelmas Term. (1) the Opening of the Law Courts which is preceded by a breakfast at the House of Lords and a special service at *Westminster Abbey,* both attended by Her Majesty's Judges and Queen's Council. (2) The newly elected Lord Mayor of London in a resplendent coach on the last leg of the Lord Mayors Show, arrives to be sworn in. (3) Quit Rents Ceremonies: probably London's oldest remaining custom is the payment of six horseshoes for a smithy plot in the parish of St Clement Danes recorded in a Pipe Roll of 1235 (see also *Public Record*

Office)-horseshoes and nails are still paid ceremoniously by the City Solicitor to the Queen's Remembrancer; at the same time, dating from the 16th century, a payment of an axe and billhook (the former having first been tested for sharpness on a bundle of faggots), is paid for a piece of land, 'The Moors' in Shropshire.

Royal Exchange, Cornhill, EC3. 1E 94 and 3G 2
Standing sentinel-like opposite the *Bank of England,* the large Corinthian portico is the public face of the third Royal Exchange to occupy this site; designed by William Tite and opened in 1844, its glass domed quadrangle now houses a financial exchange. The original exchange, set up here by Thomas Gresham in 1564, assumed the prefix 'Royal' after a visit by Elizabeth I in 1571. Following the Great Fire 1666, a second exchange was completed 1670 and subsequently burnt down in 1838. The 180ft campanile is surmounted by a gilded vane in the shape of a grasshopper—the Gresham family crest.

Royal Festival Hall, South Bank, SE1. 071-928 3002 5F 93 and 3F 3
The highly praised acoustics here have established this hall among the world's leading concert venues; performances are held throughout the year by the leading orchestras of Britain and overseas; the Festival Ballet; and international entertainers. It was specially constructed for the 1951 Festival of Britain but an improved and enlarged river frontage was added in1962-5. The wide tree-lined riverside promenade links with the Queen Elizabeth Hall, Purcell Room, Hayward Gallery, National Theatre, National Film Theatre and the rest of *South Bank;* and, via the footbridge, the *West End.*

Royal Hospital Chelsea see Chelsea

Royal Mews, Buckingham Palace Road, SW1. 1G 99 and 4D 2
The only annex of *Buckingham Palace,* besides the *Queens Gallery,* open to the public. Here in the palace stable block, it is possible to inspect the Royal horses and equipage: the State Coach designed for George III in 1762 by William Chambers and used for Coronations; the Glass State Coach bought by George V in 1910 and used in Royal weddings; the Irish State Coach bought by Queen Victoria in 1852 and used for the State Opening of Parliament. *Open Wed. and Thurs. 14.00-16.00. Admisson charge. (Not open Royal Ascot week).*

Royal Naval College see Greenwich

Royal Opera House, Bow Street, Covent Garden, WC2. 071-240 1911 1D 92 and 3E 3
Home of the Royal Opera and Royal Ballet companies who, in conjunction with famous international artistes, perform here throughout the year. The interior is of lush decoration in white, gold and deep crimson, and there are displays of memorabilia connected with historic performances and performers. The Opera House, also known as Covent Garden Theatre, is the third to occupy the site, and was not devoted to opera until 1847. The first building lasted from 1732 to 1808, the second 1808 to 1856, both being destroyed by fire. The present structure built 1856-8 incorporates Flaxman and Rossi sculptured panels in the portico from the previous building.

St. James's, SW1. 4A 92
St. James's still retains much of its 17th century exclusiveness and although no longer a community of courtiers and Royal hangers-on, is famous for gentleman's discreet clubs, high-class retailers, art and antique galleries. Brooks's, Boodle's, and White's on St James's Street are among those clubs to have originated as coffee houses, and were once notorious centres of 'society' gambling; the Athenaeum, Reform, and Travellers on Pall Mall are other eminent clubs. St James's Street and Jermyn Street are the address of bespoke makers of hats, shirts, shoes and boots; of Berry Bros & Rudd, wine merchants established in the 17th century; of Paxton & Whitfield renowned purveyors of cheese and provisions. The development of St. James's Fields was begun by Henry Jermyn soon after the restoration of Charles II in 1660, and many fashionable houses were built on his layout of streets around the spacious St. James's Square. Pall Mall is a derivative of 'pell mell', then a popular croquet-like game played here prior to 1662, when the route was paved to become the main approach to *St James's Palace* at the instigation of the King, who wished to remove interference from his own Royal pell mell alley (now The Mall). Those houses between Pall Mall and The Mall became the most sought after, their gardens overlooking *St James's Park* —John Evelyn disapprovingly noted in his 1671 diary that the King chatted to Nell Gwyn over her garden wall.

St James's Palace, Pall Mall, SW1. 6J 91
A Royal Palace since the 16th century when Henry VIII decided to build here, and, following the loss of the palace at *Whitehall* in 1698, it remained the chief London palace until the accession of Queen Victoria 1837. Foot

Guards are maintained on sentry duty, and foreign ambassadors are still accredited to the Court of St James. It is from here that the Royal Proclamation 'the King is dead, long live the King' is made after the death of a Monarch. Many Kings and Queens have been born or have died here, or have been married in the Chapel Royal. The Queen's Chapel, added 1623-7 to designs by Inigo Jones, was the private chapel of Charles I's Queen Henrietta Maria and Charles II's Queen Catherine of Braganza; Charles I spent his last night here January 1649 before walking across *St James's Park* to the *Banqueting House* and his execution.

A stroll round the courtyards can reveal glimpses of name plates of official residences and 'The Queen's Body Guard of the Yeoman of the Guard'. The Yeoman of the Guard ('Beefeaters', formed in 1485 by Henry VII) and Gentlemen at Arms (also here and formed in 1509 by Henry VIII) together comprise the Sovereigns dismounted bodyguard at State ceremonies; their uniforms are unmistakable: the former in Tudor style red emblazoned with gold and purple, the latter with white plumed helmets, white gauntlets and black boots. 1485 marks the beginning of the history of the British Army as told in the *National Army Museum*—the date of the last battle of the Wars of the Roses, when Henry VII defeated the Yorkist Richard III at the Battle of Bosworth, thereby beginning the Tudor monarchy.

St James's Park, SW1. 6A 92 and 4E 3
First enclosed by Henry VIII to provide a deer park to his Royal residences. Charles II, commissioning the French landscape gardener Le Notre to create a formal park around a central canal, turned it into a fashionable rendezvous. The present layout of charming 'naturalistic' parkland, walks and lake, the work of John Nash for George IV, date from 1827, see *Regent Street.* Duck Island is a bird sanctuary with many species of duck, geese and even pelicans; bandstand and refreshment pavilion are summer bonuses, but the much recorded views towards *Whitehall* and *Westminster* are all year round, a delight to the eye.

St Katharine's Dock,
St. Katharine-by-the-Tower, E1. 4J 95 and 3H 3
This, one of London's first free trade docks, was built in 1827 on the site of the former Hospital of St Katharine which dated back to the 10th century. Its massive and secure warehouses designed by Thomas Telford were the first such to be built in London for storing valuable cargoes from all over the world. There are now restaurants and a shopping mall, the whole complex is finished with cobbled promenades and period detailing, and focuses on a 240 mooring yacht haven

St. Martin in the Fields, Trafalgar Square. WC2.
071-930 1862 3C 92 and 1C 36
This historic church rebuilt by James Gibbs 1721-61 is famous as a landmark in Trafalgar Square, for its work with the homeless and for its concerts. Visit the Visitor's Centre, Bookshop, Fields Restaurant, Courtyard Craft

ST. JAMES'S PARK: looking towards Whitehall

market and Brass Rubbing Centre.
Open Daily. See also Trafalgar Square.

St Paul's Cathedral, St Paul's Churchyard, EC4. 071-248 2705 1B 94 and 3G 3
The *City of London's* most magnificent landmark, and, although no longer commanding the skyline as it did prior to the construction of tower blocks, the sheer boldness of its huge dome and great double columned west front are memorable. Christopher Wren's Cathedral, built 1675-1710, captures the peculiarly English trait of compromise, combining Gothic precedent and new ideals, while balancing large scale forms with human scale detail.
The cavernous octagonal intersection between nave, choir and transepts forms the internal focal point, and here, 100ft above the floor, is the famous Whispering Gallery, where whispers against the wall on one side can be heard near the wall opposite. You can ascend higher still; at the dome's balustrade level 182ft high, the Stone Gallery gives a good panoramic view over London; and, for the more adventurous, it is possible to go on up to the Golden Gallery at 281 ft, via open metal stairs between the inner and outer domes. Many other notable features include: choir stalls and organ case carved by Grinling Gibbons, ironwork by Jean Tijou, Wren's own model for his cathedral in the crypt, where there is also an exhibition of diocesan treasures; monuments to, and tombs of many famous people. Wren himself was the first person to be buried here and his simple black marble tomb carries the inscription 'Reader, if you seek his monument, look around you'. St Paul's is the seat of the Bishopric of London, and Parish Church of the Commonwealth; it is the third cathedral on the site, the first possibly dated from the ordination of Millitus by St Augustine c.604; the second, an elaborate Gothic structure, was largely destroyed in the Great Fire 1666. The last stone of Wren's building—the master being then aged 78—was placed on top of the lantern by his son.
Open 07.30-18.00 daily. East end, Crypt and Galleries 10.00-16.15 Mon. to Fri. (Sat. from 11.00); Closed Sun; Admission charges. Visiting subject to restrictions during services.

Science Museum, Exhibition Road, SW7. 071-938 8000 2H 97 and 4B 2
Here many hundreds of exhibits, supplemented by working models and reconstructions are displayed to illustrate a history of science and technology, the development of engineering, transport and important industries from their earliest beginnings. In the motive power and transportation section, exhibits include: beam engines; early locomotives 'Puffing Billy' and 'Rocket'; horse-drawn and steam vehicles; early petrol motor cars; cycles like the 'Boneshaker' and 'Penny-farthing', models of sailing and steam ships. In aeronautics, the aircraft used by Alcock and Brown on the first direct trans-Atlantic flight 1919, and the experimental vertical take- off 'Flying-Bedstead' 1954. In Space Exploration, satellites, Apollo 10 re-entry capsule, simulated lunar-scape with landing craft. In Power Production, waterwheel to nuclear

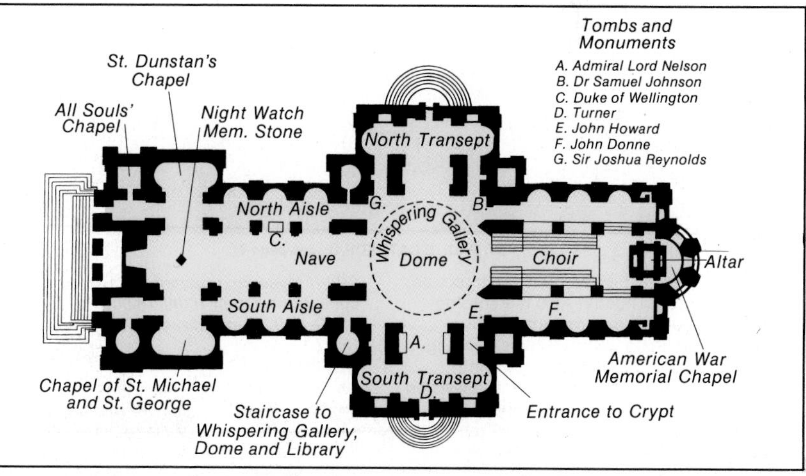

Plan of ST. PAUL'S CATHEDRAL

ST. PAUL'S CATHEDRAL: see page 27

power. In medical history, 1905 Pharmacy and 1980 Operating Theatre. Also meteorology, astronomy, time measurement, physics; metallurgy, mining, glass, textiles, printing and agricultural industries; typewriting; photography; telecommunications; television, radio, radar and so on. The Science Museum, established in 1909, stemmed from the South Kensington Museum (instigated by Prince Albert following the success of his 1851 Great Exhibition) and which, renamed the *Victoria & Albert Museum,* retained the art and craft collections. *Open 10.00-18.00 Mon. to Sat. 11.00-18.00 Sun. Admission charge.*

Scotland Yard

This name, so long associated with the police, is thought to derive from a former palace on N.E. side of *Whitehall* used by Scottish Kings when in London. Following the union of the Crowns by the accession of James 1st.,(James VI of Scotland) the site became offices destined in the 19th century to become the HQ of the Metropolitan Police. A purpose-built block, constructed with granite excavated by Dartmoor convicts, in the Scottish baronial style, to designs by Norman Shaw, was completed in 1891, overlooking the then new Victoria Embankment 3D 38; 'New Scotland Yard' became world famous through countless detective stories, particularly Arthur Conan Doyle's 'Sherlock Holmes' (see Sherlock Holmes Museum). In 1967, however, Police H.Q. moved from there to a new tower block in Broadway, SW1. 4B 38

Shakespeare Globe Museum, 1 Bear Gardens, SE1 071-928 6342 42 94 and 3G 3
Permanent exhibition of Shakespearean theatre and Bankside history. Nearby the International Shakespeare Centre and Globe Theatre are under construction.
Open 10.00-17.00 Mon. to Sat. 13.30-17.30 Sun. Admission charge.

Sherlock Holmes Museum, 221b Baker Street NW1 071-935 8866 4C 82
Portrays the life and times of Sherlock Holmes and Dr Watson as portrayed by Sir Arthur Conan Doyle. *Open 10.00-18.00 daily. Admission charge.*

Shopping, *see pages 65 to 80*
The vast range of shopping in London is a magnet for overseas visitors and day-trippers alike; from the rush of Oxford Street 3D 2, the more refined Knightsbridge 4C 2, to the very selectness of Bond Street, and Burlington Arcade 3C 35, there is something for everyone. Here are the main areas and principal stores: WEST END Oxford St. 3D 2 (Marks & Spencer, Selfridges, Debenhams, D.H. Evans, John Lewis, Top Shop, British Home Stores, C & A); Regent Street 3D 2 (Aquascutum, Dickins & Jones, Liberty, Hamleys, Chinacraft); Piccadilly 3D 2 (Simpsons, Fortnum & Mason); Charing Cross Road 3E 3 (Foyles); Haymarket 3E 3 (Burberrys); New and Old Bond Street 3D 2 (Fenwick, Saint Laurent, Asprey & Co, Gucci, Cartier, White House); Tottenham Court Road 2E 3 (Heals, Habitat, Maples, Laskys). KNIGHTSBRIDGE 4C 2 (Harrods, Harvey Nichols); Brompton Road 4C 2 (Waring & Gillow) Sloane Street 4c 2 (Jaeger). CHELSEA Kings Road 5B 2 (Peter Jones, Habitat, Reject Shop). KENSINGTON HIGH STREET 4A 2 (Barkers, Marks & Spencer, British Home Stores). COVENT GARDEN 3E 3 where in the wake of the departed wholesale market, a lively mix of small shops and boutiques have joined long established names.

Sir John Soane's Museum, Lincoln's Inn Fields, WC2. 071-405 2107 7E 85 and 2F 3
One of the smaller yet most remarkable of London's museums, it houses the personal collection of the architect John Soane 1753-1837, as displayed by him. The house is his own unique design, incorporating many of his individual ideas on the use of space, scale, proportion and mirrored surfaces. The contents include: Soanes furniture and library with his valuable collection of architectural drawings; antiquities, casts and sculpture. The sarcophagus of Pharaoh Seti I c.1370 B C purchased by Soane following the *British*

Shopping In BURLINGTON ARCADE

Museum's lack of interest; Roman architectural and sculpture fragments; Gothic fragments and casts; fragments from the old Palace of Westminster. Paintings by Turner, Canaletto and Watteau, while the Picture Room with its hinged walls, reveals William Hogarth's renowned 'Rakes Progress' and 'The Election'. *Open 10.00-17.00 Tues. to Sat.*

Smithfield, EC1. 6A 86 and 2G 3
Once known as 'smoothfield', famous for tournaments; St Bartholomews Fair (until 1840); horse and livestock markets (until 1855); and also a place of executions, burning of religious martyrs at the stake, of the murder of Wat Tyler struck down by the Lord Mayor—ending the 1381 Peasant's Revolt. 'London Central Market or 'SMITHFIELD MARKET' for dead meats opened in 1869; this vast market covering 10 acres has been suffering a decline in trade over many years although some of the bustling market atmosphere remains. There is much else of interest in close proximity: Rahere the court jester to Henry II, founded an Augustinian Priory here in 1123 of which the now famous ST BARTHOLOMEWS HOSPITAL 2A 11 formed part, with St Bartholomew the Great 1A 11 as the priory church, while St Bartholomew the Less 2A 11 founded c. 1150, is both the parish and hospital church. Another priory (Carthusian) founded nearby in the 14th century, became in 1611, the site of CHARTERHOUSE 4A 86; initially a hospital for poor brethren and school for poor boys, this grew into the famous public school, removed to Godalming in 1872. ST JOHN'S GATE, 4J 85 built 1504, is a remnant of the 12th century priory of the Knights Hospitallers of St John, founded as a chivalrous order to help pilgrims en-route to Jeruslalem, and revived in 1831 as the Order of St John-now widely known for its hospital and ambulance work. The Museum of the Order of St. John has the most comprehensive collection of relics of the medieval order outside Malta. *Open 10.00-17.00 daily, to 16.00 Sat. Closed Sun. Tours of the Gate and Norman Crypt Tue., Fri. & Sat.*

Soho, W1. 1A 92 and 3E 3
Though long associated with the 'naughty' side of life, this is a far more interesting district than that. Many of the 18th and 19th century houses have associations with famous men; William Blake, Burke, Canaletto, Chopin, Dryden, Haydn and Marx among them. Wren's church, ST ANNE SOHO 3D 37 was destroyed by World War II bombs, leaving only the 19th century steeple, but the churchyard has interesting epitaphs including those to William Hazlitt and Theodore, King of Corsica (d-1830). Wardour Street 1A 92 is a film industry centre, and nearby is Berwick Street Market 3C 37, one of the best in central London. Refugees from many countries have settled here: Greeks; Chinese-Gerrard Street 2B 92 is the High Street of 'china town'; Italians; but most notably French: both Protestant and Catholic French churches and a 'French Pub' the York Minster. A chef of Napoleon III is said to have opened a restaurant here and French restaurants now abound, along with Italian and Chinese; all helping to emphasize the multi-national atmosphere. If you are still unable to resist temptation, and willing to risk the morbid boredom of sex shows, you will never be short of company.

Somerset House, Strand, WC2. 2E 93 and 3F 3
(For Courtauld Institue Galleries see above).
Like a huge palace around a central quad, Somerset House was built 1776-86 to designs by William Chambers; the 800ft river frontage, in monumental Palladian style supported on rusticated arches, stands four-square, anchor like, in contrast to the elegant ocean liner lines of the modern National Theatre on the opposite bank of the *River Thames.* It is occupied by official offices as is the extra west wing added 1851-6, while the east wing of 1829-34 is the home of Kings College. The site was once that of a real palace, begun by the Duke of Somerset, Lord Protector of Edward VI; later occupants included Elizabeth I and the Queens by marriage, of James I, Charles I and Charles II.

South Bank, SE1.
An embankment stroll here affords first-class views of the river scene, links a number of interesting places, besides following a section of the SILVER JUBILEE WALKWAY,an eleven mile circular route around central London, created 1977 to commemorate Queen Elizabeth II's Silver Jubilee. LAMBETH PALACE 2E 100, the London residence of Archbishops of Canterbury for over 700 years, contains medieval and later buildings housing a fine collection of portraits and an important theological library (open only by appt.). Adjacent is ST MARY at LAMBETH; formerly parish church and now a *Museum of Garden History.* COUNTY HALL 6E 92, former HQ of LCC and GLC, dates from 1922. JUBILEE GARDENS 6E 92, established 1977, are on the site of the 1951 Festival of Britain, of which, the *Royal Festival Hall* and National Film Theatre are our principal legacy, forming, together with the Queen Elizabeth Hall, Purcell Room, Hayward Gallery of 1967 and National Theatre of 1976, the SOUTH BANK ARTS

CENTRE 4F 93; see the panoramic view—*Houses of Parliament* to *St Paul's Cathedral*-from a terrace of the Queen Elizabeth Hall. Further east are Bankside and Southwark see *Southwark Cathedral, HMS Belfast, Tower Bridge & Walkway.* Near GUY'S HOPSPITAL 6D 94 are *the macabre London Dungeon, Operating Theatre Museum, and George Inn,* London's only surviving 18th century galleried coaching hostelry. Bankside is an area associated with Elizabethan Theatre, in particular Shakespeare's Globe, and being outside the City jurisdiction with 16th century London low-life—stewes, bear and bull baiting rings, see the *Shakespeare Globe Museum.*

South Kensington see Kensington

Southwark Cathedral, Southwark High Street, SE1. 071-407 2939 4C 94 and 3G 3
Do not be put off by the railway lines, sheds of Borough Market, or the fact that this has been a Cathedral only since 1905; there are many interesting things to see here and the choir, built c. 1220, is perhaps the finest example in London of the simple grace of Early English Gothic architecture. The site dates back to a Saxon nunnery dissolved 852; this was followed by a Norman church built by Augustinian Canons, rebuilt in Gothic style after a fire in 1207, the Nave again being rebuilt in the 1890's, though, kept in harmony with the original. Among the many interesting monuments to survive are those to John Gower friend of Chaucer; Shakespeare and his brother, the latter being buried here. See the Harvard Chapel, restored with money donated by Harvard University in memory of John Harvard, its founder, baptised here in 1607. *Open daily.*

Sports
'Sport for all' a motto of the Sports Council, well describes sport in London. The main sports venues are: WEMBLEY STADIUM 1B 43 built for the 1924-5 British Empire Exhibition and scene of the 1948 Olympics, now of FA and League Football Cup Finals, Rugby League Finals, International Football, Hockey and Speedway; WEMBLEY ARENA: formerly Empire Pool, venue for Badminton, Basketball, Covered Court Tennis, Cycling, Gymnastics and Ice Hockey Championships, also Show Jumping and Ice Show Spectaculars. NATIONAL SPORTS CENTRE, Crystal Palace 3C 43, National and International Athletics, Basketball, Gymnastics and Swimming. RUGBY UNION GROUND Twickenham 2B 43, Internationals and many important matches. WIMBLEDON 2C 43, All England Club, Amateur Lawn Tennis Championships-the annual 'Wimbledon Fortnight' (although the Wimbledon *Lawn Tennis Museum* here, is open regularly all the year).
To augment local sports facilities provided both in Borough Parks and Royal Parks, many multi-sports centres have been built to cater for growing public participation, among them: Sobel Sports Centre, Swiss Cottage Sports Centre, Chelsea Manor Sports Centre, Harrow Leisure Centre and the National Sports Centre Crystal Palace. LEE VALLEY PARK 1C 43 a 23 mile long regional development offers extensive leisure and sports facilities including Banbury Sailing Centre, Broxbourne Lido, Eastway Sports Centre and Cycle Circuit, Lea Bridge Riding Centre, Picketts Lock Sports Centre and Springfield Marina together with County Parks, working farms, camp and caravan sites and country walks.
IMPORTANT SPORTS EVENTS: include League Football games leading up to the FA Cup Final at Wembley; County Cricket matches interspersed with Test Matches at The Oval 5F 3 and Lords 1B 2, Oxford v Cambridge Boat Race; the London Marathon; London to Brighton Walk; Henley Royal Regatta; Wimbledon Fortnight; Horse Race meetings at Ascot 3A 43 (Royal Ascot week), Epsom 3B 43 (The Derby), Kempton Park 3B 43, Sandown Park 3B 43, Royal International Horse Show and Horse of the Year Show at Wembley; details of these and other events are available from the London Visitor & Convention Bureau.

Staple Inn, Holborn, WC2. 5G 85
Remarkable survival of a 16th century 'black and white' timber building, vividly described by Dickens in 'Edwin Drood', and home of his Mr Grewgious; also in real life of Dr Johnson 1759-60. Formerly one of the nine Inns of Chancery—lesser Inns entered by Law students before passing on to one of the Inns of Court ie *Grays Inn, Lincolns Inn,* Inner or Middle *Temple.*

Stock Exchange, Old Broad Street, EC2. 071-588 2355 1E 94 and 3H 3
The London Market for stocks and shares.

Tate Gallery, Millbank, SW1. 071-821 1313 4C 100 and 5E 3
Houses the National Collection of British Painting, and modern painting and sculpture, both British and Foreign, from the Impressionists to the present day. The gallery is particularly rich in paintings by Turner, (in the purpose built Clore Gallery), water-colours, drawings and prints by William Blake, and works by the Pre-Raphaelites. Special exhibitions and retrospectives are

mounted. The gallery stems from the bequest of works by the sculptor Francis Chantrey in 1841; later bequests include that of Henry Tate, who also financed the original building opened in 1897. *Open 10.00-17.50, Sun. 14.00-17.50*

Telecom Tower, Howland Street, W1. 5H 83 and 2D 2
That aerial bedecked metal and glass column soaring over the *West End* is 620 ft. high. Formerly called the Post Office Tower, it was built to facilitate telecommunications without interference from other high buildings.

Temple, EC4. 2G 83 and 3C 14
One of London's most evocative experiences —a complex of quiet squares and courts, of quaint corners, and a feeling of exploring a private world; which is indeed the case; for the precincts comprising two Inns of Court, Inner Temple and Middle Temple, are private property although freely accessible to pedestrians.
Although land was let to lawyers and their students as early as the 14th century, this continued between the 12th and 16th centuries as the property first of the Knights Templars, then of Knights Hospitallers of St John (see St John's Gate *Smithfield).* Direct link to these early times is TEMPLE CHURCH, one of the few remaining round churches in England—the circular nave, dedicated 1185 in the presence of Henry II and his court, being built for the Knights Templars in imitation of the Church of the Holy Sepulchre in Jerusalem. The interior, including that of the chancel, added c. 1240, is well restored after serious World War II bomb damage; there are important 12th and 13th century tomb effigies and a 1682 reredos by Wren. Inner Temple Hall crypt survives from the 14th century, MIDDLE TEMPLE HALL with its elaborate double hammerbeam roof, was opened in 1576 by Elizabeth I. *Open 10.00-12.00, 15.00-16.00 Mon. to Fri.* Both Inns have important legal libraries. (see also *Grays Inn, Lincolns Inn).*
TEMPLE BAR 2C 14, has been the western boundary of the *City of London* from Medieval times, and was until 1878 the site of a gateway. The last gate, by Wren, erected in 1666, is now in Theobalds Park, Waltham Cross 1C 42, but from its Fleet Street site rises a griffin surmounted monument.

Theatre Museum, Russell Street, WC2. 071-836 7891 2D 92
History of the theatre from Elizabethan times to the present including Opera, Ballet, Music Hall, Pantomine and Pop. *Open 11.00-19.00 Tues. to Sun. Admission charge.*

Tower Bridge and **Tower Bridge Walkway,** SE1. 071-407 0922 4H 95 and 3H 3
These dramatic twin towers and drawbridge roadway are one of Londons famous visual landmarks (sometimes confused in name with *London Bridge);* built 1886-94, in Victorian

TOWER BRIDGE

Gothic style to designs by Horace Jones and John Barry. TOWER BRIDGE WALKWAY at 142ft above the Thames, provides a perfect Panoramic view-point, while the small exhibition includes some of the original hydraulic machinery. *Open 10.00-18.30, to 16.45 winter (last ticket 45 mins. earlier). Admission charge.*

Tower of London, EC3. 071-709 0765 3H 95 and 3H 3
Encased within these walls and towers are 900 years of history significant to both London and England—its precincts the haunt of many historically romantic ideas and past gruesome inhumanities; in fact the Tower of London fires the imagination of so many, that it would seem to have a magnetic quality, creating long queues at peak times during the summer. There are certain features so well known as hardly to need mentioning: the CROWN JEWELS housed in the Jewel House (closed February for cleaning); the BLOODY TOWER; the important and dazzling collections of arms and armour; Yeomen Warders, popularly known as Beefeaters; the Ravens; the

CROWN JEWELS: Tower of London

execution block reserved for Royal and noble persons, but there are many others: The great Norman Keep or WHITE TOWER, with its perfect little self contained church called the

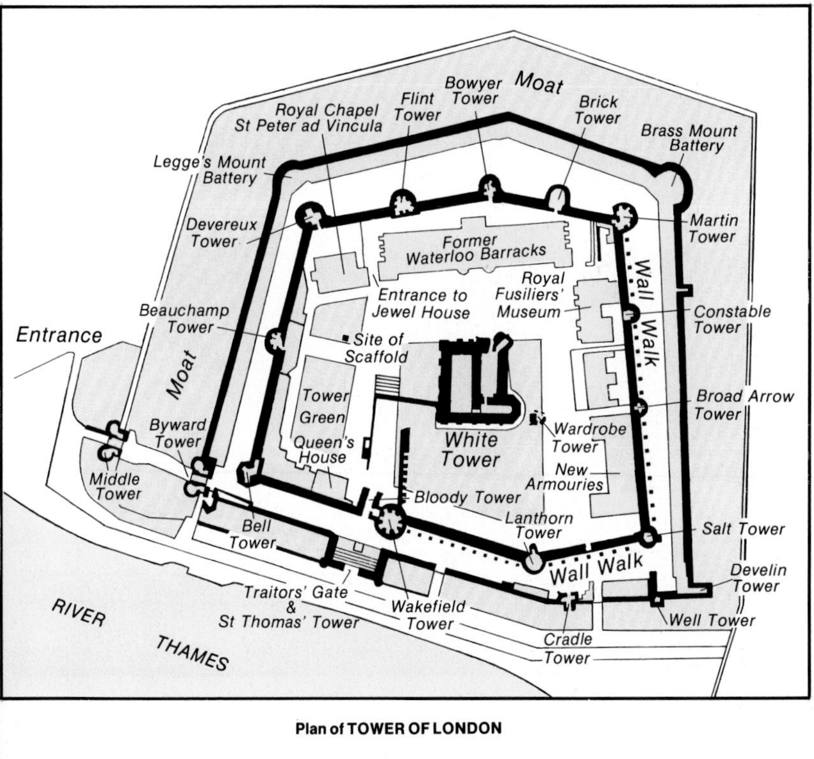

Plan of TOWER OF LONDON

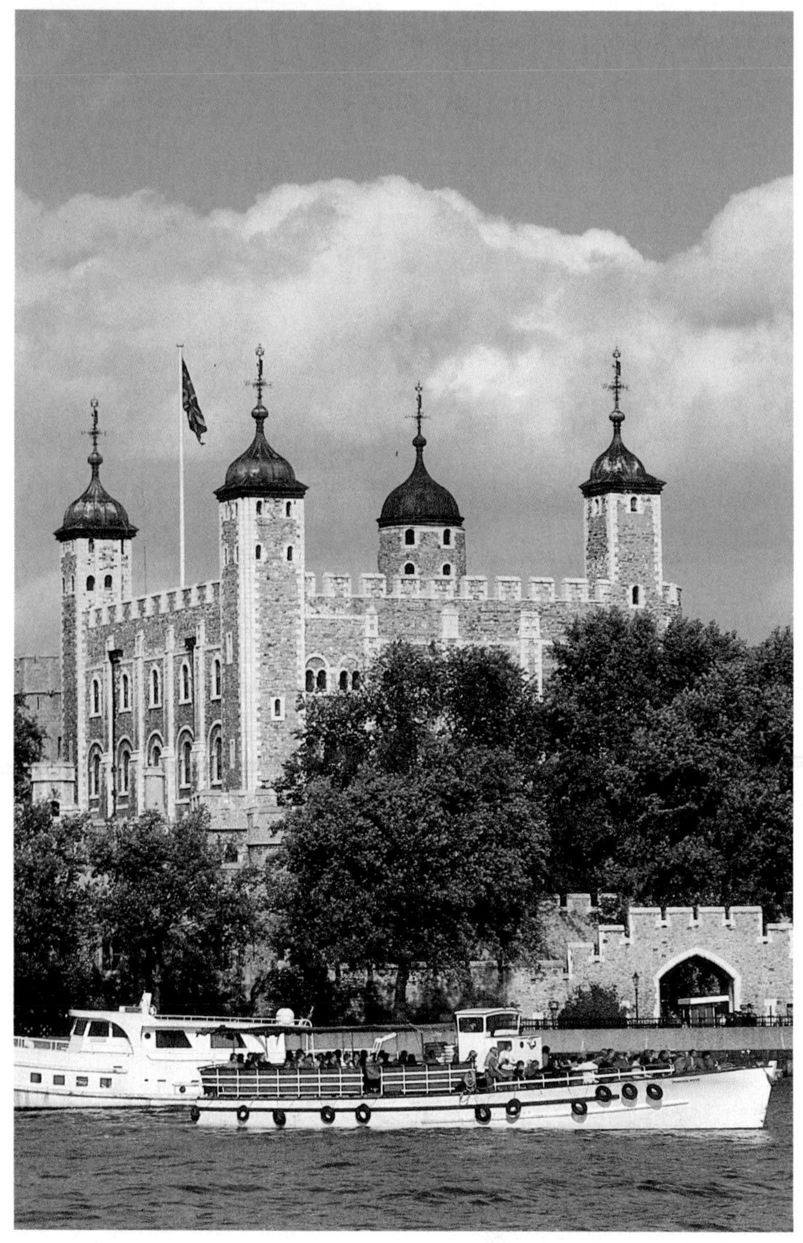

TOWER OF LONDON: from across the River Thames

Royal Chapel of St John; the HERALDS MUSEUM showing the history and development of heraldry; the WALL WALK giving good views over the tower and river; the Royal Chapel of St Peter ad Vincular with its Royal graves; the ROYAL FUSILIERS MUSEUM. Royal Salutes are fired from Tower Wharf by the Honourable Artillery Company on Royal anniversaries and important occasions. CEREMONY OF THE KEYS is enacted nightly at 22.00. when the main gates are locked and on the return of the keys a sentry challenges—"Halt! Who comes there!" The Chief Warden replies "The Keys". "Whose Keys ?"—"Queen Elizabeth's Keys". "Advance Queen Elizabeths Keys. Alls well!". (see also *Pageantry).*

First built by William the Conqueror to protect and control the *City of London,* it has continually been added to over the centuries, and, during its history has served as Fortress, Palace, and Prison, has housed the Royal Mint, Public Records, Royal Obervatory, Ordnance Survey and the Royal Menagerie (predecessor of *London Zoo).* Occupied as a palace until the reign of James I, and up to the time of Charles II, it served as traditional lodging to the monarch before a processional ride through the City to *Westminster Abbey* and the Coronation ceremony.

Open March to October 09.30-17.00 Mon. to Sat; 14.00-17.00 Sun. November to February 09.30-16.00 Mon. to Sat. only. Admission charge.

Trafalgar Square, WC2. 4B 92 and 3E 3
The grand public face of London, all monuments and monumental buildings; the view from the portico of the *National Gallery* takes in not only the whole square, but

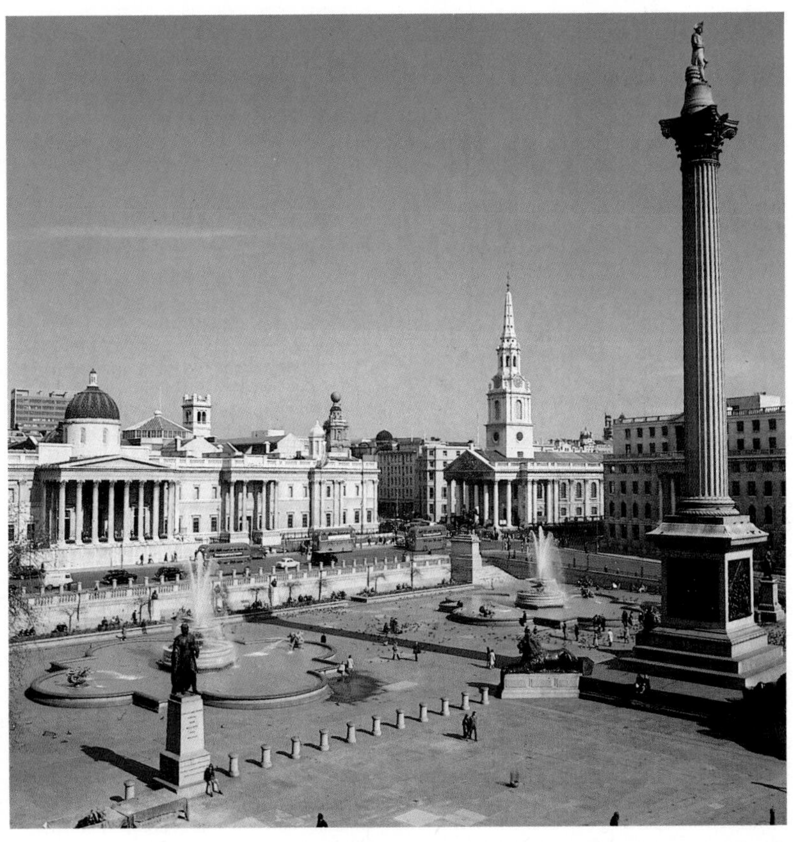

TRAFALGAR SQUARE

Whitehall and the nucleus around *Parliament Square* Laid out 1829-41 as a memorial to Nelson and his victory at Trafalgar, it is only right that the dominating feature should be NELSON'S COLUMN—184ft 10ins. high traditionally to allow the statue of Nelson a view of the sea. Landseer's bronze Lions were added in 1868 and the fountains, the scene of many a New Years Eve frolic, date from 1948. Trafalgar Square is much used for open-air meetings and demonstrations, a roosting place for the ubiquitous pigeon, and is decorated annually with a Christmas tree gift from Norway. Foremost among the statuary is that of Charles I, an equestrian piece cast in 1633 by Hubert Le Sueur, fortunately kept in hiding during the Commonwealth and set up here at 'Charing Cross' in 1675 (the scene of an annual ceremony in January to commemorate the King's execution 1649). Once the location of the village of Charing, this site was chosen in 1291 as the site for the last of twelve crosses erected by Edward I, to commemorate the funeral journey of his dead Queen Eleanor—from Nottinghamshire to *Westminster Abbey;* a replica of the cross stands in Charing Cross station forecourt. *St. Martin-in-the-Fields* with its famous Corinthian portico, steps and spire is an 18th century rebuild by James Gibbs on ancient foundations (see also *Churches*). Its interior features include a font of 1689 from the previous church, Royal box and Admiralty pews, both *Buckingham Palace* and *Admiralty* being within the parish, also old memorials to those buried here including Chippendale, John Hunter and Nell Gwyn; among the famous baptized here have been John Hampden, Francis Bacon and Charles II.

Victoria and Albert Museum, Cromwell Road, SW7. 071-938 8500 2H 97 and 4C 2
One of the world's most extensive collections of fine and applied art: within these many galleries, halls and courts are masterpieces of craftsmanship design and imagination from all parts of the world and periods of time. Collections are arranged into two groups 1)PRIMARY: all arts brought together by style, period or nationality. 2)DEPARTMENTAL: exhibits grouped under type: sculpture, textiles, pottery, woodwork, glass, costume, timepieces, arms, armour, metalwork, photography and so on. Two of the most impressive set-pieces are the Architectural Galleries with whole house fronts on display; and the Victorian Cast Court including a two part cast of Trajan's Column (erected in Rome AD 113).
The Museum grew out of the Museum of Manufactures opened in 1852 under the inspiration of Prince Albert, which later became the South Kensington Museum and from 1909, the V & A (when the scientific exhibits were moved to their own premises see *Science Museum)* The V & A buildings, designed by Aston Webb, incorporate the National Art Library. *Open 10.00-17.50. Sun. 14.30-17.50. Admission by voluntary donation.*

Wallace Collection, Hertford House, Manchester Square, W1. 071-935 0687
7D 82 and 2C 2
Tucked away just behind Selfridges, this—one of the great 19th century private collections—was amassed by the fourth Marquess of Hertford and his son Sir Richard Wallace. The interiors are sumptuous settings for fine French furniture (some from the Royal Palaces of Versailles and Fontainbleau bought after the French Revolution) and ceramics, European and Oriental arms and armour, and paintings of the British, French, Dutch, Flemish, Italian and Spanish Schools including masterpieces by Velazquez, Rubens, Rembrandt, Holbein, Gainsborough, Watteau. Originally built as Manchester House 1776-78 for the 4th Duke of Manchester, Hertford House and its contents were bequeathed to the Nation in 1877 by Lady Wallace.
Open 10.00-17.00. Sun. 14.00-17.00.

Wellington Museum see Apsley House

Wesley's Chapel, House and Museum of Methodism, City Rd., EC1. 071-253 2262
3E 86 and 2H 3
John Wesley lived here for 12 years and died in this house in 1791. His own rooms and furniture are preserved; he is buried in the graveyard behind the chapel. *House and Museum open 10.00-16.00 Mon. to Sat. Chapel 08.00-18.00 Mon. to Sat.*

West End, 3D 2—3E 3 and see page 37
'West End' has become synonymous with shopping and entertainment—such is the sheer profusion of retail shopping, restaurants, theatres, cinemas and night-spots. The West End 'High Street' is Oxford Street 1D 90, over a mile of shops with many large department stores including the emporium Selfridges. From Oxford Circus another great shopping avenue Regent Street 1H 91 links via the bright lights of *Piccadilly Circus* with the night-life centre Leicester Square 3B 92, where appropriately there are statues of William Shakespeare and Charlie Chaplin. See also *Entertainment, Mayfair, Restaurants, Shopping, Soho.*

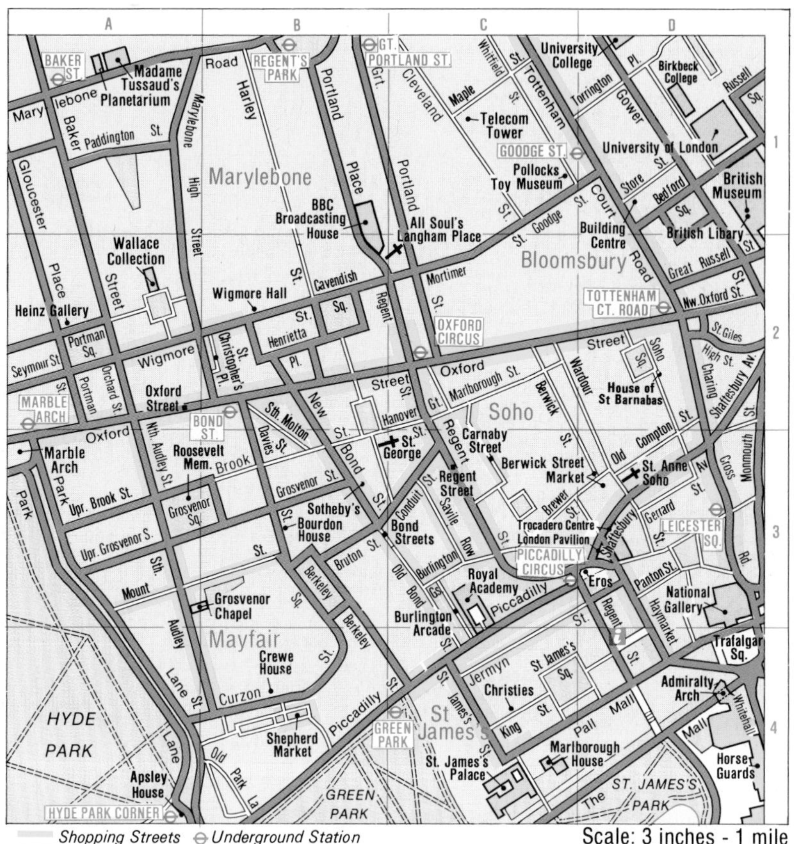

THE WEST END

Westminster, 4D 2—4E 3 and see page 38 Westminster is the most important area of central London for visitors to explore; with the lush greenery of *St James's Park* as a central point, you can find in a few minutes many of London's highlights: *Buckingham Palace, St James's Palace, Trafalgar Square, National Gallery, Horse Guards, Whitehall, Houses of Parliament, Westminster Abbey.* Interspersed are to be found a great many other interesting places, among them to the north of the park are: Lancaster House 6H 91, a Victorian mansion of the Duke of York; Clarence House 6J 91, home of H.R.H. the Queen Mother; Marlborough House 5J 91, 1709-11 by Wren, now the Commonwealth Conference Centre. Also, flanking the Duke of York's Column 5A 92 is Carlton House Terrace, a typical imposing Nash design 1827-32 like an open-air stage setting (see also *Regent Street).* To the south of the park are Wellington Barracks 7J 91, see *Guards Museum* illustrating 300 years of Guards history; also the modern *Guards Chapel* its predecessor destroyed in 1944 by a flying-bomb during morning service with great loss of life; notable Georgian houses in Queen Anne's Gate 7A 92, CENTRAL HALL 7B 92, the London HQ of the Methodist Church and venue in 1946 for the first session of the United Nations General Assembly. The City of Westminster has grown from the founding of a Saxon monastery called Westminster (or West Monastery ie: west of the *City of London*); this being refounded and rebuilt by Edward the Confessor and consecrated in 1065. Possibly to be close enough to oversee his *Westminster Abbey* work, Edward also founded the Palace of Westminster (see *Houses of Parliament*),

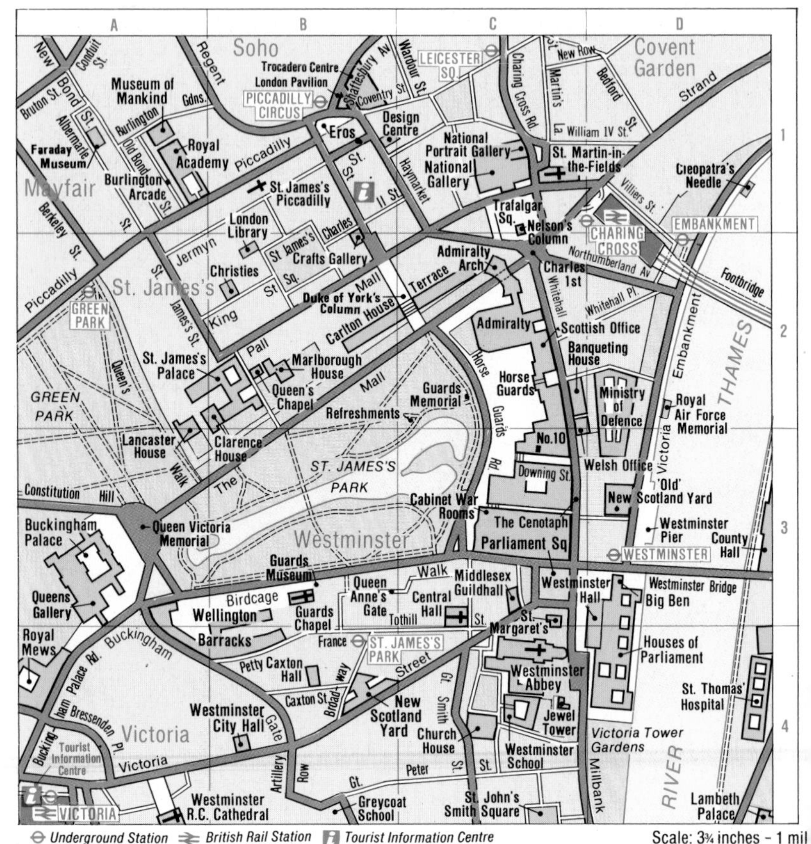

WESTMINSTER: see page 37

the first permanent Royal home and a principal Royal palace until the 16th century when Henry VIII favoured more modern palaces including *Whitehall, St James's, Hampton Court* and *Greenwich.* See also *Westminster Hall,* added 1097-9 and once a meeting place of the Great Council, the precursor of modern Parliament.

Westminster Abbey, Parliament Square, SW1. 071-222 5152 1C 100 and 4E 3
Although not of cathedral status, one of England's great churches. Neither the Archbishop of Canterbury nor the Bishop of London have any authority here—like St George's Chapel *Windsor,* this is a Royal Peculiar, run by Dean and Chapter subject only to the Crown. All English Sovereigns from William I (1066) to Elizabeth II (1953) were crowned here except Edward V and VIII (who abdicated before his Coronation). Most, from Henry III (d.1272) to George II (d.1760) are also buried here.
Only two fragments remain of the Abbey consecrated in 1065 by Edward the Confessor the Chamber of the Pyx, and the Undercroft; the abbey church itself being rebuilt for Henry II and rededicated 1269. Its creators Henry of Rheims, John of Gloucester and Robert of Beverley moulded the ethereal simplicity of Early English architecture with French Gothic ideas—most easily seen in the radiating apse chapels; the nave (at 102ft England's highest Gothic vault) was completed in keeping with

WESTMINSTER ABBEY: from Deans Yard

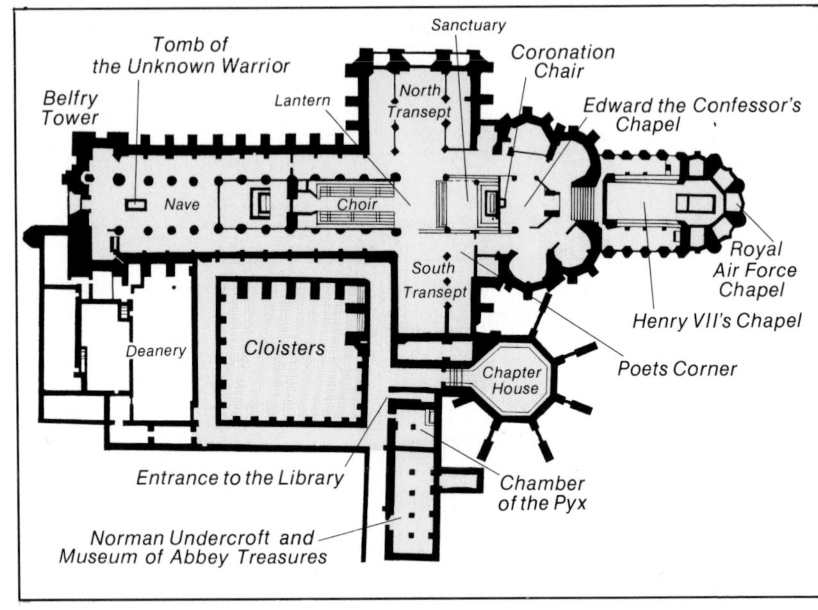

Plan of WESTMINSTER ABBEY

the original style during the late 13th and early 14th centuries partly under Henry Yevele, architect of *Westminster Hall* and Canterbury Cathedral nave. Major additions to the Medieval work are: firstly the resplendent Henry VII Chapel 1503-19—a high point in late Perpendicular architecture with its carving and profuse decoration, (including banners of Knights of the Order of the Bath), culminating in an awe inspiring fan vault roof; secondly the twin West Towers—18th century additions by Nicholas Hawksmoor, a pupil of Wren.
On a tour of the Abbey you will see very many memorials and monuments to those famous men and women buried here and many more who are buried elsewhere; notably in POETS' CORNER, STATESMANS AISLE and the ROYAL CHAPELS; the latter focus on the Chapel of Edward the Confessor with its once jewel bedecked 13th century shrine and Coronation Chair. All round and through the Henry VII Chapel are tombs of Kings, Queens and noble families, while that of the UNKNOWN WARRIER is at the opposite end of the Abbey, just inside the entrance. The octagonal CHAPTER HOUSE c 1250 built for Henry III, is closely connected with the origins of Parliament; and where the King's Great Council met in 1257, and the Commons, following its separation from the Lords in the reign of Edward I met 1352-1547. The 11th century Undercroft, now housing the remarkable WESTMINSTER ABBEY MUSEUM, is approached via the 13th and 14th century cloisters. Some of the Medieval monks' quarters are now occupied by the famous WESTMINSTER SCHOOL 4C 38, which, like CHURCH HOUSE 4C 38, the HQ of the General Synod, is approached via Deans Yard.
Open: Nave open daily (Sundays between services only). Royal Chapels, Poets' Corner, Choir and Statesmens' Aisle Mon. to Sat. only; Admission charge. Chapter House and Museum daily; Admission charge.

Westminster Cathedral, Ashley Place, SW1. 071-834 7452 2H 99 and 4D 2
England's premier Roman Catholic Cathedral seat of Cardinal Archbishop of Westminster and scene of the first mass ever celebrated by a Pope on English soil—Pope Paul II, May 1982. This great Early Christian Byzantine style edifice was built 1895-1903 to designs by J. F Bentley, its exterior of alternate brick and stone bands dominated by the 284ft campanile

WESTMINSTER CATHEDRAL: and Piazza

is beautifully off set by modern architecture and piazza. The interior, 342ft long is divided into three domed bays with low relief carvings—Stations of the Cross—by Eric Gill; the eleven side chapels illustrate the intended interior design when completed, lavish surface decoration in marble and mosaic. The Campanile provides ineffable views over *Westminster. Open 07.00-20.00 daily. Tower 09.00-17.00. Summer only.*

Westminster Hall, Parliament Square, SW1. 7C 92
Main fragment of the Medieval Palace of Westminster to have survived destruction by fire in 1834; other parts are St Stephens Chapel crypt and the nearby moated *Jewel Tower* built 1365-6 to store the Kings private treasure; the *Houses of Parliament* now occupy the remainder of the site. Westminster Hall was added to Edward the Confessor's Royal Palace for William Rufus 1097-1099, although the present hall is in fact a 1394-99 reconstruction by Henry Yevele for Richard II. It is chiefly famous for its great oak hammerbeam roof spanning 240ft x 28ft. Decorations include Richard's coat of arms in repeat pattern, and also full size statues of Medieval Kings.
As the Great Hall of the Royal Palace, this would be the place of assembly for the King's Great Council—out of which grew the Courts of Justice and Parliament. By the end of the 13th century its principal function was to house the various Law Courts and here they remained until 1882 when they moved into the then new *Royal Courts of Justice.* The hall has been the scene of historic trials including William Wallace 1305, Thomas More 1535, Duke of Somerset the Lord Protector 1551, Guy Fawkes 1606, Charles I 1649 and the rebel Scottish Lords 1715 & 1745. In more recent years the hall has been used for State Ceremonies and the lying-in-State of Kings and the eminent, such as Winston Churchill (1965).

Whitehall, 5C 92 and 3E 3
At one and the same time both a centre and an important link—a centre of 'official' Westminster, with its brass plaque name plated government departments; also a broad, grand processional way linking *Trafalgar Square* and *Parliament Square,* the route used for Royal ceremonial drives to and from *Buckingham Palace.* Amongst the many interesting features are *Admiralty; Horse Guards; Banqueting House;* Scottish Office (Dover House); Welsh Office (Gwydyr House); *Downing Street;* two great blocks of 'Imperial' classical style offices—the lavish Foreign and Commonwealth office by George Gilbert Scott (1873) and the Edwardian Treasury; the *Cenotaph;* and many statues including those of Charles I, Duke of Cambridge, Earl Haig; Walter Raleigh, General Montgomery.
Whitehall is named after the once large and important Royal Palace of Whitehall. Originally 'York Place' the town house of the Archbishop of York, this became enlarged and embellished by Cardinal Wolsey into so luxurious a palace as to rouse Henry VIII's envy (see also *Hampton Court),* who, after taking possession, continued to enlarge it, and created two impressive linking gateways over the Charing Cross-Westminster thoroughfare and renamed it 'Whitehall', and it was here in Whitehall Palace that he died in 1547.
It continued as focus of court life through the reigns of Elizabeth and the Stuart Kings, but in 1698 most of the buildings were destroyed by fire, only the famous *Banqueting House* surviving.

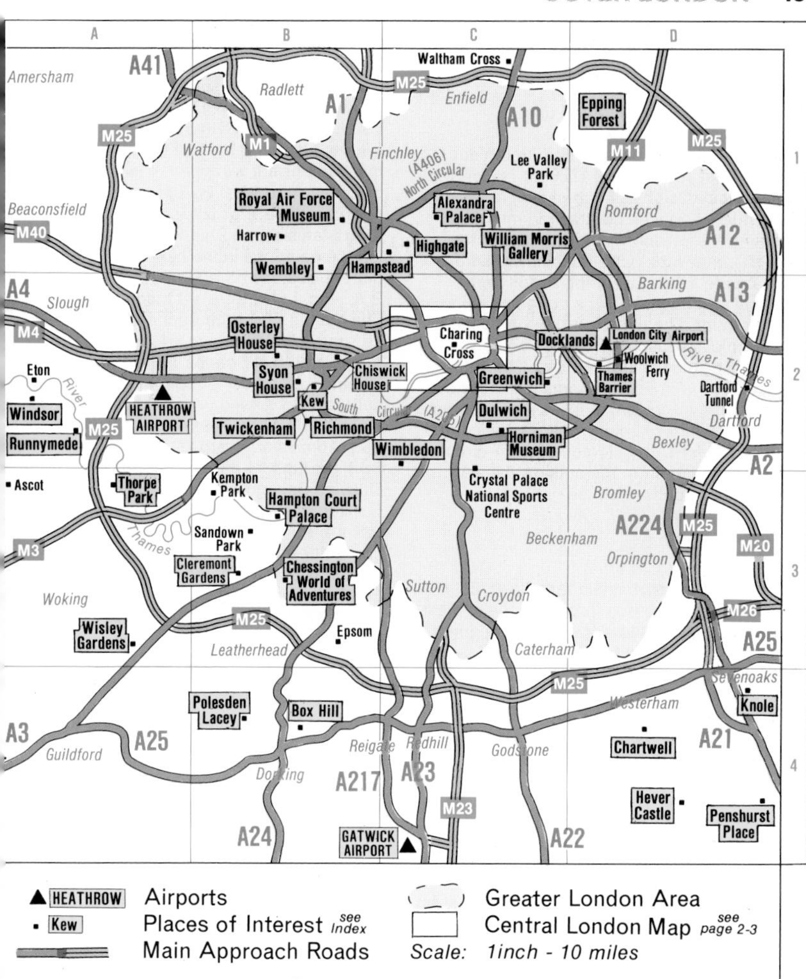

Box Hill, Surrey 4B 43 (General Enquiries 0306-885502)
800 acres of National Trust woods and chalk downland famous for its magnificent views to the South Downs. Rising to 400 ft., this is a designated Country Park with nature walks; the summit buildings include an exhibition room and 1890's fort. *Open: free access to countryside all year.*

Chartwell, near Westerham, Kent. 0732-866368 4D 43
This is the famous home of Sir Winston Churchill from 1924 to his death. Its rooms, studio and gardens are now maintained as they were in his lifetime by the National Trust; two rooms form a museum of memorabilia. Nearby are three other historic places of interest open to the public—the 15th and 17th century mansion Knole, family home of the Sackvilles, also in care of the National Trust; Penshurst Place the Medieval and Tudor stately home of the Sidney family, and the outstanding Medieval Hever Castle, where Henry VIII courted Anne Boleyn. *Open: House Garden and Studio 12.00-17.30 Tues. Wed. &*

Thurs. (11.00-17.30 Sat. & Sun.) April to Oct. House only March and Nov. 11.00-16.00 Sat. Sun. & Wed. Admission charge

Chiswick House, Burlington Lane, W4. 081-995 0508 2B 43
This Palladian villa by Lord Burlington and William Kent constructed 1720-30, is a perfect symmetrical design built up of simple geometric forms with contrasting intricate detailing; the gardens—a forerunner of the English Landscape park—also designed by Kent, create a natural setting as foil to the classical architecture, like a cut gem set in a subtle mount. The main front is composed of two double approach stairways flanking a dominant portico at first floor level; the interior is a series of connecting rooms with sensitive decoration by Kent which takes into account the relationships of linking spaces; the central room has a clerestory pierced by semi-circular windows, which, from the outside visually echo the surmounting dome.
Open 10.00-18.00, to 14.00 winter months. Admission charge.

Cleremont Garden, Portsmouth Road, Esher 3B 43 A National Trust property, the earliest surviving English landscape garden begun prior to 1720 extended and remodelled by William Kent and Capability Brown. Includes lake, grotto, avenues and viewpoints.
Open daily 09.00-19.00 April to Oct. (to 17.00 or sunset Nov. to March). House not open. Admission charge

Docklands *Information 071-512 3000*
The Port of London was once one of the worlds largest ports occupying the banks of the River Thames from the Tower of London to Woolwich; during the 1960's and 70's industrial strife and new technologies bought about their decline and replacement by modern facilities at Tilbury. Since 1981 when the London Docklands Development Corporation was formed, some eight and a half square miles of derelict or underused land and water has undergone a remarkable transformation. The Docklands Light Railway-automated and driverless-snakes through the acres of new development, many attracting architectural awards. Features of particular interest include: St Katharine's Dock; Design Museum at Butlers Wharf; shopping centres at Hay's Galleria-London Bridge City, Tobacco Dock and Surrey Quays; Canary Wharf Financial Centre with Britains tallest tower block (800ft); New Billingsgate Fish Market; London Arena; Sailing Centre and Marina; North Woolwich Station Railway Museum; London City Airport.

Dulwich, SE21. 2C 43
One of London's villages, which like Hampstead, manages to retain something of its old character, despite being surrounded by suburbia. The DULWICH COLLEGE PICTURE GALLERY College Rd., SE21 081-693 5254 houses a remarkable fine art collection with many important works representing the principal schools of European painting; some of which, were originally collected together for King Stanislaus of Poland, whose abdication left the paintings in the hands of his French picture-dealer who left them to P. F. Bourgeois R A; who, in his turn, left them to the College. The building by John Soane, opened in 1814 as London's first public art gallery, is a rare example of Soanes' individual style; the galleries are so designed that the whole collection is viewed only by daylight.
Open 11.00-17.00 Tues. to Sat. 14.00-17.00 Sun. Admission charge.
Both the Gallery and the famous boys school, Dulwich College, are run by a trust, fomerly the College of God's Gift, founded in 1619 by Edward Allyn, an actor-manager contemporary with Shakespeare. Other buildings of interest include the 17th century Old College Chapel and Almshouses, the 19th century Italianate College and London's last toll-gate.

Epping Forest, between Chingford and Epping 1D 43
A relic of the ancient Royal hunting forest of Waltham, now extends about 11 miles north to south by about 1-2 miles broad. The woods were saved from complete destruction by the Commons Preservation Society in 1871. Lovely forest walks are to be enjoyed. *Open at all times*

Greenwich, SE10. 2C 43 and below
Tourist Information Centre: 071-858 6376
Royal Greenwich—birthplace, favourite residence and seaport of Tudor monarchs—its outstanding river frontage of Royal Naval College and Queen's House with Greenwich Park as a backdrop, is one of London's most inspired views. The great double wings of the ROYAL NAVAL COLLEGE 081-858 2154 stand on the site of the 15th century Palace of Placentia, birthplace of Henry VIII and his daughters Mary and Elizabeth (both subsequent Queens). Rebuilt by a succession of architects including Wren, the palace became Greenwich Hospital in 1705; (the naval equivalent of the Royal Hospital for soldiers at Chelsea); and afterwards, in 1873, a college for the higher education of Naval Officers; its Chapel and Painted hall are both open to the public. *14.30-17.00 daily, closed*

Thurs. Admission charge. Tea clipper CUTTY SARK 081-853 3589 dominates the river front in a totally different way with its towering masts and filligree rigging; adjacent is the diminutive GIPSY MOTH IV, Francis Chichester's round the world yacht. *Open 10.00-18.00, Sundays 14.00-18.00 (Closed 17.00 winter). Admission charge.* Set back, from the river the NATIONAL MARITIME MUSEUM 081-858 4422 has modern and stimulating galleries displaying exhibits ranging from ships models to actual boats, sections devoted to all aspects of ships, seafaring and seafarers; historical events and characters eg. Nelson, Trafalgar, Captain Cook. Collections are enhanced by being housed in some exceptional buildings including QUEEN'S HOUSE; commissioned by James 1st, this is a design by Inigo Jones, which, with his *Banqueting House* Whitehall,

GREENWICH MAP and VIEW FROM THE RIVER THAMES

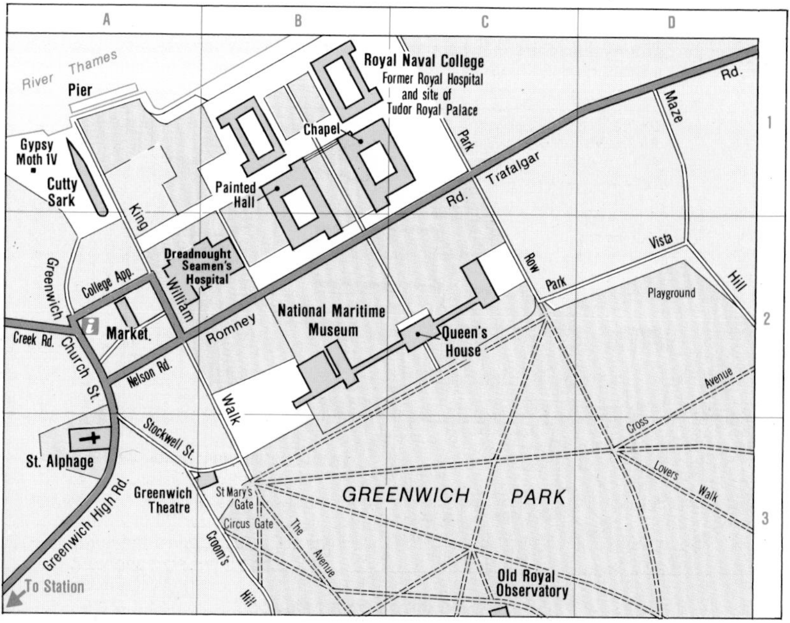

A B C D
1 2 3
River Thames
Pier
Royal Naval College
Former Royal Hospital and site of Tudor Royal Palace
Chapel
Gypsy Moth IV
Cutty Sark
Painted Hall
King
Park Row
Trafalgar Rd.
Maze Hill
Vista
Park
Playground
Dreadnought Seamen's Hospital
William
Greenwich
College App.
Market
Creek Rd.
Church St.
Nelson Rd.
Romney Rd.
National Maritime Museum
Queen's House
Walk
Avenue
Cross
Stockwell St.
St. Alphage
Greenwich High Rd.
Greenwich Theatre
St Mary's Gate
Circus Gate
The Avenue
Croom's Hill
GREENWICH PARK
Lovers Walk
Old Royal Observatory
To Station

marks the introduction of the classical ideals of Palladian architecture into England. Astronomical and navigation collections are housed in the OLD ROYAL OBSERVATORY Greenwich Park; buildings include the Meridian Building where zero meridian longitude is marked by a brass strip, and Flamsteed House by Wren, with its time-ball falling 13.00 daily. *Open 10.00-18.00 Mon. to Sat, 14.00-18.00 Sun. (Closed 17.00 winter). Admission charge.* RANGER'S HOUSE, Chesterfield Walk. SE10 081-853 0035 (can be reached through the park) has a remarkable long gallery of portraits—Elizabethan to Georgian; also the Dolmetsch collection of musical instruments. *Open 10.00-18.00 summer, to 16.00 winter.*

Ham House, Ham, Nr Richmond
081-940 1950 2B 43 (National Trust)
Fine Stuart house built c.1610 with lavish Baroque interior much as left by the Duke of Lauderdale a favorite of Charles II. *Open 11.00-17.30 Tues. to Sun. Admission charge.*

Hampstead, NW3. 2C 43
A hill-top community that in parts, still retains something of a village character, with its maze of small streets and alleys providing surprise views and architectural settings. To be found here are famous pubs: The Old Bull and Bush, Jack Straws Castle and Spaniards Inn; KEATS HOUSE, Keats Grove, NW3 071-435 2062 *Open daily;* home of John Keats 1818-21, a plaque in the garden marks the spot where he wrote 'Ode To a Nightingale'; FENTON HOUSE (National Trust) Hampstead Grove, NW3 071-435 3471 *Open 11.00-18.00. Sat. to Wed. April to Oct. Admission charge.* A fine Queen Anne building known for its collection of early keyboard instruments; HAMPSTEAD HEATH is a great tract of undulating, informal parkland and among its many delights are Parliament Hill with its kite flyers and superb views over London, bathing ponds, bank holiday fairs and to the north, KENWOOD, Hampstead Lane, NW3. 081 348 1286 *open daily;* the gracious stately home re-modelled by Robert Adam 1764-73 for the first Earl of Mansfield. It houses the Iveagh Bequest, an important collection of Old Master and English paintings. FREUD MUSEUM 20 Maresfield Gardens NW3. 071-353 2002 *open 12.00-17.00 Wed. to Sun. Admission charge.*

Hampton Court Palace, Hampton, Middlesex. 081-977 8441 3B 43
This, the largest and grandest of England's Tudor Palaces, is one of London's most popular tourist attractions; its great range of mellow brick buildings are beautifully offset against Hampton Court Park, Bushey Park and 'Old Father Thames' himself. Built with a magnificence that outshone even the Royal Palaces, Cardinal Wolsey's Hampton Court, by rousing the jealousy of Henry VIII, contributed to his downfall from high office.
Wolseys buildings are those around the west front—Base Court and Clock Court; some like his Closet still have the original furnishings. For Henry VIII, much was rebuilt and added new wings and courts, including the Great

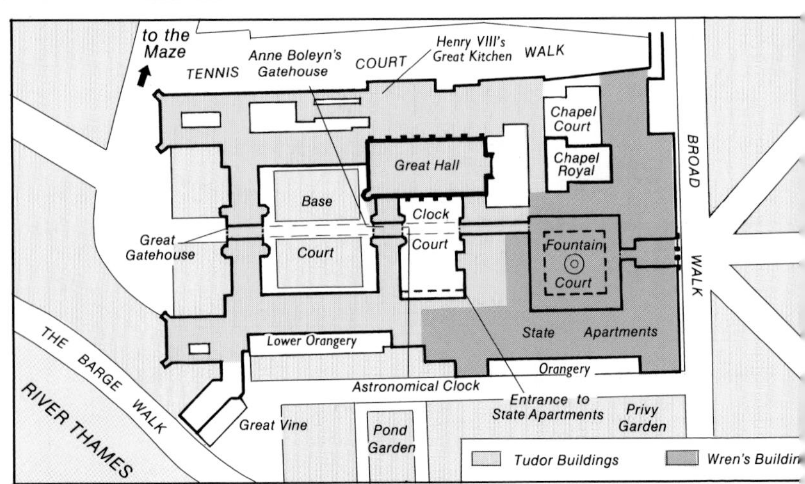

Plan of **HAMPTON COURT PALACE**

HAMPTON COURT PALACE: the Great Gatehouse

Hall. For William and Mary, Christopher Wren added the east wing State Apartments and Orangery; for Queen Anne, the Banqueting House. Features of interest are almost numberless and much time is needed to see everything. Some of the most important are: 16th century panelling, sumptuous wood carving by Grinling Gibbons, stone carving by Cibber, ironwork by Tijou, frescoes by Verrio; and outstanding art collection (part of the Royal Collection), including the Mantegna cartoons bought by Charles 1st; 16th and 17th century tapestries; Anne Boleyn's Gateway; the Haunted Gallery; Tudor Kitchens and tennis courts; Astronomical Clock (1540); Great Vine (1768); The Maze, formal gardens and landscape park. *Open daily 09.30-18.00 Summer; to 16.30 winter. Admission charge.*

Hever Castle, Hever, Nr. Edenbridge Kent 0732 865224 4D 43
A romantic 13th century moated castle, childhood home of Anne Boleyn. The castle was restored and filled with treasures by William Waldorf Astor in 1903. Exhibition on the life and times of Anne Boleyn; Regimental Museum. 30 acres of beautiful gardens including an Italian garden and antique statuary and sculpture; also fine topiary and maze; 35 acre lake. Adventure playground for children. *Open 12.00-18.00 (Garden from 11.00) daily end of March to early November. Admission charge.*

Hogarth's House, Hogarth La., W4. 081-944 6757 nr. Chiswick House 2B 43
Queen Anne country home of artist Hogarth, now a museum of his drawings and engravings. *Closed Tuesdays; 1st two weeks Sept., last three weeks Dec. and New Year. Open 11.00-18.00; 14.00-18.00 Sun. April to Sept. until 16.00 Oct. to March.*

Horniman Museum and Gardens, 100 London Rd., SE23. 081-699 2339 2C 43
Devoted to the world's living heritage and natural environment; also arts and craft and musical instruments, Gardens with children's zoo, aquarium and nature trails. *Open 10.30-17.50 Mon. to Sat. 14.00-17.50 Sun.*

Kew, Richmond upon Thames 2B 43
ROYAL BOTANICAL GARDENS
(Kew Gardens), Kew Road, 081-940 1171 2B 43 were founded in 1759 by Princess Augusta and are now an important identification and research institution. The 300 acres of specimen gardens, parkland, lake, water gardens and hot-houses are enhanced by several architectural delights : 18th century works by William Chambers include a 'ruined' arch, pagoda and set of temples; the soaring Palm House—erected 1844-8 and designed by Richard Turner and Decimus Burton—is a precursor of modern functional design, all curving glass and iron frames with a simplicity akin to that of the plant forms within;

KEW GARDENS: the Palm House, see page 47

KEW PALACE (or Dutch House) of 1631, a royal residence from 1734 to the death of Queen Charlotte in 1818, is the setting for Queen's Garden containing only plants grown in this country in the 17th century. *Open daily. Admission charge.*

Kew Bridge Steam Museum, Green Dragon Lane, Brentford 081-568 4757
Steam pumping engines, working beam engines etc. *Open 11.00-17.00 daily (in steam weekends & Bank Holiday Mondays). Admission charge.*

Knole, Sevenoaks, Kent 0732 450608 4D 43
One of England's largest private houses, dating from 1456, enlarged in 1603 by Thomas Sackville 1st Earl of Dorset, to whom it was granted by Elizabeth 1st; and whose descendants gave the house to the National Trust. This, the childhood home of Vita Sackville-West, displays a fascinating series of galleries, apartments and state rooms, hardly changed since their creation. Formal gardens open 1st Wed. in month only. Set in extensive rolling deer park. *Open 11.00-17.00 Wed. to Sat. 14.00-17.00 Sun. April to Oct. Admission charge.*

London Airport, Heathrow 2A 43
For those attracted to aircraft and the romance of exotic destinations, London's Heathrow Airport, as one of the worlds busiest, is a must. Public viewing is from a roof garden where arrivals and departures are announced. An Interdenominational Chapel, 24 hours refreshment and banking are among the many facilities. For public transport to and from central London see page 63

Marble Hill House, Richmond Rd., Twickenham 081-892 5115
Built 1728 for Henrietta Howard, mistress of George II, a small Palladian style villa in Thames side parkland. *Open 10.00-18.00 summer, to 16.00 winter.*

Musical Museum, 368 High Street, Brentford 081-560 8108 Large collection of mechanical musical machines from music boxes to ochestrions. *Open 14.00-17.00 Sat. & Sun. April to Oct. Admission charge.*

Osterley Park House, Osterley. 081-560 3918 2B 43
Now a National Trust property and administered by the *Victoria and Albert Museum,* Osterley was begun as an Elizabethan Mansion (1560's) for Thomas Gresham, founder of the *Royal Exchange,* Elizabeth I being entertained here in 1576. The house was remodelled, including new encasing walls, by Wiliam Chambers from about 1756 until Robert Adam took over as architect in 1762. Besides adding the portico, Adam designed the magnificent interiors—plasterwork, fireplaces, doors etc., and furniture to match; little altered, this is considered by some amongst Adam's finest work. The stables and parkland remain largely Elizabethan, except for the addition of the elevated M4 motorway. *Open 11.00-17.00 Tues. to Sun. March to end December. Park 10.00-20.00 or dusk. Admission charge.*

Penshurst Place, Penshurst, Nr. Tonbridge Kent 0892-870307 4D 43
Magnificent Stately Home; includes fine state

rooms and famous 60ft. high medieval Great Hall. Family home of the Sidney family since it was granted to Sir Philip Sidney by Edward VI in 1552; Sir Philip Sidney, Elizabethan poet, courtier and soldier was born here in 1554. Ten acres of walled garden within parkland. Venture playground for children, nature trail, farm museum. *Open 12.30-18.00 Tues. to Sun. (and Bank Hol. Mons.) April to Oct. Admission charge.*

Polesden Lacy, Nr. Dorking, Surrey
0372 58203 4B 43
National Trust house, orginally an 1820's Regency Villa, remodelled in 1906; contains a fine collection of furniture, pictures, porcelain and silver. Extensive grounds and gardens. *Open 13.30-16.30 Wed. to Sun. April to end Oct. (Sat. and Sun. only March to Oct.) Admission charge.*

Richmond upon Thames, 2B 43
One of London's best known riverside 'villages'. Contributiing to its individuality are many factors: its narrow shopping streets and alleys; fine Georgian Houses including those around Richmond Green; the Tudor gateway to Henry VIII's palace; Richmond Bridge, the only 18th century London Bridge left, built 1774-77 in the classical style with five graduating arches; the view immortalised by Turner's painting from Richmond Terrace. RICHMOND PARK, a Royal Park enclosed by Charles 1 in 1637, is a landscape of forest trees and undergrowth big enough to get temporarily lost in, roamed by herds of deer and other wild animals. Within are: Isabella Plantation, a noted woodland garden; Pen Ponds for angling; Adam's Pond for model boats; White Lodge, built 1727-29 for George II, the birthplace in 1894 of uncrowned Edward VIII, and now houses the Royal Ballet School (lower); Pembroke Lodge c.1800, now a restaurant.

Royal Air Force Museum, Grahame Park Way, Hendon, NW9. 081-205 2266 1B 43
An excitingly displayed collection of 60 aircraft and galleries telling the story of over 100 years of aviation from the balloonists onwards, and the history of the R.A.F. Exhibits include technical equipment, uniforms, photographs, personalia, medals, weapons, models and dioramas, transport, simulated workshop scenes and of course the aircraft themselves. Battle of Britain Hall has a specific collection of aircraft, equipment, memorabilia and vivid displays devoted to those who were involved in the battle for the supremacy of the sky over Gt Britain in 1940 when, to quote Winston Churchill 'never in the field of human conflict was so much owed by so many to so few!' Bomber Command Hall tells the story of Bomber Command and the development of aerial bombing from World War 1 to the present day, aircraft include, Halifax, Wellington, Avro Lancaster, Avro Vulcan and Valiant. *Open 10.00-18.00 daily. Admission charge.*

Runnymede, nr. Egham, Surrey 2A 43
188 acres of historic National Trust Thameside meadows where King John traditionally signed Magna Carta in 1215. There are memorials also to John F. Kennedy and the Air Forces. 110 acres of wooded slopes overlooking give fine views. *Open: free access to the meadows.*

ROYAL AIR FORCE MUSEUM

Syon House and Park, London Road, Brentford. 081-560 0882 2B 43
Set in 55 acres of riverside parkland, this, the summer house of the Duke of Northumberland, looks across the Thames to *Kew Gardens.* its origins date back to 1415 when Henry V founded a convent here; taken over by Henry VIII at the Dissolution, his Queen Catherine Howard was later confined here prior to her execution. The great Tudor house—built by the Duke of Somerset, Lord Protector to Henry's son Edward VI—was granted by James I to Henry Percy, the ninth Earl of Northumberland and his heirs in perpetuity. The interior transformation by Robert Adam 1762-69 for the first Duke—a series of delicately contrasted colour schemes and elaborate plaster detailing—is recognised as a masterpiece. The gardens famous even in the 16th century for rare, ornamental trees and shrubs were enhanced by the landscape design of Capability Brown, the addition of such features as a six acre rose garden and also the Great Conservatory by Robert Fowler 1820, one of the earliest large iron and glass structures. The gardens now incorporate a walk-through *London Butterfly House,* the historic *Heritage Motor Museum* with its collection of over 100 display cars illustrating the development of the British motor industry. *Open: HOUSE 12.00-17.00 Sun. to Thurs. April to Sept. Sundays only in Oct. Admission charge. PARK 10.00-18.00 or dusk in winter.*

William Morris Gallery, Lloyd Park, Forest Rd. E17. 081-527 5544 1C 43
Devoted to the life and work of Morris, his followers and the Morris Company.
Open 10.00-13.00; 14.00-17.00 Tues. to Sat. and 1st Sun. in each month.

Wimbledon Lawn Tennis Museum, All England Club, Church Rd, SW19. 081-946 6131 2C 43
History of Lawn Tennis. *Open 11.00-17.00 14.00-17.00 Sun. Admission charge.*

Windsor, 2A 43
Tourist Information Centre: 0753 852010
A traditional Thames-side home of English Monarchs, dominated by WINDSOR CASTLE established here by William the Conqueror,

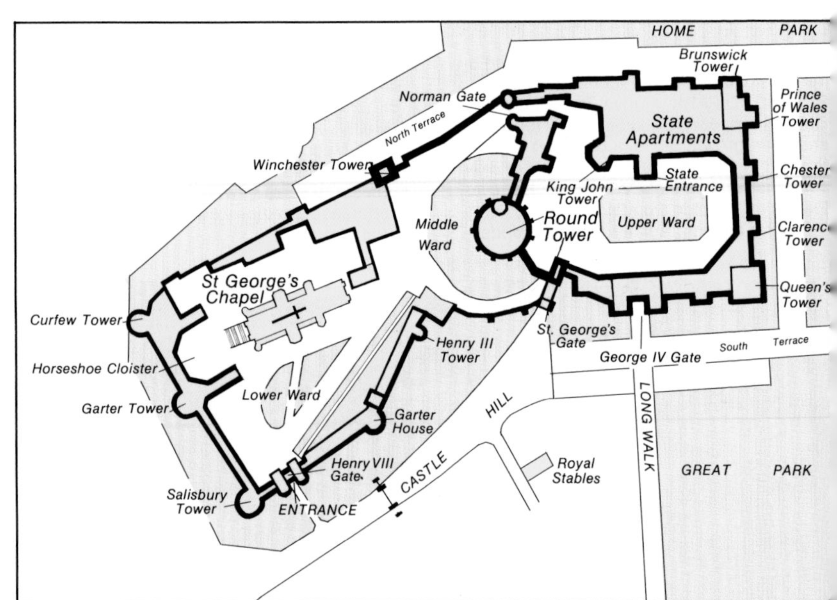

Plan of WINDSOR CASTLE

WINDSOR CASTLE from across the River Thames

and rebuilt in stone by Henry II. Since then many additions have been made by consecutive Sovereigns making this now the largest castle in England.Its main points of interest are (1) STATE APARTMENTS, Upper Ward; mainly of Charles II and 19th century origin containing carvings by Gibbons, ceiling paintings by Verrio, superlative Royal collections of armour, furniture, and fine art (in particular Leonardo da Vinci sketches and Holbein drawings); (2) the Middle Ward ROUND TOWER rebuilt in stone by Henry II overlooking (3) the Lower Ward with its famous ST GEORGE'S CHAPEL, a Royal Peculiar (see *Westminster Abbey),* the Chapel of the Dean and Canons of Windsor, and Order of the Garter, with its wonderful fan vault roof and elaborate stalls, their plates recording Knights of the Garter since 1390.
Telephone 0753 868286 *Open daily; (State Apartments closed when the Queen is in residence). Admission charge.*

Close-by, and not to be missed are: the Guildhall Museum; Madame Tussauds *Royalty & Empire* exhibition; the Household Cavalry Museum; Home Park with Frogmore—the Royal Mausoleum of Victoria and Albert; Windsor Great Park encompassing Savill Gardens, Virginia Water and *Windsor Safari Park;* Eton, with its famous public school Eton College, founded 1440 by Henry VI.

Wisley Gardens, Wisley, Surrey 3A 43
The gardens of the Royal Horticultural Society; 250 acres of beautiful British garden landscapes. A wide variety of garden types are represented—tree, shrub, flower gardens; also model fruit and vegetable gardens and greenhouses. *Open 10.00-17.00 or sunset if earlier Mon. to Sat. (Sundays for members and their guests only). Admission charge.*

HOUSES OF PARLIAMENT: from the South Bank

Barbican Arts Centre Tour, Silk Street, EC2. 5C 86
Tours behind the scenes (excluding the Theatre). Bookings 071-638 4141. The Arts Centre is the London equivalent of the Lincoln Center New York or the Centre Pompidou Paris; its wide range of facilities include: Barbican Hall, Barbican Theatre, The Pit studio theatre, Barbican Library, art gallery, sculpture court, cinemas, conference and trade exhibition areas, roof top conservatory, restaurants, bars and car park. *Open: 09.00-23.00 Mon. to Sat. 12.00-23.00 Sun. See also page 5.*

Boat Trips. Riverboat Information Service 071-730 4812
There are regular daily trips from three piers: Westminster Pier 6D 92, Charing Cross Pier 4E 92, Tower Pier 4G 95. Boats go downstream to Greenwich and the Thames Barrier; upstream to Kew Gardens, Richmond and Hampton Court Palace.

Canal boat trips are operated by Jenny Wren Canal Trips, 250 Camden High Street NW1 071-485 6210 1D 2 : Jason's Trip, Little Venice W2 071-286 3428 2B 2 : London Waterbus Company, Little Venice W2 071-482 2550 2B 2

Day boats are for hire on boating lakes in Hyde Park 6B 90 and Regent's Park 2C 82

Brass Rubbing
1. St. Martin in the Fields, Trafalgar Sq, WC2 071-437 6023 3C 92 *Open 10.00-18.00 Mon. to Sat. 12.00-18.00 Sun.*
2. All Hallows by the Tower, Byward St, EC3 071-481 2928 3G 95 *Open 11.00-16.00. Sun. 13.00-16.00. Summer Season only.*
3. Westminster Abbey, Parliament Sq. SW1 071-222 2085 7C 92 *Open 09.00-17.00 Mon. to Sat.*

Cabaret Mechanical Theatre, 33-34 The Market, Covent Garden WC2 071-379 7961 2D 92
Contemporary automata, 50 bush button displays. *Open 10.00-18.30 Tues. to Sun. Admission charge.*

Changing the Guard and **Horse Guards**
One of the Capital's great traditions with impeccable displays of pageantry, military precision, colour and music, always well attended so arrive early for the best view- especially with children. The Changing of the Queen's Guard takes place at *Buckingham Palace* every morning at 11.30 during the summer, on alternate days in winter months. The ceremony is carried out by one of the five regiments of Foot Guards marching to a military band (no band in wet weather). The Changing of the Queen's Life Guard takes place in the small courtyard of *Horse Guards* daily at 11.00 (Sundays 10.00) carried out by the Household Cavalry. See also page 8.

Chessington World of Adventures,
Leatherhead Road, Chessington 03727 727227 3B 43 Theme park and fun fair with over 100

attractions and rides; also zoo and circus world; skyway monorail. *Open: zoo all year daily; theme park March to October only. Admission charge.*

Court Dress Collection, Kensington Palace 071-937 9561 5D 88
Colourful collection of historical costumes worn at Court 1750 to the 1930's. The Palace State Apartments are also open, see also page 16 *Open 09.00-17.00 Mon. to Sat. 13.00-17.00 Sun. Admisson charge.*

Docklands Light Railway, Passenger enquiries 071-222 1234
A spectacular ride from Tower Gateway Station 2J 95 over the developing docklands to Island Gardens; (pedestrian tunnel under the Thames gives access to Greenwich).

Guinness World of Records, Trocadero Centre, Piccadilly Circus W1 071-439 7331 3A 92 and 3E 3
An exhibition designed to transform the "Book of Records" into a three dimensional presentation. *Open 10.00-22.00 daily. Admission charge.*

Heritage Motor Museum, Syon Park, London Road, Brentford 081-560 1378 2B 43
Over a hundred historic motor vehicles showing the development of the British Motor Industry. The British Motor Industry Heritage Trust make periodic changes to the displays drawing on its extensive reserve collection covering dozens of famous by long-gone marques. See also Syon House and London Butterfly House. *Open daily. Admission charge.*

Highgate Cemetery, Swains Lane N6 081-340 1834 1C 43
Eastern side (Karl Marx is buried here). *Open daily summer months.* Western side with catacombs by guided tour only.

Horniman Museum, 100 London Rd., SE23 081-699 2339 2C 43
Experience the world's living heritage in the unique Horniman Museum; arts and crafts, musical instruments from around the world, but especially the natural environment. Enjoy one of the best views of London from the Horniman Gardens, with animals, nature trails and picnic area. To open in 1991. "Living Waters", a unique conservation-minded aquarium experience. *Open 10.30-17.50 Mon. to Sat. 14.00-17.050 Sun.*

Imperial War Museum, Lambeth Road, SE1 071-735 8922 2H 101
For those interested in guns, and most children seem to be, this museum displays every variety of them, tanks, howitzers, a battle ship gun turret; there are aircraft, torpedos, a German one man submarine and lots more. There are also dramatic recreations with sounds, smells and special effects, WW1 "Trench Experience" and WWII "Blitz Experience". *Open 10.00-18.00 daily. Admisson charge, free on Fridays. See also page 16.*

Laserium, London Planetarium, Marylebone Rd, NW1 4D 82 and 2C 2
Laser Light concerts most evenings; 071-486 2242 for details.

London Butterfly House, Syon Park, London Rd., Brentford 081-560 7272 2B 43
Large undercover tropical garden set with pools and water cascades, filled with colourful flowers and hundreds of free-flying butterflies, their caterpillars and pupae; also tropical birds, reptiles and fish. Additional displays of exotic insects, spiders and a seasonal British butterfly house. See also Syon House and Heritage Motor Museum. *Open daily. Admission charge.*

London Diamond Centre, 10 Hanover St., W1 071-629 5511 1G 91
Exhibition of diamond working and tour of workshops. *Open 09.30-17.30 Mon. to Fri. to 13.00 Sat.*

London Dungeon, 28-34 Tooley Street, SE1 071-403 0606 5E 95 and 4H 3
An exhibition of gruesome and macabre events, not recommended by the management to the nervous or unaccompanied children. *Open 10.00-17.30 (to 16.30 winter). Admission charge.*

London Ecology Centre, 45 Shelton Street, WC2 071-379 4324 1C 92
Exhibitions on ecological themes, information service on matters "green"; gift shop & National Trust Shop. *Open 10.30-18.00 Mon. to Fri.*

London Transport Museum, Covent Garden, WC2 071-379 6344 2D 92
If you've always wanted to sit in the driving seat of a double decker London bus or underground train, here's your chance; surrounded by an evocative display of all those old buses, trams and trollybuses you usually only see in photo's and films, *Open 10.00-18.00 daily. Admission charge. See also page 18*

London Zoo, Regents Park, NW1 071-722 3333 off 1E 82
For a day with a difference you can wander round one of Central Londons green oasis-Regent's Park, and yet be within eyeshot, ear-shot and camera shot of thousands of animals from around the world. There's also a 'Childrens Zoo', various rides and animal feeding can be seen at advertised times. *Open*

March to Oct. 09.00-18.00, (19.00 Sun. & Bank Hols.); Nov. to Feb. 10.00-Dusk. Admission charge. See also page 18/19

Lord's Cricket Ground Tours St John's Wood Rd., NW8 1B 2
Tours include The Long Room, Mound Stand, and Museum. Bookings 071-266 3825

Madame Tussauds, Marylebone Road, NW1
071-935 6861 4D 82
An old favourite for a family visit; the best known and most visited waxwork exhibition in the world. This is probably the closest you will ever come to meeting royalty, famous superstars and politicians-possibly too close in some cases. *Open: 10.00-17.30 daily (from 09.00 summer months, from 09.30 weekends). Admission charge, See also page 18.*

Museum of the Moving Image, South Bank Arts Centre, SE1 071-928 3232 4F 92
Take a journey back in time from the moving images of today's films and TV, to the shadow plays of 2500 BC. Participate in film and video processes, everything from the silent movie techniques of Charlie Chaplin to the modern television studio. *Open 10.00-20.00 Tues. to Sat. 10.00-18.00 Sun. Closed Mondays. Admission charge. See also page 21*

National Maritime Museum, Romney Road, Greenwich SE19 081-858 4422 2C 43
Ideally sited between Greenwich Park and the River Thames; here the story of Britain's maritime history is told. Good displays of boats and barges, models, paintings, navigational instruments; galleries devoted to Cook, Nelson and Trafalgar. Planetarium gives educational and public performances during school holidays. Nearby are the Cutty Sark and Gipsy Moth IV. *Open 10.00-18.00 Mon. to Sat. 14.00-18.00 Sun. (closes 17.00 winter). Admission charge. See also page 44/45*

National Theatre Tours, Upper Ground SE1
4F 93
Tour the backstage areas and auditoriums. Bookings 071-633 0880

Natural History Museum,Cromwell Road, SW7 071-589 6323 2G 67
Exciting exhibitions invite you to discover a new way of looking at natural history, Origin of Species, Dinosaurs and their living relatives, Discovering Mammals, Man's Place in Evolution-and much more. The traditional displays include everything from huge exhibits like the Whale and Elephant to tiny birds and insects. The Children's Centre will provide trail sheets for an indoor nature trail. *Open 10.00-18.00 Mon. to Sat. 11.00-18.00 Sun. Admission charge. See also page 21.*

Planetarium, Marylebone Road, NW1
071-486 1121 4D 82
Regular daily performances 11.00-18.00. *Admission charge.* For description see London Planetarium

Pollock's Toy Museum, 1 Scala Street, W1
071-636 3452 5J 83
Toy theatres, dolls, teddy bears, games, toys of all kinds. Theatre kits for sale. *Open 10.00-17.00 Mon. to Sat. Admission charge.*

Rock Circus, London Pavilion, Piccadilly Circus, 3A 92 and 3C 3
An exhibition and audio-visual experience presenting the story of rock and pop music from the 1950's onwards; features both the stars and their music. *Open 10.00-22.00 daily. Admission charge.*

Royal Air Force Museum, Grahame Park Way, Hendon, NW9 081-205 2266 1B 43
An exciting display of aircraft, equipment, bombs, missiles—bringing over 100 years of aviation history to life. *Open 10.00-18.00 daily. Admission charge. See also page 49*

Royal Mews, Buckingham Palace Road, SW1
1G 99
You can inspect all those lovely carriages and coaches that you last saw in a Royal Wedding procession, only warn your little children there won't be anyone inside waving! the horses can also be seen in the stable block. *Open Wed. and Thurs. 14.00-16,00. Admisson charge. (not open Royal Ascot week). See also page 25*

Royalty and Empire, Thames St., Windsor
0753 857837 2A 43
A Madame Tussaud's animated exhibition recreating Queen Victorias Diamond Jubilee in 1897; includes sumptuous settings with life size figures, and audio show. *Open daily. Admission charge.*

Rugby Football Union Tours, Rugby Road, Twickenham 2B 43
Tours behind the scenes, Museum; includes audio-visual show. Bookings 081-892 8161

Science Museum, Exhibiton Road, SW7
071-938 8000 2H 87
Historical collections showing the development of transport, communications, industry. 'The Sciences' but also much more including exploration of space; an interactive gallery "Launch Pad" with things to do for children of all ages. Hundreds of working models with knobs to press and handles to turn. *Open 10.00-18.00 Mon. to Sat. 11.00-18.00 Sun. Admission charge. See also page 27.*

Ships
1. HMS Belfast : see page 6
2. Cutty Sark : see Greenwich page 44
3. Kathleen and May : St. Mary Overie Dock, Cathedral St., SE1 071-403 3965 4D 94. The last "three masted" topsail wooden schooner. *Open 10.00-17.00 Mon. to Fri. 11.00-16.00 Sat. & Sun.*
4. Tobacco Dock : Two replica 18th century ships; The Three Sisters with history of piracy exhibition and The Sea Lark with an audio-visual presentation of Treasure Island.

Telecom Technology Showcase, Baynard House, Queen Victoria St., EC4 071-248 7444 2A 94.
The story of telecommunications; working exhibits and video presentations. *Open 10.00-17.00 Mon. to Fri.*

Thames Barrier, Unity Way, Woolwich SE18 081-854 1373 2D 43
Exhibition, viewing platform, audio-visual presentation, shop, riverside walk. *Open 10.35-17.00 daily. Admission charge.*

Theatre, professional theatre for young audiences
1. Little Angel Marionette Theatre, 14 Dagmar Passage, Cross St. N1 071-226 1787
2. Polka Childrens Theatre, 240 Broadway SW19 081-543 4888
3. Unicorn Theatre for Young People, Gt. Newport St., WC2 071-836 3334

Thorpe Park, Staines Road, Chertsey 0932-562633 3A 43
Theme park and fun fair with over 70 attractions around a lakeland setting. *Open summer months. Admission charge.*

Tower Bridge and Tower Bridge Walkway, SE1 071-407 0922 4H 95
Walk over the River 142ft. up, along a glass sided walkway for a dramatic view, also see the exhibiton of the original machinery. *Open 10.00-18.30 daily; to 16.45 winter (last ticket 45 mins. earlier). Admission charge. See also page 32.*

Tower of London, EC3 071-709 0765 3H 95
You can sense the 900 years of history encased within these ancient walls, the political intrigue, the doom of those incarcerated or executed here in times past. In present times these walls enclose no less than four separate museums, The Crown Jewels, The Royal Armouries, The Heralds Museum and The Royal Fusiliers Museum; but the ancient walls and towers, dungeons and chapels are the prime attraction. *Open March to Oct. 09.30-17.00 Mon. to Sat. 14.00-17.00 Sun. Nov. to Feb. 09.30-16.00 Mon. to Sat. only. Admission charge. See also page 32-35*

YEOMAN WARDER: Tower of London

Toy Museums, see
London Toy and Model Museum
Bethnal Green Museum of Childhood
Pollock's Toy Museum

Views.
1. The Monument : views over the City of London from 202 ft, see page 20
2. Queens Tower : Imperial College Rd., SW7 1G 97 Views over central London from 287 ft. clock tower, all that remains of the Imperial Institute. *Open 10.00-17.30 July, Aug, Sept.*
3. St. Paul's Cathedral : views from the Stone Gallery at 182 ft. and the Golden Gallery at 281ft. see page 27/28
4. Tower Bridge Walkway : views from 142 ft. walkway over the River Thames and City, see page 32
5. Westminster Cathedral : views over Westminster from 284 ft. Campanile see page 40/41
6. Panoramic View: from the South Bank Centre 4F 93, you can enjoy a sweeping view from the Houses of Parliament to St. Paul's Cathedral.

Wembley Stadium Tours, Empire Way. 1B 43
Tour behind the scenes, dressing rooms, Royal Box Steps; includes audio-visual show. Bookings 081-902 8833

Windsor Safari Park, Winkfield Road, Windsor 0753-830866 2A 43
This 'African Adventure' includes the famous drive through reserves to view giraffes, rhinos, zebra, camels, baboon, tigers and lions; safari bus rides are available. Additional enclosures include a cliff side Elephant Garden with 'Tree Tops' viewing platform; Seaworld Show with performing dolphins, Tropical House, Birds of Prey with demonstration flights etc. Family fun rides. *Open daily. Admission charge.*

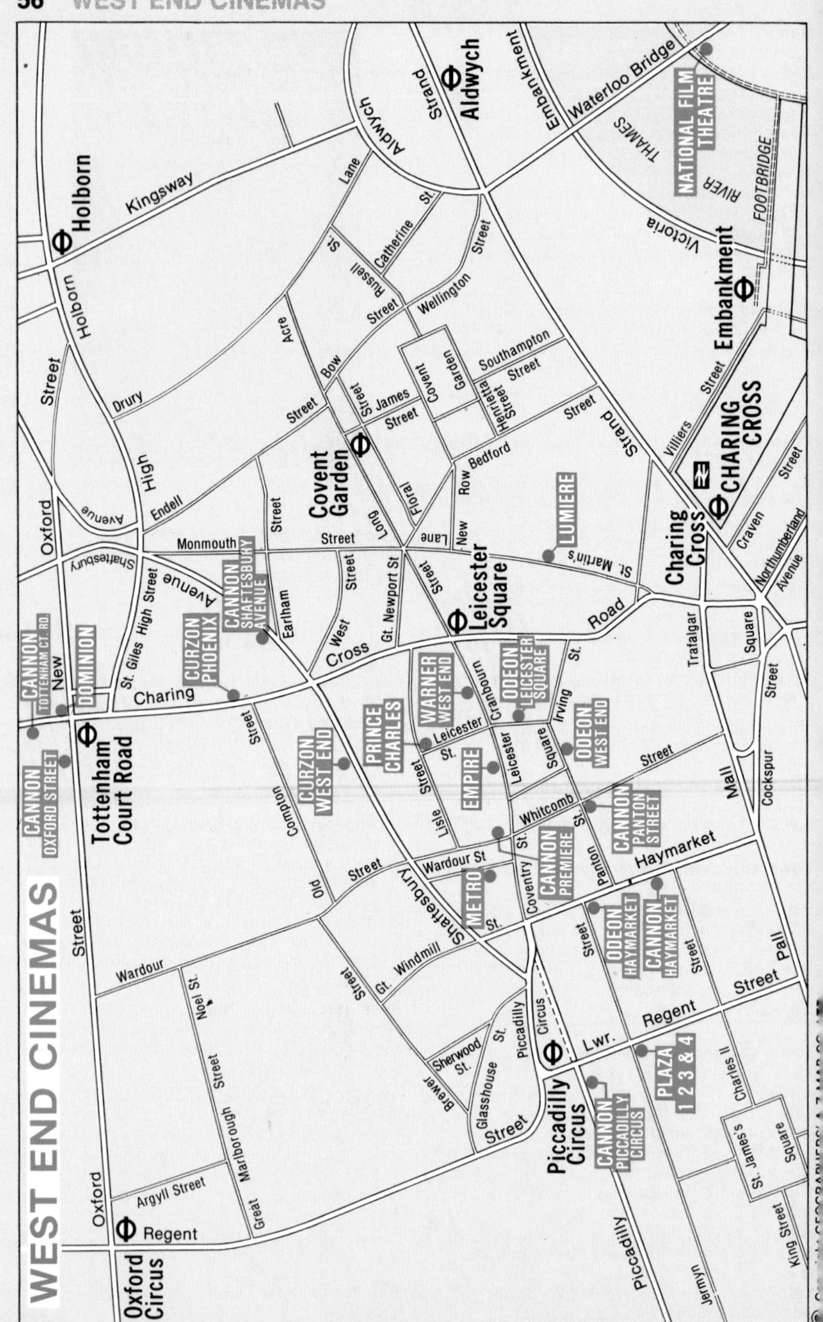
WEST END CINEMAS
CANNON TOTTENHAM CT. RD.
DOMINION
CANNON OXFORD STREET
CURZON PHOENIX
CANNON SHAFTESBURY AVENUE
CURZON WEST END
PRINCE CHARLES
WARNER WEST END
EMPIRE
ODEON LEICESTER SQUARE
ODEON WEST END
LUMIERE
CANNON PANTON STREET
CANNON PREMIERE
METRO
ODEON HAYMARKET
CANNON HAYMARKET
PLAZA 1 2 3 & 4
CANNON PICCADILLY CIRCUS
NATIONAL FILM THEATRE
Holborn
Aldwych
Covent Garden
Leicester Square
Tottenham Court Road
Charing Cross
CHARING CROSS
Embankment
Piccadilly Circus
Oxford Circus
RIVER THAMES
FOOTBRIDGE
Waterloo Bridge
Victoria Embankment
Kingsway
Strand
Oxford Street
New Oxford Street
Charing Cross Road
Shaftesbury Avenue
Long Acre
Drury Lane
High Holborn
Endell Street
Monmouth Street
St. Giles High Street
Earlham Street
Gt. Newport St
West Street
St. Martin's Lane
Bow Street
Russell St.
Catherine St.
Wellington Street
James Street
Floral Street
Henrietta Street
Southampton Street
Bedford Street
New Row
Cranbourn Street
Leicester Square
Irving St.
Lisle Street
Leicester St.
Wardour Street
Wardour St
Old Compton Street
Whitcomb Street
Coventry St.
Panton St.
Haymarket
Gt. Windmill St.
Brewer Street
Sherwood St.
Glasshouse Street
Piccadilly
Piccadilly Circus
Lwr. Regent Street
Charles II Street
St. James's Square
King Street
Jermyn Street
Pall Mall
Cockspur Street
Trafalgar Square
Northumberland Avenue
Craven Street
Villiers Street
Noel St.
Great Marlborough Street
Argyll Street
Regent Street

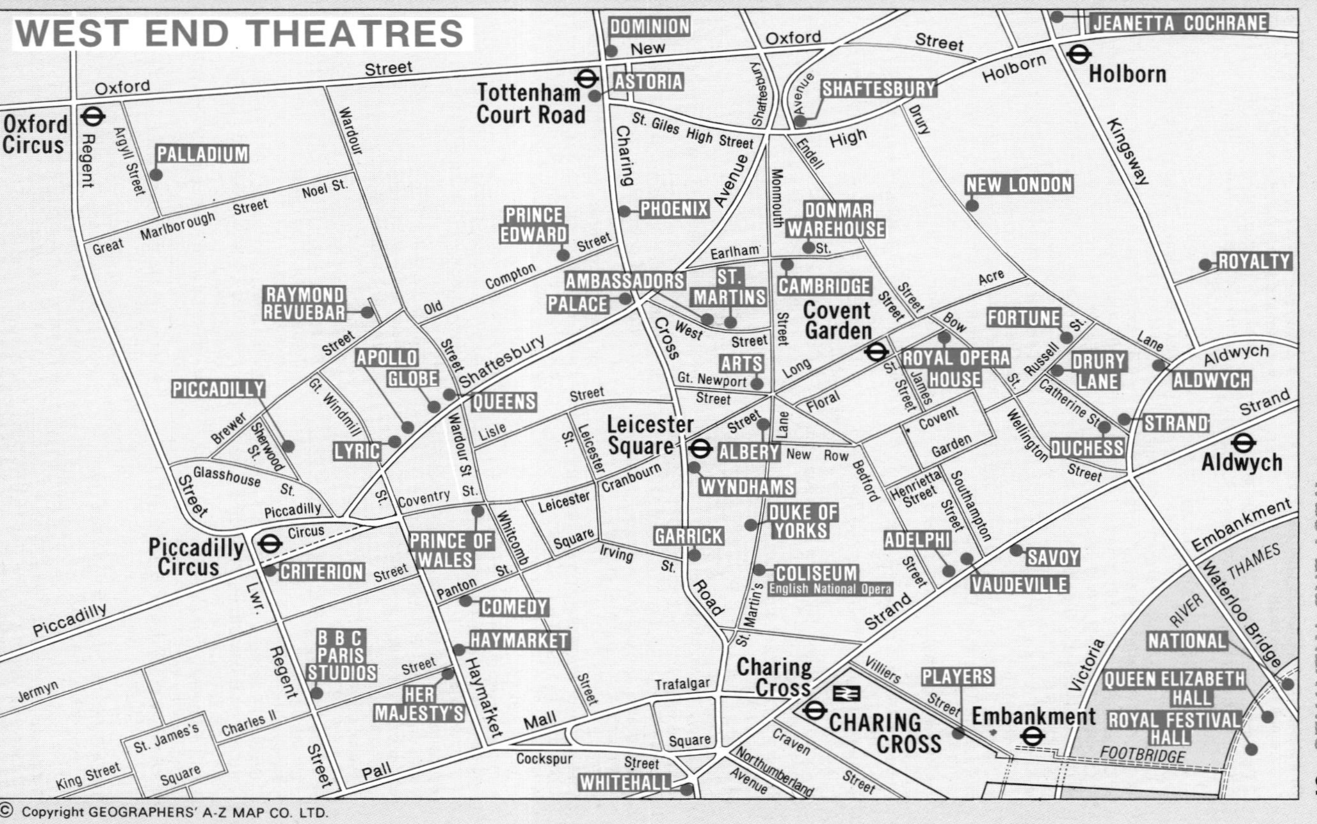
WEST END THEATRES
DOMINION
JEANETTA COCHRANE
ASTORIA
SHAFTESBURY
PALLADIUM
NEW LONDON
PHOENIX
PRINCE EDWARD
DONMAR WAREHOUSE
ROYALTY
AMBASSADORS
ST. MARTINS
CAMBRIDGE
PALACE
RAYMOND REVUEBAR
FORTUNE
ARTS
ROYAL OPERA HOUSE
DRURY LANE
ALDWYCH
APOLLO
GLOBE
PICCADILLY
QUEENS
STRAND
LYRIC
ALBERY
DUCHESS
WYNDHAMS
DUKE OF YORKS
GARRICK
ADELPHI
PRINCE OF WALES
SAVOY
CRITERION
COLISEUM
English National Opera
VAUDEVILLE
COMEDY
HAYMARKET
NATIONAL
B B C PARIS STUDIOS
PLAYERS
QUEEN ELIZABETH HALL
HER MAJESTY'S
ROYAL FESTIVAL HALL
WHITEHALL
Oxford Circus
Tottenham Court Road
Holborn
Covent Garden
Leicester Square
Aldwych
Piccadilly Circus
Charing Cross
CHARING CROSS
Embankment
New Oxford Street
Oxford Street
Holborn
Kingsway
Regent Street
Argyll Street
Great Marlborough Street
Noel St.
Wardour Street
Charing Cross Road
St. Giles High Street
Shaftesbury Avenue
Endell Street
High Holborn
Drury Lane
Monmouth Street
Earlham St.
Old Compton Street
Long Acre
West Street
Gt. Newport Street
Bow Street
Russell St.
Catherine St.
Wellington Street
Floral Street
James Street
Covent Garden
Henrietta Street
Southampton Street
Bedford Street
New Row
St. Martin's Lane
Lisle Street
Leicester Street
Cranbourn Street
Leicester Square
Irving St.
Wardour St
Gt. Windmill Street
Brewer Street
Sherwood St.
Glasshouse St.
Piccadilly Circus
Coventry St.
Whitcomb Street
Panton St.
Piccadilly
Lwr. Regent Street
Jermyn Street
Haymarket
Charles II Street
St. James's Square
King Street
Pall Mall
Cockspur Street
Trafalgar Square
Strand
Villiers Street
Craven Street
Northumberland Avenue
Victoria Embankment
Waterloo Bridge
RIVER THAMES
FOOTBRIDGE
© Copyright GEOGRAPHERS' A-Z MAP CO. LTD.

CINEMAS ★ indicates on West End Cinemas Map page 56

Barbican, Silk Street EC2 071-638 8891
Cannon Baker Street, Marylebone Rd., NW1 071-935 9772
Cannon Chelsea, 279 Kings Road, SW3 071-352 5096
Cannon, Fulham Rd., SW10 071-370 2636
★ **Cannon,** Haymarket SW1 071-839 1527
★ **Cannon,** Oxford St., W1 071-636 0310
★ **Cannon,** Panton St., SW1 071-930 0631
★ **Cannon Piccadilly Circus,** Piccadilly W1 071-437 3561
★ **Cannon Premiere,** Leicester Sq., W1 071-439 4470
★ **Cannon,** Shaftesbury Av., W1 071-379 7025
★ **Cannon,** Tottenham Court Road, W1 071-636 6148
Chelsea Cinema, 206 Kings Road, SW3 071-351 3742
Curzon Mayfair, Curzon St., W1 071-499 3737
★ **Curzon Phoenix,** Charing Cross Rd., WC2 071-240 9661
★ **Curzon West End,** 93 Shaftesbury Av., W1 071-439 4805
★ **Dominion,** Tottenham Court Rd., W1 071-580 9562
★ **Empire,** Leicester Sq., WC2 071-437 1234
Institute of Contemporary Arts (ICA). The Mall SW1 071-930 3647
★ **Lumiere,** St. Martins La., WC2 071-836 0691
★ **Metro,** Rupert St., W1 071-437 0757
Mezzanine, see Odeon Leicester Square
Minema, 45 Knightsbridge SW1 071-235 4225
Museum of the Moving Image (MOMI) South Bank SE1 071-401 2636
★ **National Film Theatre** South Bank SE1 071-928 3232
★ **Odeon,** Haymarket SW1 071-839 7697
Odeon, Kensington High Street, W8 071-602 6644
★ **Odeon,** Leicester Square, WC2 071-930 6111
Odeon, Marble Arch W1 071-723 2011
★ **Odeon West End,** Leicester Sq., WC2 071-930 5252
★ **Plaza,** Lower Regent Street SW1 071-437 1234
★ **Prince Charles,** Leicester Sq., WC2 071-437 8181
Renoir, Brunswick Sq., WC1 071-837 8402
Scala, 275 Pentonville Rd., N1 071-278 0051
Screen on Baker Street, 96 Baker St., NW1 071-935 2772
UCI Whiteleys, Whiteleys Centre, Queensway W2 071-792 3303
★ **Warner West End,** Leicester Sq., WC2 071-439 0791

THEATRES ★ indicates on West End Theatres Map page 57

★ **Adelphi,** Strand WC2 071-836 7611
★ **Albery,** St. Martin's La., WC2 071-867 1115
★ **Aldwych,** The Aldwych WC2 071-836 6404
★ **Ambassadors,** West St., WC2 071-836 1171
★ **Apollo,** Shaftesbury Av., WC2 071-437 2663
Apollo Victoria, 17 Wilton Rd., WC1 071-630 6262
★ **Arts,** Gt. Newport St., WC2 071-836 2132
★ **Astoria,** Charing Cross Rd., WC2 071-434 0403
Barbican, Silk St., EC2 071-638 8891
★ **BBC Paris Theatre/Studios** Lower Regent St., SW1
Bloomsbury, 15 Gordon St., WC1 071-387 9629
★ **Cambridge,** Earlham St., WC2 071-379 5299
★ **Comedy,** Panton St., SW1 071-930 2578
★ **Cottesloe**-see National Theatre
★ **Criterion,** Piccadilly Circus, W1 071-867 1117
★ **Dominion,** Tottenham Court Rd., W1 071-580 9562
★ **Donmar Warehouse,** 41 Earlham St., WC2 071-240 8230
★ **Drury Lane,** Catherine St., WC2 071-836 8108
★ **Duchess,** Catherine St., WC2 071-836 8243
★ **Duke of York's,** St. Martin's La., WC2 071-836 5122
★ **Fortune,** Russell St., WC2 071-836 2238
★ **Garrick,** Charing Cross Rd., WC2 071-379 6107
★ **Globe,** Shaftesbury Av., W1 071-437 3667
★ **Haymarket,** Haymarket SW1 071-930 9832
★ **Her Majesty's,** Haymarket SW1 071-839 2244
Institute of Contemporary Arts (ICA) The Mall SW1 071-930 3647
Jeanetta Cochrane, Theobalds Rd., WC1 071-242 7040
★ **Lyric,** Shaftesbury Av., W1 071-437 3686
★ **Lyttlelton** see National Theatre
Mermaid, Puddle Dock EC4 071-236 5568
★ **National Theatre,** Upper Ground, South Bank SE1 071-928 2252
★ **New London,** Parker Street, WC2 071-405 0072
Old Vic, Waterloo Rd., SE1 071-928 7616
★ **Olivier** see National Theatre
Open Air Theatre, Regents Park, NW1 071-935 5756
★ **Palace,** Shaftesbury Av., W1 071-434 0909
★ **Paladium,** Argyll St., W1 071-437 7373
★ **Phoenix,** Charing Cross Rd., W1 071-836 2294
★ **Piccadilly,** Denman St., W1 071-867 1118
Playhouse, Northumberland Av., WC2 071-839 4401
★ **Prince Edward,** Old Compton St., W1 071-734 8951
★ **Prince of Wales,** Coventry St., W1 071-839 5972
★ **Queen's,** Shaftesbury Av., W1 071-734 1166
Royal Court, Sloane Sq., SW1 071-730 1745
Royal Shakespeare Company, see Barbican
★ **Royalty,** Portugal St., WC2 071-831 0660
★ **St. Martin's,** West St., WC2 071-836 1443
★ **Savoy,** Strand WC2 071-836 8888

★ **Shaftesbury,** Shaftesbury Av., WC2 071-379 5399
Shaw, 100 Euston Rd., NW1 071-388 1394
★ **Strand,** Aldwych WC2 071-836 2660
★ **Theatre Royal Drury Lane,** see Drury Lane
★ **Theatre Royal Haymarket,** see Haymarket
★ **Vaudeville,** Strand, WC2 071-836 5645
Victoria Palace, Victoria St., SW1 071-834 1317
Westminster, Palace St., SW1 071-834 0283
★ **Whitehall,** 14 Whitehall SW1 071-867 1119
★ **Wyndhams,** Charing Cross Rd., WC2 071-836 3028

FRINGE THEATRE Selected Venues.

Albany Empire, Douglas Way SE8 081-691 3333
Almeida Theatre, 1a/1b Almeida Street N1 071-359 4404
Battersea Arts Centre, Lavender Hill SW11 071-223 8413
Boulevard Theatre, Walkers Court W1 071-437 2661
Bush Theatre, Bush Hotel, Shepherd's Bush Green W12 081-743 3388
Cafe Theatre, Bear and Staff, 37 Charing Cross Rd., WC2 071-240 9582
Canal Cafe Theatre, Bridge Ho., Delamere Terrace, Little Venice W2 071-289 6054
Comedy Store, 28a Leicester Sq., WC2 071-839 6665
Corner Theatre, Hen and Chicken, Highbury Corner N1 071-226 3724
Finborough Theatre Club, Finborough Arms, Finborough Rd., SW10 071-373 3842
Gate Theatre Club, Prince Albert Pub, 11 Pembridge Rd., W11 071-229 0706
Greenwich Studio Theatre, Prince of Orange, Greenwich High Rd., SE10 081-858 2862
Hackney Empire, 291 Mare Street E8 081-985 2424
Half Moon Theatre, 213 Mile End Rd., E1 071-790 4000
Hampstead Theatre Club, Swiss Cottage Centre, Avenue Rd., NW5 071-722 9301
I C A The Mall SW1 071-930 3647
Kings Head Theatre Club, 115 Upper Street N1 071-226 1916
Lyric Hammersmith, King Street, W6 071-741 2311
Man in the Moon, 392 Kings Road, SW3 071-351 2876
Old Red Lion Theatre, 418 St. John Street, EC1 071-833 3053
Oval House Arts Centre, 54 Kennington Oval, SE11 071-582 7680
Riverside Studios, Crisp Road, W6 081-748 3354
Royal Court, Sloane Square, SW1 071-730 1745
Soho Poly Theatre Club, 16 Riding House Street, W1 071-636 9050
Tabard Theatre, 2 Bath Road, W4 081-995 6035
Theatre Royal Stratford East, Gerry Raffles Square E15 081-537 0310
Watermans Arts Centre, 40 High Street, Brentford 081-568 1176
Young Vic, 66 The Cut, SE1 071-928 6363

EXHIBITION HALLS AND CENTRES.

Alexandra Palace and Park, Wood Green, N22 081-365 2121
Barbican Centre, Silk St., EC2 071-638 4141
Building Centre, 26 Store St., WC1 (enquiries Winkfield Row 884999)
Business Design Centre, 52 Upper St., N1 071-359 3535
Central Hall, Storeys Gate SW1 071-222 8010
Commonwealth Institute, 230 Kensington High St. W8 071-603 4535
Contemporary Applied Arts-Crafts Centre, 43 Earlham St., WC2 071-836 6993
Crafts Gallery, 12 Waterloo Place SW1 071-930 4811
Design Centre, 28 Haymarket SW1 071-839 8000
Earls Court Exhibiton Halls, Warwick Rd., SW5 071-385 1200
London Arena, Limeharbour, E14 071-583 8880
Olympia Exhibition Halls, Hammersmith Rd., W14 071-603 3344
Royal Horticultural Society Halls, Vincent Sq., SW1 071-630 0770
Sandown Exhibition Centre, Sandown Park, Esher, Surrey 0372 67540
Wembly Arena, Conference and Exhibition Centre, Empire Way, 081-902 8833
Westminster Exhibition Centre-see Royal Horticultural Society Halls.

CONCERT HALLS, OPERA, BALLET & DANCE VENUES.

Barbican, Silk St., EC2 071-638 8891
Coliseum, St. Martin's La., WC2 071-836 3161
Dominion, Tottenham Court Rd., WC1 071-580 9562
English National Opera, see Coliseum
Purcell Room, as for Royal Festival Hall
Queen Elizabeth Hall, as for Royal Festival Hall
Riverside Studios, Crisp Rd:, W6 081-748 3354
Royal Albert Hall, Kensington Gore SW7 071-589 8212
Royal Festival Hall, Belvedere Rd., South Bank SE1 071-928 8800
Royal Opera House, Bow St., WC2 071-240 1066
Sadler's Wells Theatre, Rosebery Av., EC1 071-278 8916
St. John's Smith Square, Smith Sq., SW1 071-222 1061
The Place, 17 Dukes St., WC1 071-380 1268
Wigmore Hall, 36 Wigmore St., W1 071-935 2141

CONFERENCE AND TRADE EXHIBITION CENTRES.

Alexandra Palace and Park, Wood Green, N22 071-365 2121
B.A.F.T.A. Conference Centre, 195 Piccadilly W1 071-734 0022
Barbican Conference & Exhibition Centre, Silk St., EC2 071-638 4141
Brewery, The. Whitbread & Co. Chiswell St., EC1 071-606 4455
Business Centre, London City Airport, King George V Dock, Silvertown E16 071-476 3999
Business Design Centre, 52 Upper Street N1 071-359 3535
Butchers Hall 87 Bartholomew Close EC1 071-600 5777
Cafe Royal 68 Regent Street W1 071-437 9090
CBI. Centre Point, New Oxford St., W1 071-379 7400
Central Hall, Storey's Gate SW1 071-222 8010
Centre 257, 257 Liverpool Street N1 071-609 8454
CFS. Conference Centre, 22 Portman Cl., W1 071-486 4152
Church House, Deans Yard, Westminster SW1 071-222 2348
City Conference Centre, 76 Mark La., EC3 071-488 1854
City University, Northampton Sq., EC1 071-253 4399
Civils, The. Conference Centre, Inst. of Civil Engineers, Gt. George St., SW1 071-222 7722
Commonwealth Institute, Kensington High St., W8 071-603 4535
Conference Forum, Sedgwick Centre, E1 071-481 5204
Crosby Hall, Cheyne Walk SW3 071-352 9663
Earls Court, Warwick Rd., SW5 071-385 1200
English Speaking Union, Dartmouth House 37 Charles Street W1 071-495 6108
Glaziers Hall, 9 Montague Close SE1 071-403 3300
Gresham Suite, Level 12, Frobisher Crescent, Barbican EC2 071-920 0111
Hop Exchange, 24 Southwark Street SE1 071-403 2573
Hurlingham Club, Ranelagh Gardens SW6 071-736 8411
Imperial College, Conference Office, Exhibition Rd. SW7 071-589 5111
Institute of Directors, 116 Pall Mall SW1 071-839 1233
Kempton Park Conference & Business Centre, Sunbury-on-Thames, Middlesex 0932 786199
Kensington Town Hall, Hornton St., W8 071-937 5464
London Arena, Limeharbour E1 071-538 8880
London Press Centre, 76 Shoe La., EC4 071-353 6211
London School of Economics, Houghton Street WC2 071-405 7686
Lords Banqueting & Conference Centre, St. John's Wood Road, NW8 071-621 0315
Olympia and Olympia 2, Hammersmith Rd., W14 071-603 3344
Olympia Conference Centre see above
Podium, The. Market Towers, 1 Nine Elms La. SW8 071-720 9200
Polytechnic of Central London, 309 Regent Street W1 071-580 2020
Polytechnic of North London, James Leicester Hall, Market Rd., N7 071-607 3250
Queen Elizabeth II Conference Centre, Broad Sanctuary SW1 071-222 5000
Queen Mary College, 98-110 High Road, E18 081-504 9282
Regent's College, Regent's Park NW1 071-487 7540
Regus Conference Centre, 1 Northumberland Av., WC2 071-872 5959
Royal Albert Hall, Kensington Gore, SW7 071-589 8212
Royal Festival Hall, Belvedere Rd., SE1 071-928 8800
Royal Society of Arts, 8 John Alan St., WC2 071-930 5115
Sandown Park Conference & Business Centre, Portsmouth Road Esher, Surrey 0372-65292
Wembley Arena & Conference Centre, Empire Way 081-902 8833
World Trade Centre, St. Katherine by the Tower, E1 01-488 2400

GALLERIES Main Collections & Public Galleries

☐ indicates see guide section for description

Barbican Art Gallery Level 8, Silk St., EC2 071-638 4141
Canada House Gallery, Trafalgar Square SW1 071-629 9492
Clore Gallery, see Tate Gallery
☐ **Courtauld Institute Galleries** Somerset House, Strand 071-873 2777
Crafts Gallery, 12 Waterloo Place, SW1 071-930 4811
☐ **Dulwich Picture Gallery,** College Road, SE21 081-693 5254
Hayward Gallery, South Bank Centre, Belvedere Road, SW1 071-928 3144
I C A The Mall SW1 071-930 0493
☐ **Iveagh Bequest,** Kenwood House, Hampstead Lane, NW3 081-348 1286
☐ **Leighton House,** 12 Holland Park Rd., W14 071-602 3316
London Institute Gallery, 388-396 Oxford Street, W1 071-491 8533 (entrance in Bird Street)
☐ **National Gallery,** Trafalgar Square WC2 071-839 3321
☐ **National Portrait Gallery,** St. Martin's Place WC2 071-930 1552
Orleans House Gallery, Riverside, Twickenham 081-892 0221
Photographer's Gallery, 5 & 8 Great Newport Street WC2 071-831 1772
☐ **Queen's Gallery,** Buckingham Palace Rd., SW1 071-930 4832
R I B A, Heinz Gallery, 21 Portman Square, W1

071-580 5533
☐ **Royal Academy of Arts,** Burlington House, Piccadilly W1 071-439 7438
Saatchi Collection 98a Boundary Rd., NW8 071-624 8299
Serpentine Gallery, Kensington Gardens, W2 071-402 6075
☐ **Tate Gallery,** Millbank SW1 071-821 1313
☐ **Wallace Collection,** Hertford House, Manchester Square Square W1 071-935 0687
Whitechapel Galleries, Whitechapel High Street E1 071-377 0107
Woodlands Art Gallery, 90 Mycenae Road SE3 081-858 4631

Selection of Commercial Galleries

Abbot and Holder, 30 Museum Street WC1 071-637 3931
Addison Ross, 40 Eaton Terrace SW1 071-730 1536
Africa Centre, 38 King Street WC2 071-836 1973
Agnew's, 43 Old Bond Street, W1 071-629 6176
Air Gallery, 6 & 8 Rosebery Avenue EC1 071-278 7751
Albemarle Gallery, 18 Albemarle Street W1 071-355 1880
Anderson O'Day, 255 Portobello Road, W11 071-221 7592
Angela Flowers Gallery, 11 Tottenham Mews W1 071 637 3089
Annely Juda Fine Art, 11 Tottenham Mews W1 071-637 5517
Anthony d'Offay, 23 Dering Street, W1 071-499 4100
Bankside Gallery, 48 Hopton Street, SE1 071-928 7521
Belgrave Gallery, 22 Mason's Yard, SW1 071-930 0294
Ben Uri Art Society, 21 Dean Street W1 071-437 2852
Berkeley Square Gallery, 23a Bruton Street, W1 071-493 7939
Boundary Gallery, 98 Boundary Road, NW8 071-624 1126
Browse & Darby, 19 Cork Street, W1 071-734 7984
Bury Street Gallery, 11 Bury Street, SW1 071-930 2902
C C A Galleries, 8 Dover Street W1 071-499 6701
Colnaghi 14 Old Bond Street W1 071-491 7408
Contemporary Applied Arts, Crafts Centre, 45 Earlham St., WC2 071-836 6993
Curwen Gallery, 4 Windmill Street W1 071-636 1459
Douwes Fine Art, 38 Duke Street SW1 071-839 5795
Drian Galleries, 7 Porchester Place W2 071-723 9473
Fine Art Society, 148 New Bond Street W1 071-629 5116
Fischer Fine Art, 30 King Street SW1 071-839 3942
Gimpel Fils, 30 Davies Street, W1 071-493 2488
Grosvenor Gallery, 48 South Molton Street W1 071-629 0891
Lefevre Gallery, 30 Bruton Street W1 071-493 2107
Leger Galleries, 13 Old Bond Street W1 071-629 3538
Leggatt Brothers, 17 Duke Street SW1 071-930 3772
Lumley Gazalet, 24 Davies Street W1 071-491 4767
Marlborough Fine Art, 6 Albermarle Street, W1 071-629 5161
New Art Centre, 41 Sloane Street, SW1 071-235 5844
Paton Gallery, 2 Langley Court, WC2 071-379 7854
Piccadilly Gallery, 16 Cork Street, W1 071-629 2875
Portal Gallery, 16a Grafton Street, W1 071-629 3506
Redfern, 20 Cork Street, W1 071-734 1732
Richard Green, 4 New Bond Street & Dover Street W1 071-493 3939
Sally Hunter Fine Art, Halkin Arcade, Motcomb Street SW1 071-235 0934
Spink & Sons, 5/7 King Street SW1 071-930 7888
Thumb Gallery, 38 Lexington Street, W1 071-439 7343
Waddington Galleries, Cork Street W1 071-437 8611
Wildenstein, 147 New Bond Street, W1 071-629 0602

CHURCHES/PLACES OF WORSHIP

ARMENIAN Armenian Church of St Sarkis, Iverna Gdns., W8 071-937 0152
AUSTRIAN Austrian Catholic Centre, 29 Brook Grn., W6 071-603 2697
BAPTIST Bloomsbury Baptist, Shaftesbury Av., WC2 071-836 6843
BELGIAN Our Lady of Hal, 165 Arlington Rd., NW1 071-485 2727
BUDDHIST London Buddhist Centre, 51 Roman Rd., E2 081-981 1225
CHINESE Chinese Church, 4 Earlsfield Rd., SW18 081-870 2251
CHRISTIAN SCIENCE First Church of Christ Scientist, Sloane Terrace SW1 071-730 8584
CHURCH OF ENGLAND Selection of: including historic City Churches.
All Hallows by the Tower, Byward St., EC3 071-481 2928
All Hallows London Wall, London Wall EC4 071-638 0971
All Saints, Margaret St., W1 071-636 1788
All Souls Langham Place, Langham Pl., W1 071-580 4357
Chelsea Old Church, Cheyne Walk SW3 071-352 5627

Christ Church Spitalfields, Commercial St., E1 071-247 7202
Grosvenor Chapel, South Audley St., W1 071-499 1684
Guards Chapel, Wellington Barracks SW1 071-930 4466
Holy Sepulchre, Holborn Viaduct EC4 071-248 1660
Holy Trinity, Sloane Street SW1 071-730 7270
St. Andrew Holborn, Holborn Circus EC1 071-353 3544
St. Andrew by the Wardrobe, Queen Victoria St., 071-248 7546
St. Andrew Undershaft, St. Mary Axe EC3 071-283 7382
St. Anne and St. Agnes, Gresham St., EC2 071-373 5566
St. Bartholomew the Great, Smithfield EC1 071-606 5171
St. Bartholomew the Less, St. Bartholomew's Hospital EC1 071-600 9000
St. Benet Guild Church, Queen Victoria Street EC4 071-723 3104
St. Botolph Aldersgate, Aldersgate St., EC1
St. Botolph Aldgate, Aldgate High St., EC3 071-283 1670
St. Botolph Bishopsgate, Bishopgate EC2 071-588 1053
St. Bride, Bride Lane EC4 071-353 1301
St. Clement Danes, Strand WC2 071-242 8282
St. Clement Eastcheap, King William St., EC4 071-248 6121
St. Dunstan in the West, Fleet St., EC4 071-242 6027
St. Edmund the King, Lombard St., EC3 071-623 6970
St. Ethelburga, Bishopsgate EC3 071-588 3596
St. George Bloomsbury, Bloomsbury Way WC1
St. George-in-the-East, Cannon Street Rd., E1 071-481 1345
St. George Hanover Square, St. George St., W1 071-629 0874
St. Giles Cripplegate, Fore St., EC2 071-606 3630
St. Helen Bishopsgate, St Helen's Place, EC3 071-283 2231
St. James Garlickhythe, Garlick Hill EC4 071-236 1719
St. James's Piccadilly, Piccadilly W1 071-734 4511
St. Katherine Cree, Leadenhall St., EC3 071-283 5733
St. Lawrence Jewry, Gresham St., EC3 071-600 9478
St. Magnus the Martyr, Lower Thames St., EC3 071-626 4481
St. Margaret Lothbury, Lothbury EC2 071-606 8330
St. Margaret Pattens, Rood Lane EC2 071-623 6630
St. Margaret's Westminster, Parliament Square SW1 071-222 6382
St. Martin-in-the-Fields, Trafalgar Square WC2 071-930 0089
St. Martin Ludgate, Ludgate Hill EC4 071-248 6054
St. Mary Abchurch, Abchurch Lane EC4 071-626 0306
St. Mary Aldermary, Queen Victoria St., EC4
St. Mary at Hill, Lovat Lane EC3 071-626 4184
St. Mary le Bow, Cheapside EC2 071-248 5139
St. Mary-le-Strand, Strand WC2 071-836 3126
St. Mary Woolnoth, Lombard Street EC3 071-626 9701
St. Michael Paternoster Royal, College St., EC4 071-248 5208
St. Michael-upon-Cornhill, Cornhill EC3 071-626 8841
St. Nicholas Cole Abbey, Queen Victoria St: EC4 071-248 5213
St. Olave Hart Street, Hart St., EC3 071-488 4318
St. Paul Covent Garden, Inigo Place WC2 071-836 5221
St. Paul's Cathedral, St Paul's Churchyard, EC4 071-248 2705
St. Peter Cornhill, Cornhill EC3 071-626 9483
St. Stephen Walbrook, Walbrook EC4 071-283 3400
St. Vedast, Foster Lane EC2 071-606 3998
Savoy Chapel, Savoy St., WC2 071-836 7221
Southwark Cathedral, Southwark High Street SE1 071-407 2939
Temple Church, Inner Temple Lane EC4 071-353 1736
Westminster Abbey, Broad Sanctuary SW1 071-222 5152

CHURCH OF SCOTLAND Crown Court Church, Russell St., WC1 071-836 5643
DANISH Danish Church, St. Katherine's Precinct NW1 071-935 7584
DUTCH Dutch Church, Austin Friars EC2 071-588 1684
FRENCH Eglise Catholique de Notre Dame de France 5 Leicester Place WC2 071-437 9363
Eglise Protestants Francaise de Londres 9 Soho Square W1 071-437 5311
GERMAN Deutsche Evangelische Christus Kirche 19 Montpelier Place SW7 071-589 5305
Deutsche Luthersiche St. Marien Kirche, Sandwich Street WC1 071-794 4207
GREEK ORTHODOX St. Sophia's, Moscow Rd., W2 071-723 4787
HINDU Hindu Centre, 39 Grafton Terrace, NW5 071-485 8200
HUNGARIAN Hungarian Reformed Church, 17 Dunstan's Rd., W6 081-748 8858
INDEPENDENT EVANGELICAL Westminster Chapel Buckingham Gate SW1 071-834 1731
INTER-DENOMINATIONAL Whitefield Memorial Church (American Church in London), 79 Tottenham Court Rd., W1 071-580 2791
ITALIAN St. Peter's, Black Hill EC1 071-837 1528
JEHOVAH'S WITNESSES Kingdom Hall, 7 Pratt Mews NW1

JEWISH West End Great Synagogue 21 Dean St., W1 071-437 1873
LITHUANIAN Lithuanian Church, 21 The Oval E2 071-739 8735
LUTHERAN St. John's Lutheran Church, St. Anne & St. Agnes, Gresham Street EC2 071-904 2849
METHODIST Central Hall, Storey's Gate SW1 071-222 8553
Wesley's Chapel, City Road, EC1 071-353 2262
MOSLEM London Central Mosque 146 Park Rd., NW8 071-723 7613
NORWEGIAN St. Olav's, 1 Albion Street SE16 071-237 5587
PENTECOSTAL Assemblies of God 141 Harrow Rd., W2 071-286 9261
POLISH St. Andrew Bubola's R.C. Church, 1 Leysfield Road, W12 081-743 8843
ROMAN CATHOLIC Selection of central area churches.
Oratory The, Brompton Road SW3 071-589 4811
St. Etheldreda, Ely Place EC1 071-405 1061
St. George's Roman Catholic Cathedral, St. George's Road SE1 071-928 5256
St. James, Spanish Place, George St., W1 071-935 0943
Westminster Cathedral, Ashley Place SW1 071-834 7452
ROMANIAN St. Dunstan in the West, Fleet Street EC4 071-242 6027
RUSSIAN All Saints Russian Cathedral, Ennismore Gardens SW7 071-584 0096
SALVATION ARMY Regent Hall, 275 Oxford Street W1 071-629 5424
SERBIAN Serbian Orthodox Church, Lancaster Rd., W1 071-727 8367
SEVENTH DAY ADVENTISTS New Gallery Centre 123 Regent St., W1 071-734 8888
SOCIETY OF FRIENDS (QUAKERS) Westminster Meeting House, 52 St. Martin's Lane WC2 071-836 7204
SPANISH Spanish Catholic Chaplaincy 47 Palace Court W2 071-229 8315
SWEDISH Swedish Protestant Lutheran Church, 6 Harcourt St., W1 071-723 5681
SWISS Swiss Church in London, 79 Endell St., WC2 071-340 9740
UKRAINIAN Catholic Cathedral, 21 Binney St., W1 071-629 1534
UNITARIAN Essex Church, Palace Gardens Terrace W8 071-727 8920
UNITED REFORMED City Temple, Holborn Viaduct EC1 071-583 5532
WELSH St. Benet Guild Church, Queen Victoria St., EC4 071-723 3104

TRANSPORT INFORMATION

LONDON TRANSPORT 24 hour travel enquiries 071-222 1234
for enquiries on buses, underground trains and Docklands Light Railway services
Travelcheck 071-222 1200 (24 hours) recorded message on how bus and rail services are running.

BRITISH TRAVEL CENTRE 12 Lower Regent St., SW1 071-730 3400 4A 92
What to see/where to stay in England, Wales Scotland and N. Ireland. Information service linked to B.R. Ticket Office, American Express Travel Office for Bureau de change, coach tours or tickets.

BRITISH RAIL Principal London train Terminals
Charing Cross, Strand WC2 071-928 5100 4C 92
Euston, Euston Rd., NW1 071-387 7070 2A 84
Kings Cross, Euston Rd., NW1 071-278 2477 1D 84
Liverpool St., EC3 071-928 5100 6F 87
Paddington, Praed St., W2 071-262 6767 1G 89
St. Pancras, Euston Rd., NW1 071-387 7070 1C 84
Victoria, Buckingham Palace Rd., SW1 071-928 5100 3G 99
Waterloo, Waterloo Rd., SE1 071-928 5100 6G 93

COACH SERVICES Victoria Coach Station, Buckingham Palace Rd., SW1 4F 99
National Express, Coach Service Information 071-730 0202
Details of other operators on 071-823 6567

AIRPORTS
Gatwick Airport, Gatwick, West Sussex 0293 28822
Heathrow Airport, Hounslow, Middlesex 081-759 4321
London City, Silvertown E16 071-474 5555
Luton Airport, Luton, Bedfordshire 0582 405100
Stansted Airport, Stansted, Essex 0279 502380

AIRPORT LINKS
Gatwick-Central London
1. British Rail Victoria to Gatwick Airport
2. Flightline 777 coach; Victoria (Buckingham Palace Rd.,) to Gatwick Airport.

Heathrow-Central London
1. Airbus: A1 from Victoria (Grosvenor Gdns.). Airbus A2 from Russell Square via Euston Station.

2. Flightline 767 coach; Victoria Coach Station to Heathrow Airport.
3. Underground train; Piccadilly line to Terminals 1 2 3 or 4

Stansted-Central London
1. British Rail Liverpool Street Station to Stansted Airport.
2. Premier 38 coach service from Victoria Coach Station.

Luton-Central London
1. Flightline 757 coach; Victoria (Eccleston Bridge) to Luton Airport.
2. British Rail St. Pancras Station to Luton (via Bus or Taxi to Luton Airport).

LOST PROPERTY

Buses and Underground Trains, Lost Property Office, 200 Baker St., NW1 4C 82 *Open 09.30-14.00 Mon. to Fri.*
British Railways, visit lost property office at Terminus.
Taxis, visit lost property office. 15 Penton St., N1.

TOURIST INFORMATION

LONDON TOURIST BOARD

London Information 071-730 3488 *Open 09.00-18.00 Mon. to Fri.*
Accommodation and Tours 071-824 8844 *Open 09.00-18.00 Mon. to Fri. (credit card holders only)*
Riverboat Information 071-730 4812
Written enquiries-LTB 26 Grosvenor Gdns., SW1

TOURIST INFORMATION CENTRES

Victoria Station Forecourt, SW1 3G 99 *Open daily*
Tower of London Tower Hill EC3 3G 95 *Open April to Oct.*
British Travel Centre Lower Regent St., SW1 071-720 3400 4A 92 *Open daily.*
Bloomsbury, 35-36 Woburn Pl., WC1 071-580 4599 4C 84 *Open daily.*
City of London, St. Paul's Churchyard, EC4 071-606 3030 1B 94 *Open daily summer months; not Sun. or Sat. pm. winter months.*
Clerkenwell, 35 St. John's Sq., EC1 071-250 1039 4J 85 *Open 10.00-17.00 Mon. to Fri.*
Docklands 3 Limeharbour, E14 071-512 3000 *Open 09.00-18.00 Mon. to Fri. 10.30-16.30 Sat. & Sun.*
Greenwich 46 Greenwich Church St., SE10 071-858 6376 *Open 10.00-17.00 daily; to 18.00 summer.*
Harrods, Knightsbridge SW1 1B 98 Basement. *Open shop hours.*
Heathrow Airport. Open daily
Liverpool Street Station, 6F 87 *Open 09.00-18.00 Mon. to Sat. 8.30-15.30 Sun.*
Selfridges, Oxford St., W1 1D 90 Basement. Open shop hours.
Windsor Central Station, Thames St., 0753-852010 *Open 09.30-18.30 (10.00-18.00 Sun.) summer. 09.30-17.00 (10.00-16.00) winter.*

BEAUCHAMP PLACE, BURLINGTON ARCADE, JERMYN AND SLOANE STREETS Page 66—67 Four select, high-class shopping areas made up of small specialist shops, people who make and sell shirts, shoes, pipes, chocolates or perfume, many up-to-date fashion boutiques, jewellery, gift and furniture shops, antiques everywhere.

BOND STREETS Page 68
New and Old Bond Streets are essentially concerned with quality, where goods often go unmarked and prices left to the imagination. Fashion, jewellery, antiques, fine art abound; other specialists include beauty salons, watches, optical equipment.

CARNABY STREET Page 69
Made a big noise in fashion during the late 1960's, now a Union Jack tourist attraction, pedestrianized with coloured pavement.

CHARING CROSS ROAD, TOTTENHAM COURT ROAD Page 70—71
None of the glitter and show of other popular shopping streets, these provide a basic service. Charing Cross Rd. is a centre for book shops, also newsagents stocking foreign newspapers; music, musical instruments and record shops. Tottenham Court Rd. features modern furniture and accessories, electrical, Hi-Fi and optical goods.

COVENT GARDEN Page 72—73
Since the departure of the wholesale fruit and vegetable market to Nine Elms, Covent Garden has been transformed. The restored central market hall and piazza are now a pedestrian shopping centre, here and in the surrounding small streets are a wide variety of shops: food, crafts, books, fashion, gifts, perfumiers, herbalists and art galleries; also many restaurants and pubs.

KENSINGTON HIGH STREET Page 74
Multiple use High Street of stores and small shops, a lively fashion centre extending into Kensington Church Street, a centre for antique shops.

KINGS ROAD Page 75
As much of a parade as a place to buy trendy clothes with the pubs providing a grandstand for the elite. Towards the south antique shops take over from clothes including the Chelsea Antique Market.

KNIGHTSBRIDGE, BROMPTON ROAD AND FULHAM ROAD Page 76—77
The fashionable Knightsbridge and northern Brompton Rd. focus on two exclusive department stores, surrounded by quality fashion and shoe shops, hairdressers and specialists in oriental carpets. Brompton Rd. begins with fashion boutiques, Fulham Rd. ends with antiques and restaurants, in between is a fast-growing shopping centre where local food shops, hairdressers, florists etc. still rub shoulders with the 20th-cent. affluent image.

OXFORD STREET Page 78—79
Perhaps the most popular and well-known shopping area. Vast range of clothing shops from the trendy boutiques through the established chain stores to the renowned department stores. Many shoe shops, jewellers, record shops and places for refreshment.

PICCADILLY Page 69
A deverse mixture of quality fashion and food stores, small specialist shops, i.e. leather and travel goods, tobacconists, hotels, airline and tourist offices and showrooms. Open-air market beside Green Park weekends.

REGENT STREET Page 80
Planned and built in the 19th cent. by John Nash as a processional way for the Prince Regent. Regent Street has a quality of grace and refinement reflected in its many fashion, china, jewellery and gift shops.

REFERENCE TO SHOPPING ROUTE MAPS

☆ **Banks**
⋇ **Books**
Clothing
● Female ♣ Children
○ Male □ Shoes
◐ Uni-sex
■ **Department Store**
⦀ **Hi-Fi, Radio, TV, Video**
❖ **Jewellery**
☒ **Photographic, Optical, Scientific**
➡ **Public House**
⊛ **Records**
▣ **Restaurant ,Cafe**
* **Souvenirs, Gifts**
⊖ **Underground Stations**

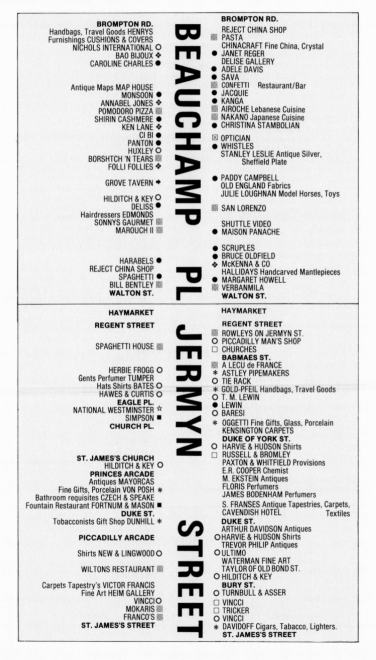

BEAUCHAMP PL

BROMPTON RD.
Handbags, Travel Goods HENRYS
Furnishings CUSHIONS & COVERS
NICHOLS INTERNATIONAL ○
BAO BIJOUX ❖
CAROLINE CHARLES ●
Antique Maps MAP HOUSE
MONSOON ●
ANNABEL JONES ❖
POMODORO PIZZA ▩
SHIRIN CASHMERE ●
KEN LANE ❖
CI BI ●
PANTON ●
HUXLEY ○
BORSHTCH 'N TEARS ▩
FOLLI FOLLIES ❖
GROVE TAVERN ➡
HILDITCH & KEY ○
DELISS ●
Hairdressers EDMONDS
SONNYS GAURMET ▩
MAROUCH II ▩
HARABELS ●
REJECT CHINA SHOP
SPAGHETTI ●
BILL BENTLEY ▩
WALTON ST.

BROMPTON RD.
REJECT CHINA SHOP
▩ PASTA
CHINACRAFT Fine China, Crystal
● JANET REGER
DELISE GALLERY
● ADELE DAVIS
● SAVA
▩ CONFETTI Restaurant/Bar
● JACQUIE
● KANGA
▩ AIROCHE Lebanese Cuisine
▩ NAKANO Japanese Cuisine
● CHRISTINA STAMBOLIAN
⊠ OPTICIAN
● WHISTLES
STANLEY LESLIE Antique Silver, Sheffield Plate
● PADDY CAMPBELL
OLD ENGLAND Fabrics
JULIE LOUGHNAN Model Horses, Toys
▩ SAN LORENZO
SHUTTLE VIDEO
● MAISON PANACHE
● SCRUPLES
● BRUCE OLDFIELD
❖ McKENNA & CO
HALLIDAYS Handcarved Mantlepieces
● MARGARET HOWELL
▩ VERBANMILA
WALTON ST.

JERMYN STREET

HAYMARKET
REGENT STREET
SPAGHETTI HOUSE ▩
HERBIE FROGG ○
Gents Perfumer TUMPER
Hats Shirts BATES ○
HAWES & CURTIS ○
EAGLE PL.
NATIONAL WESTMINSTER ☆
SIMPSON ■
CHURCH PL.
ST. JAMES'S CHURCH
HILDITCH & KEY ○
PRINCES ARCADE
Antiques MAYORCAS
Fine Gifts, Porcelain VON POSH ✱
Bathroom requisites CZECH & SPEAKE
Fountain Restaurant FORTNUM & MASON ■
DUKE ST.
Tobacconists Gift Shop DUNHILL ✱
PICCADILLY ARCADE
Shirts NEW & LINGWOOD ○
WILTONS RESTAURANT ▩
Carpets Tapestry's VICTOR FRANCIS
Fine Art HEIM GALLERY
VINCCI ○
MOKARIS ▩
FRANCO'S ▩
ST. JAMES'S STREET

HAYMARKET
REGENT STREET
▩ ROWLEYS ON JERMYN ST.
○ PICCADILLY MAN'S SHOP
□ CHURCHES
BABMAES ST.
▩ A LECU de FRANCE
✱ ASTLEY PIPEMAKERS
○ TIE RACK
✱ GOLD-PFEIL Handbags, Travel Goods
○ T. M. LEWIN
● LEWIN
○ BARESI
✱ OGGETTI Fine Gifts, Glass, Porcelain
KENSINGTON CARPETS
DUKE OF YORK ST.
○ HARVIE & HUDSON Shirts
□ RUSSELL & BROMLEY
PAXTON & WHITFIELD Provisions
E.R. COOPER Chemist
M. EKSTEIN Antiques
FLORIS Perfumers
JAMES BODENHAM Perfumers
S. FRANSES Antique Tapestries, Carpets, Textiles
CAVENDISH HOTEL
DUKE ST.
ARTHUR DAVIDSON Antiques
○ HARVIE & HUDSON Shirts
TREVOR PHILIP Antiques
○ ULTIMO
WATERMAN FINE ART
TAYLOR OF OLD BOND ST.
○ HILDITCH & KEY
BURY ST.
○ TURNBULL & ASSER
□ VINCCI
□ TRICKER
○ VINCCI
✱ DAVIDOFF Cigars, Tabacco, Lighters.
ST. JAMES'S STREET

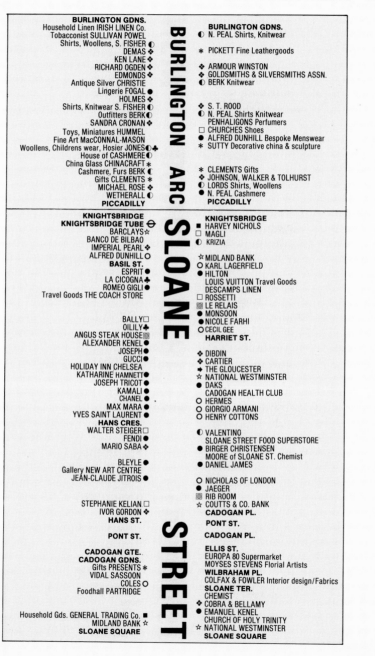

BURLINGTON ARC

BURLINGTON GDNS.
Household Linen IRISH LINEN Co.
Tobacconist SULLIVAN POWEL
Shirts, Woollens, S. FISHER ◐
DEMAS ❖
KEN LANE ❖
RICHARD OGDEN ❖
EDMONDS ❖
Antique Silver CHRISTIE
Lingerie FOGAL ●
HOLMES ❖
Shirts, Knitwear S. FISHER ◐
Outfitters BERK ◐
SANDRA CRONAN ❖
Toys, Miniatures HUMMEL
Fine Art MacCONNAL-MASON
Woollens, Childrens wear, Hosier JONES ◐ ♣
House of CASHMERE ◐
China Glass CHINACRAFT ∗
Cashmere, Furs BERK ◐
Gifts CLEMENTS ∗
MICHAEL ROSE ❖
WETHERALL ◐
PICCADILLY

BURLINGTON GDNS.
◐ N. PEAL Shirts, Knitwear
∗ PICKETT Fine Leathergoods
❖ ARMOUR WINSTON
❖ GOLDSMITHS & SILVERSMITHS ASSN.
◐ BERK Knitwear
❖ S. T. ROOD
◐ N. PEAL Shirts Knitwear
PENHALIGONS Perfumers
□ CHURCHES Shoes
● ALFRED DUNHILL Bespoke Menswear
∗ SUTTY Decorative china & sculpture
∗ CLEMENTS Gifts
❖ JOHNSON, WALKER & TOLHURST
◐ LORDS Shirts, Woollens
● N. PEAL Cashmere
PICCADILLY

SLOANE STREET

KNIGHTSBRIDGE
KNIGHTSBRIDGE TUBE ⊖
BARCLAYS ☆
BANCO DE BILBAO
IMPERIAL PEARL ❖
ALFRED DUNHILL ○
BASIL ST.
ESPRIT ●
LA CICOGNA ♣
ROMEO GIGLI ●
Travel Goods THE COACH STORE
BALLY □
OILILY ♣
ANGUS STEAK HOUSE ▣
ALEXANDER KENEL ●
JOSEPH ●
GUCCI ●
HOLIDAY INN CHELSEA
KATHARINE HAMNETT ●
JOSEPH TRICOT ●
KAMALI ●
CHANEL ●
MAX MARA ●
YVES SAINT LAURENT ●
HANS CRES.
WALTER STEIGER □
FENDI ●
MARIO SABA ❖
BLEYLE ●
Gallery NEW ART CENTRE
JEAN-CLAUDE JITROIS ●
STEPHANIE KELIAN □
IVOR GORDON ❖
HANS ST.
PONT ST.
CADOGAN GTE.
CADOGAN GDNS.
Gifts PRESENTS ∗
VIDAL SASSOON
COLES ○
Foodhall PARTRIDGE
Household Gds. GENERAL TRADING Co. ■
MIDLAND BANK ☆
SLOANE SQUARE

KNIGHTSBRIDGE
■ HARVEY NICHOLS
□ MAGLI
◐ KRIZIA
☆ MIDLAND BANK
○ KARL LAGERFIELD
● HILTON
LOUIS VUITTON Travel Goods
DESCAMPS LINEN
□ ROSSETTI
▣ LE RELAIS
● MONSOON
● NICOLE FARHI
○ CECIL GEE
HARRIET ST.
❖ DIBDIN
❖ CARTIER
➡ THE GLOUCESTER
☆ NATIONAL WESTMINSTER
● DAKS
CADOGAN HEALTH CLUB
○ HERMES
○ GIORGIO ARMANI
○ HENRY COTTONS
◐ VALENTINO
SLOANE STREET FOOD SUPERSTORE
● BIRGER CHRISTENSEN
MOORE of SLOANE ST. Chemist
● DANIEL JAMES
○ NICHOLAS OF LONDON
● JAEGER
▣ RIB ROOM
☆ COUTTS & CO. BANK
CADOGAN PL.
PONT ST.
CADOGAN PL.
ELLIS ST.
EUROPA 80 Supermarket
MOYSES STEVENS Florial Artists
WILBRAHAM PL.
COLFAX & FOWLER Interior design/Fabrics
SLOANE TER.
CHEMIST
❖ COBRA & BELLAMY
● EMANUEL KENEL
CHURCH OF HOLY TRINITY
☆ NATIONAL WESTMINSTER
SLOANE SQUARE

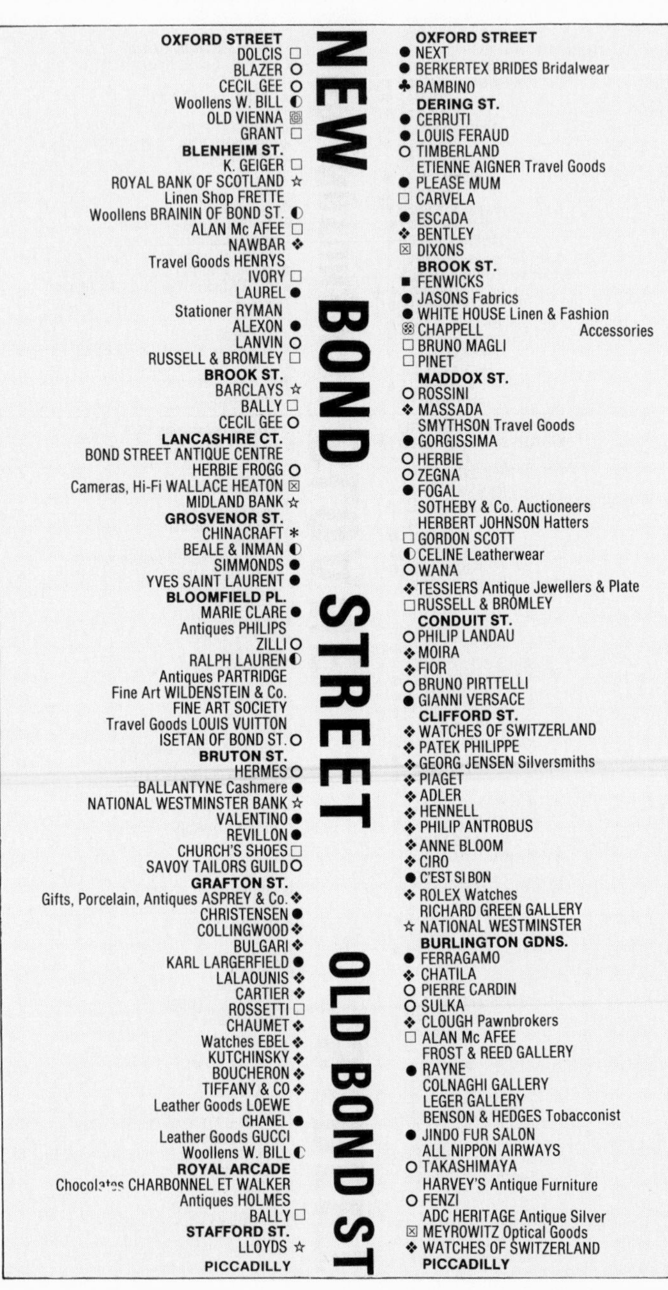
NEW BOND STREET
OLD BOND ST
OXFORD STREET
DOLCIS □
BLAZER ○
CECIL GEE ○
Woollens W. BILL ◐
OLD VIENNA
GRANT □
BLENHEIM ST.
K. GEIGER □
ROYAL BANK OF SCOTLAND ☆
Linen Shop FRETTE
Woollens BRAININ OF BOND ST. ◐
ALAN Mc AFEE □
NAWBAR ❖
Travel Goods HENRYS
IVORY □
LAUREL ●
Stationer RYMAN
ALEXON ●
LANVIN ○
RUSSELL & BROMLEY □
BROOK ST.
BARCLAYS ☆
BALLY □
CECIL GEE ○
LANCASHIRE CT.
BOND STREET ANTIQUE CENTRE
HERBIE FROGG ○
Cameras, Hi-Fi WALLACE HEATON ⊠
MIDLAND BANK ☆
GROSVENOR ST.
CHINACRAFT *
BEALE & INMAN ◐
SIMMONDS ●
YVES SAINT LAURENT ●
BLOOMFIELD PL.
MARIE CLARE ●
Antiques PHILIPS
ZILLI ○
RALPH LAUREN ◐
Antiques PARTRIDGE
Fine Art WILDENSTEIN & Co.
FINE ART SOCIETY
Travel Goods LOUIS VUITTON
ISETAN OF BOND ST. ○
BRUTON ST.
HERMES ○
BALLANTYNE Cashmere ●
NATIONAL WESTMINSTER BANK ☆
VALENTINO ●
REVILLON ●
CHURCH'S SHOES □
SAVOY TAILORS GUILD ○
GRAFTON ST.
Gifts, Porcelain, Antiques ASPREY & Co. ❖
CHRISTENSEN ●
COLLINGWOOD ❖
BULGARI ❖
KARL LARGERFIELD ●
LALAOUNIS ❖
CARTIER ❖
ROSSETTI □
CHAUMET ❖
Watches EBEL ❖
KUTCHINSKY ❖
BOUCHERON ❖
TIFFANY & CO ❖
Leather Goods LOEWE
CHANEL ●
Leather Goods GUCCI
Woollens W. BILL ◐
ROYAL ARCADE
Chocolates CHARBONNEL ET WALKER
Antiques HOLMES
BALLY □
STAFFORD ST.
LLOYDS ☆
PICCADILLY
OXFORD STREET
● NEXT
● BERKERTEX BRIDES Bridalwear
♣ BAMBINO
DERING ST.
● CERRUTI
● LOUIS FERAUD
○ TIMBERLAND
ETIENNE AIGNER Travel Goods
● PLEASE MUM
□ CARVELA
● ESCADA
❖ BENTLEY
⊠ DIXONS
BROOK ST.
■ FENWICKS
● JASONS Fabrics
● WHITE HOUSE Linen & Fashion Accessories
CHAPPELL
□ BRUNO MAGLI
□ PINET
MADDOX ST.
○ ROSSINI
❖ MASSADA
SMYTHSON Travel Goods
● GORGISSIMA
○ HERBIE
○ ZEGNA
● FOGAL
SOTHEBY & Co. Auctioneers
HERBERT JOHNSON Hatters
□ GORDON SCOTT
◐ CELINE Leatherwear
○ WANA
❖ TESSIERS Antique Jewellers & Plate
□ RUSSELL & BROMLEY
CONDUIT ST.
○ PHILIP LANDAU
❖ MOIRA
❖ FIOR
○ BRUNO PIRTTELLI
● GIANNI VERSACE
CLIFFORD ST.
❖ WATCHES OF SWITZERLAND
❖ PATEK PHILIPPE
❖ GEORG JENSEN Silversmiths
❖ PIAGET
❖ ADLER
❖ HENNELL
❖ PHILIP ANTROBUS
❖ ANNE BLOOM
❖ CIRO
● C'EST SI BON
❖ ROLEX Watches
RICHARD GREEN GALLERY
☆ NATIONAL WESTMINSTER
BURLINGTON GDNS.
● FERRAGAMO
❖ CHATILA
○ PIERRE CARDIN
○ SULKA
❖ CLOUGH Pawnbrokers
□ ALAN Mc AFEE
FROST & REED GALLERY
● RAYNE
COLNAGHI GALLERY
LEGER GALLERY
BENSON & HEDGES Tobacconist
● JINDO FUR SALON
ALL NIPPON AIRWAYS
○ TAKASHIMAYA
HARVEY'S Antique Furniture
○ FENZI
ADC HERITAGE Antique Silver
⊠ MEYROWITZ Optical Goods
❖ WATCHES OF SWITZERLAND
PICCADILLY

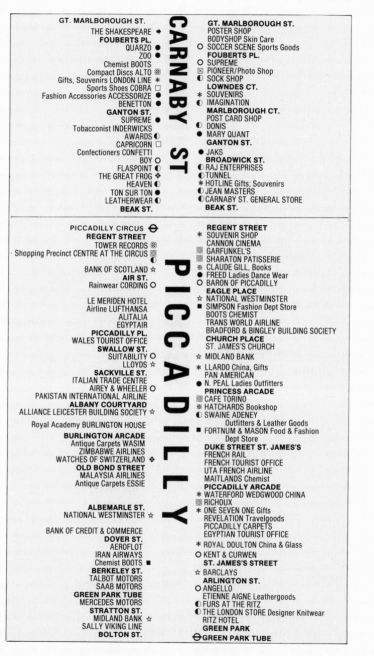

CARNABY ST

GT. MARLBOROUGH ST.
THE SHAKESPEARE ➡
FOUBERTS PL.
QUARZO ●
ZOO ●
Chemist BOOTS
Compact Discs ALTO ⊛
Gifts, Souvenirs LONDON LINE ✱
Sports Shoes COBRA ☐
Fashion Accessories ACCESSORIZE ●
BENETTON ●
GANTON ST.
SUPREME ●
Tobacconist INDERWICKS
AWARDS ◐
CAPRICORN ☐
Confectioners CONFETTI
BOY ○
FLASPOINT ◐
THE GREAT FROG ❖
HEAVEN ◐
TON SUR TON ●
LEATHERWEAR ◐
BEAK ST.

GT. MARLBOROUGH ST.
POSTER SHOP
BODYSHOP Skin Care
○ SOCCER SCENE Sports Goods
FOUBERTS PL.
○ SUPREME
⊠ PIONEER/Photo Shop
◐ SOCK SHOP
LOWNDES CT.
✱ SOUVENIRS
◐ IMAGINATION
MARLBOROUGH CT.
POST CARD SHOP
◐ DONIS
● MARY QUANT
GANTON ST.
● JAKS
BROADWICK ST.
◐ RAJ ENTERPRISES
◐ TUNNEL
✱ HOTLINE Gifts; Souvenirs
◐ JEAN MASTERS
◐ CARNABY ST. GENERAL STORE
BEAK ST.

PICCADILLY

PICCADILLY CIRCUS ⊖
REGENT STREET
TOWER RECORDS ⊛
Shopping Precinct CENTRE AT THE CIRCUS ▣ ◐
BANK OF SCOTLAND ☆
AIR ST.
Rainwear CORDING ○
LE MERIDEN HOTEL
Airline LUFTHANSA
ALITALIA
EGYPTAIR
PICCADILLY PL.
WALES TOURIST OFFICE
SWALLOW ST.
SUITABILITY ○
LLOYDS ☆
SACKVILLE ST.
ITALIAN TRADE CENTRE
AIREY & WHEELER ○
PAKISTAN INTERNATIONAL AIRLINE
ALBANY COURTYARD
ALLIANCE LEICESTER BUILDING SOCIETY ☆
Royal Academy BURLINGTON HOUSE
BURLINGTON ARCADE
Antique Carpets WASIM
ZIMBABWE AIRLINES
WATCHES OF SWITZERLAND ❖
OLD BOND STREET
MALAYSIA AIRLINES
Antique Carpets ESSIE
ALBEMARLE ST.
NATIONAL WESTMINSTER ☆
BANK OF CREDIT & COMMERCE
DOVER ST.
AEROFLOT
IRAN AIRWAYS
Chemist BOOTS ■
BERKELEY ST.
TALBOT MOTORS
SAAB MOTORS
GREEN PARK TUBE
MERCEDES MOTORS
STRATTON ST.
MIDLAND BANK ☆
SALLY VIKING LINE
BOLTON ST.

REGENT STREET
✱ SOUVENIR SHOP
CANNON CINEMA
▣ GARFUNKEL'S
▣ SHARATON PATISSERIE
※ CLAUDE GILL, Books
● FREED Ladies Dance Wear
○ BARON OF PICCADILLY
EAGLE PLACE
☆ NATIONAL WESTMINSTER
■ SIMPSON Fashion Dept Store
BOOTS CHEMIST
TRANS WORLD AIRLINE
BRADFORD & BINGLEY BUILDING SOCIETY
CHURCH PLACE
ST. JAMES'S CHURCH
☆ MIDLAND BANK
✱ LLARDO China, Gifts
PAN AMERICAN
● N. PEAL Ladies Outfitters
PRINCESS ARCADE
▣ CAFE TORINO
※ HATCHARDS Bookshop
◐ SWAINE ADENEY Outfitters & Leather Goods
■ FORTNUM & MASON Food & Fashion Dept Store
DUKE STREET ST. JAMES'S
FRENCH RAIL
FRENCH TOURIST OFFICE
UTA FRENCH AIRLINE
MAITLANDS Chemist
PICCADILLY ARCADE
✱ WATERFORD WEDGWOOD CHINA
▣ RICHOUX
✱ ONE SEVEN ONE Gifts
REVELATION Travelgoods
PICCADILLY CARPETS
EGYPTIAN TOURIST OFFICE
✱ ROYAL DOULTON China & Glass
○ KENT & CURWEN
ST. JAMES'S STREET
☆ BARCLAYS
ARLINGTON ST.
○ ANGELLO
ETIENNE AIGNE Leathergoods
◐ FURS AT THE RITZ
◐ THE LONDON STORE Designer Knitwear
RITZ HOTEL
GREEN PARK
⊖ **GREEN PARK TUBE**

CHARING CROSS ROAD

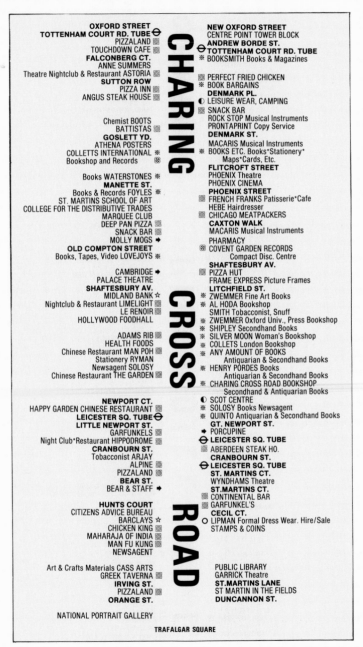

OXFORD STREET
TOTTENHAM COURT RD. TUBE
PIZZALAND
TOUCHDOWN CAFE
FALCONBERG CT.
ANNE SUMMERS
Theatre Nightclub & Restaurant ASTORIA
SUTTON ROW
PIZZA INN
ANGUS STEAK HOUSE
Chemist BOOTS
BATTISTAS
GOSLETT YD.
ATHENA POSTERS
COLLETTS INTERNATIONAL
Bookshop and Records
Books WATERSTONES
MANETTE ST.
Books & Records FOYLES
ST. MARTINS SCHOOL OF ART
COLLEGE FOR THE DISTRIBUTIVE TRADES
MARQUEE CLUB
DEEP PAN PIZZA
SNACK BAR
MOLLY MOGS
OLD COMPTON STREET
Books, Tapes, Video LOVEJOYS
CAMBRIDGE
PALACE THEATRE
SHAFTESBURY AV.
MIDLAND BANK
Nightclub & Restaurant LIMELIGHT
LE RENOIR
HOLLYWOOD FOODHALL
ADAMS RIB
HEALTH FOODS
Chinese Restaurant MAN POH
Stationery RYMAN
Newsagent SOLOSY
Chinese Restaurant THE GARDEN
NEWPORT CT.
HAPPY GARDEN CHINESE RESTAURANT
LEICESTER SQ. TUBE
LITTLE NEWPORT ST.
GARFUNKELS
Night Club*Restaurant HIPPODROME
CRANBOURN ST.
Tobacconist ARJAY
ALPINE
PIZZALAND
BEAR ST.
BEAR & STAFF
HUNTS COURT
CITIZENS ADVICE BUREAU
BARCLAYS
CHICKEN KING
MAHARAJA OF INDIA
MAN FU KUNG
NEWSAGENT
Art & Crafts Materials CASS ARTS
GREEK TAVERNA
IRVING ST.
PIZZALAND
ORANGE ST.
NATIONAL PORTRAIT GALLERY

NEW OXFORD STREET
CENTRE POINT TOWER BLOCK
ANDREW BORDE ST.
TOTTENHAM COURT RD. TUBE
BOOKSMITH Books & Magazines
PERFECT FRIED CHICKEN
BOOK BARGAINS
DENMARK PL.
LEISURE WEAR, CAMPING
SNACK BAR
ROCK STOP Musical Instruments
PRONTAPRINT Copy Service
DENMARK ST.
MACARIS Musical Instruments
BOOKS ETC. Books*Stationery* Maps*Cards, Etc.
FLITCROFT STREET
PHOENIX Theatre
PHOENIX CINEMA
PHOENIX STREET
FRENCH FRANKS Patisserie*Cafe
HEBE Hairdresser
CHICAGO MEATPACKERS
CAXTON WALK
MACARIS Musical Instruments
PHARMACY
COVENT GARDEN RECORDS Compact Disc. Centre
SHAFTESBURY AV.
PIZZA HUT
FRAME EXPRESS Picture Frames
LITCHFIELD ST.
ZWEMMER Fine Art Books
AL HODA Bookshop
SMITH Tobacconist, Snuff
ZWEMMER Oxford Univ., Press Bookshop
SHIPLEY Secondhand Books
SILVER MOON Woman's Bookshop
COLLETS London Bookshop
ANY AMOUNT OF BOOKS Antiquarian & Secondhand Books
HENRY PORDES Books Antiquarian & Secondhand Books
CHARING CROSS ROAD BOOKSHOP Secondhand & Antiquarian Books
SCOT CENTRE
SOLOSY Books Newsagent
QUINTO Antiquarian & Secondhand Books
GT. NEWPORT ST.
PORCUPINE
LEICESTER SQ. TUBE
ABERDEEN STEAK HO.
CRANBOURN ST.
LEICESTER SQ. TUBE
ST. MARTINS CT.
WYNDHAMS Theatre
ST.MARTINS CT.
CONTINENTAL BAR
GARFUNKEL'S
CECIL CT.
LIPMAN Formal Dress Wear. Hire/Sale
STAMPS & COINS
PUBLIC LIBRARY
GARRICK Theatre
ST.MARTINS LANE
ST MARTIN IN THE FIELDS
DUNCANNON ST.

TRAFALGAR SQUARE

TOTTENHAM COURT ROAD

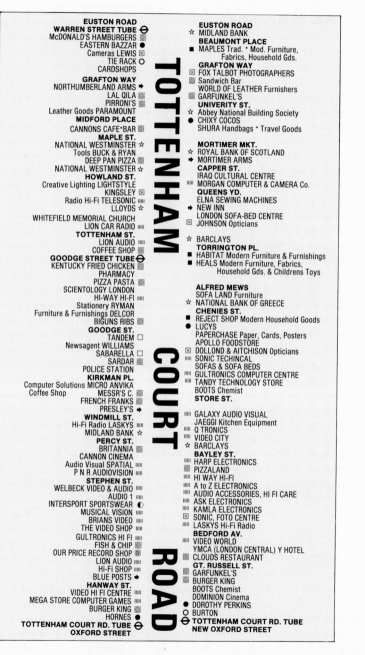

EUSTON ROAD
WARREN STREET TUBE
McDONALD'S HAMBURGERS
EASTERN BAZZAR
Cameras LEWIS
TIE RACK
CARDSHOPS
GRAFTON WAY
NORTHUMBERLAND ARMS
LAL QILA
PIRRONI'S
Leather Goods PARAMOUNT
MIDFORD PLACE
CANNONS CAFE*BAR
MAPLE ST.
NATIONAL WESTMINSTER
Tools BUCK & RYAN
DEEP PAN PIZZA
NATIONAL WESTMINSTER
HOWLAND ST.
Creative Lighting LIGHTSTYLE
KINGSLEY
Radio Hi-Fi TELESONIC
LLOYDS
WHITEFIELD MEMORIAL CHURCH
LION CAR RADIO
TOTTENHAM ST.
LION AUDIO
COFFEE SHOP
GOODGE STREET TUBE
KENTUCKY FRIED CHICKEN
PHARMACY
PIZZA PASTA
SCIENTOLOGY LONDON
HI-WAY HI-FI
Stationery RYMAN
Furniture & Furnishings DELCOR
BIGUNS RIBS
GOODGE ST.
TANDEM
Newsagent WILLIAMS
SABARELLA
SARDAR
POLICE STATION
KIRKMAN PL.
Computer Solutions MICRO ANVIKA
Coffee Shop MESSR'S C.
FRENCH FRANKS
PRESLEY'S
WINDMILL ST.
Hi-Fi Radio LASKYS
MIDLAND BANK
PERCY ST.
BRITANNIA
CANNON CINEMA
Audio Visual SPATIAL
P N R AUDIOVISION
STEPHEN ST.
WELBECK VIDEO & AUDIO
AUDIO 1
INTERSPORT SPORTSWEAR
MUSICAL VISION
BRIANS VIDEO
THE VIDEO SHOP
GULTRONICS HI FI
FISH & CHIP
OUR PRICE RECORD SHOP
LION AUDIO
Hi-Fi SHOP
BLUE POSTS
HANWAY ST.
VIDEO HI FI CENTRE
MEGA STORE COMPUTER GAMES
BURGER KING
HORNES
TOTTENHAM COURT RD. TUBE
OXFORD STREET

EUSTON ROAD
MIDLAND BANK
BEAUMONT PLACE
MAPLES Trad. * Mod. Furniture, Fabrics, Household Gds.
GRAFTON WAY
FOX TALBOT PHOTOGRAPHERS
Sandwich Bar
WORLD OF LEATHER Furnishers
GARFUNKEL'S
UNIVERITY ST.
Abbey National Building Society
CHIXY COCOS
SHURA Handbags * Travel Goods
MORTIMER MKT.
ROYAL BANK OF SCOTLAND
MORTIMER ARMS
CAPPER ST.
IRAQ CULTURAL CENTRE
MORGAN COMPUTER & CAMERA Co.
QUEENS YD.
ELNA SEWING MACHINES
NEW INN
LONDON SOFA-BED CENTRE
JOHNSON Opticians
BARCLAYS
TORRINGTON PL.
HABITAT Modern Furniture & Furnishings
HEALS Modern Furniture, Fabrics, Household Gds. & Childrens Toys
ALFRED MEWS
SOFA LAND Furniture
NATIONAL BANK OF GREECE
CHENIES ST.
REJECT SHOP Modern Household Goods
LUCYS
PAPERCHASE Paper, Cards, Posters
APOLLO FOODSTORE
DOLLOND & AITCHISON Opticians
SONIC TECHINCAL
SOFAS & SOFA BEDS
GULTRONICS COMPUTER CENTRE
TANDY TECHNOLOGY STORE
BOOTS Chemist
STORE ST.
GALAXY AUDIO VISUAL
JAEGGI Kitchen Equipment
Q TRONICS
VIDEO CITY
BARCLAYS
BAYLEY ST.
HARP ELECTRONICS
PIZZALAND
HI WAY HI-FI
A to Z ELECTRONICS
AUDIO ACCESSORIES, HI FI CARE
ASK ELECTRONICS
KAMLA ELECTRONICS
SONIC, FOTO CENTRE
LASKYS Hi-Fi Radio
BEDFORD AV.
VIDEO WORLD
YMCA (LONDON CENTRAL) Y HOTEL
CLOUDS RESTAURANT
GT. RUSSELL ST.
GARFUNKEL'S
BURGER KING
BOOTS Chemist
DOMINION Cinema
DOROTHY PERKINS
BURTON
TOTTENHAM COURT RD. TUBE
NEW OXFORD STREET

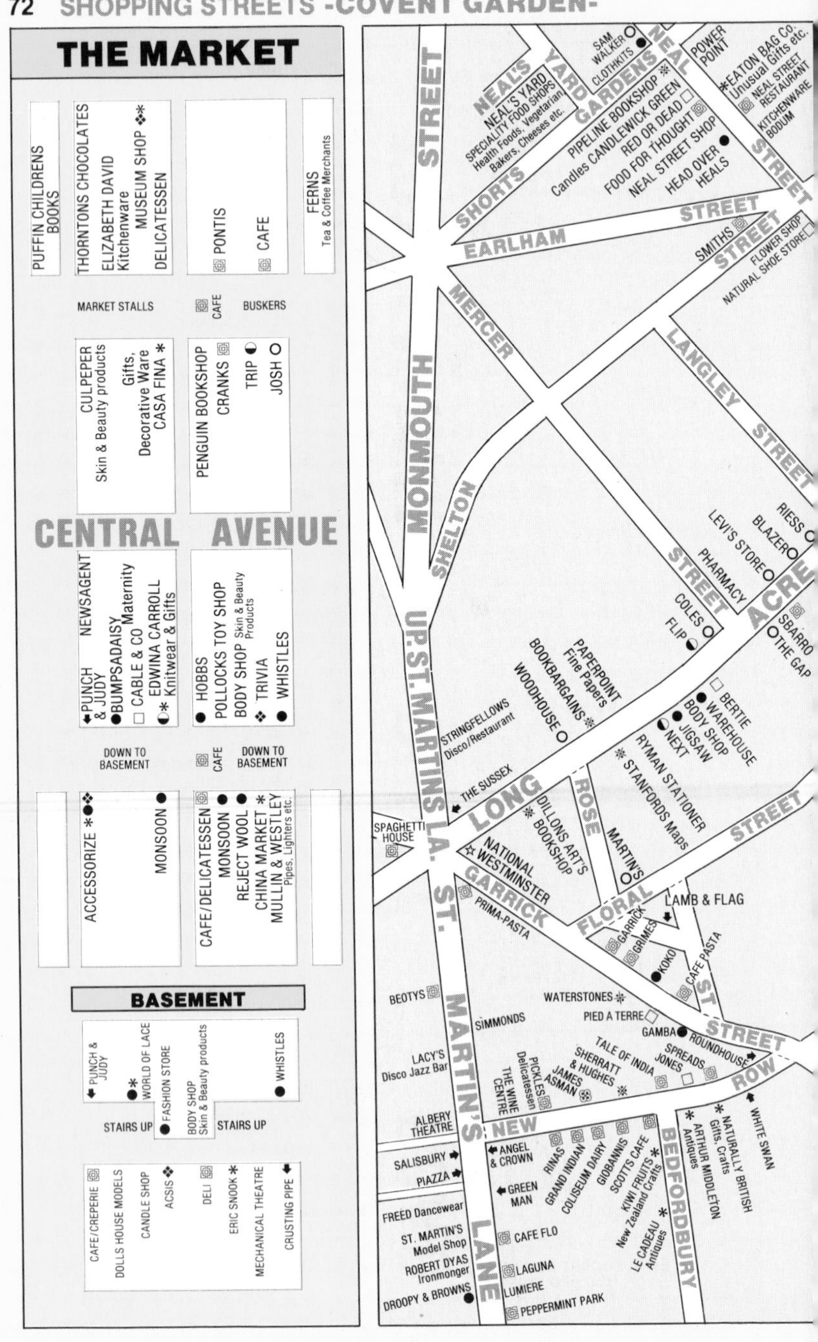
THE MARKET
PUFFIN CHILDRENS BOOKS
THORNTONS CHOCOLATES
ELIZABETH DAVID Kitchenware
MUSEUM SHOP
DELICATESSEN
PONTIS
CAFE
FERNS Tea & Coffee Merchants
MARKET STALLS
CAFE
BUSKERS
CULPEPER Skin & Beauty products
Gifts, Decorative Ware
CASA FINA
PENGUIN BOOKSHOP
CRANKS
TRIP
JOSH
CENTRAL AVENUE
PUNCH & JUDY
NEWSAGENT
BUMPSADAISY Maternity
CABLE & CO
EDWINA CARROLL Knitwear & Gifts
HOBBS
POLLOCKS TOY SHOP
BODY SHOP Skin & Beauty Products
TRIVIA
WHISTLES
DOWN TO BASEMENT
CAFE
DOWN TO BASEMENT
ACCESSORIZE
MONSOON
CAFE/DELICATESSEN
MONSOON
REJECT WOOL
CHINA MARKET
MULLIN & WESTLEY Pipes, Lighters etc.
BASEMENT
PUNCH & JUDY
WORLD OF LACE
FASHION STORE
BODY SHOP Skin & Beauty products
WHISTLES
STAIRS UP
STAIRS UP
CAFE/CREPERIE
DOLLS HOUSE MODELS
CANDLE SHOP
ACSIS
DELI
ERIC SNOOK
MECHANICAL THEATRE
CRUSTING PIPE
STREET
NEAL'S
NEAL'S YARD
SPECIALITY FOOD SHOPS Health Foods, Vegetarian, Bakers, Cheeses etc.
YARD
SAM WALKER
CLOTHKITS
GARDENS
NEAL
PIPELINE BOOKSHOP
Candles CANDLEWICK GREEN
RED OR DEAD
FOOD FOR THOUGHT
NEAL STREET SHOP
HEAD OVER HEALS
POWER POINT
EATON BAG Co. Unusual Gifts etc.
NEAL STREET RESTAURANT
KITCHENWARE BODUM
STREET
SHORTS
EARLHAM
STREET
SMITHS
STREET
FLOWER SHOP
NATURAL SHOE STORE
MERCER
MONMOUTH
LANGLEY
STREET
SHELTON
RIESS
BLAZER
LEVI'S STORE
PHARMACY
STREET
ACRE
COLES
FLIP
SBARRO
THE GAP
UP. ST. MARTINS LA.
PAPERPOINT Fine Papers
BOOKBARGAINS
WOODHOUSE
BERTIE
WAREHOUSE
BODY SHOP
JIGSAW
NEXT
RYMAN STATIONER
STANFORDS Maps
STRINGFELLOWS Disco/Restaurant
THE SUSSEX
LONG
DILLONS ART'S BOOKSHOP
ROSE
MARTIN'S
STREET
SPAGHETTI HOUSE
NATIONAL WESTMINSTER
GARRICK
PRIMA-PASTA
FLORAL
LAMB & FLAG
GARRICK
GRIMES
KOKO
CAFE PASTA
ST.
BEOTYS
WATERSTONES
PIED A TERRE
SIMMONDS
GAMBA
ROUNDHOUSE
STREET
MARTIN'S
LACY'S Disco Jazz Bar
TALE OF INDIA
SPREADS
JONES
SHERRATT & HUGHES
JAMES ASMAN
PICKLES Delicatessen
THE WINE CENTRE
ROW
WHITE SWAN
NATURALLY BRITISH Gifts, Crafts
ARTHUR MIDDLETON Antiques
ALBERY THEATRE
NEW
ANGEL & CROWN
RINAS
GRAND INDIAN
COLISEUM DAIRY
GIOBANNIS
SCOTTS CAFE
KIWI FRUITS New Zealand Crafts
LE CADEAU Antiques
BEDFORDBURY
SALISBURY
PIAZZA
GREEN MAN
FREED Dancewear
ST. MARTIN'S Model Shop
ROBERT DYAS Ironmonger
DROOPY & BROWNS
CAFE FLO
LAGUNA
LUMIERE
PEPPERMINT PARK
LANE

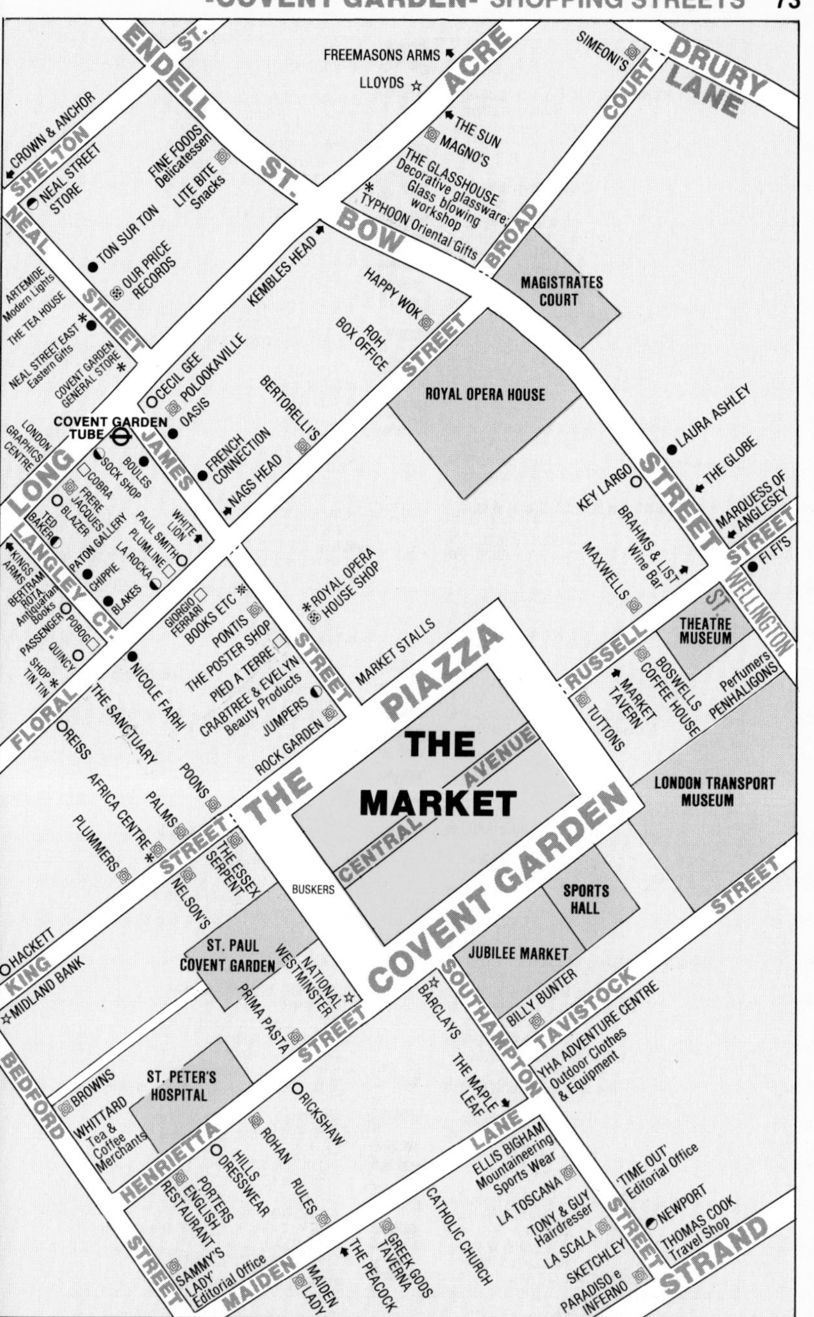

THE MARKET
ROYAL OPERA HOUSE
MAGISTRATES COURT
THEATRE MUSEUM
LONDON TRANSPORT MUSEUM
SPORTS HALL
JUBILEE MARKET
ST. PAUL COVENT GARDEN
ST. PETER'S HOSPITAL
COVENT GARDEN TUBE
ENDELL ST.
ACRE
DRURY LANE
COURT
SHELTON
NEAL STREET
BOW STREET
BROAD
JAMES STREET
LONG
LANGLEY CT.
FLORAL
STREET
RUSSELL
WELLINGTON
ST.
THE PIAZZA
CENTRAL AVENUE
COVENT GARDEN
KING STREET
BEDFORD
HENRIETTA STREET
SOUTHAMPTON
TAVISTOCK
STREET
MAIDEN LANE
STRAND
FREEMASONS ARMS
LLOYDS
SIMEONI'S
THE SUN
MAGNO'S
THE GLASSHOUSE Decorative glassware; Glass blowing workshop
TYPHOON Oriental Gifts
CROWN & ANCHOR
NEAL STREET STORE
FINE FOODS Delicatessen
LITE BITE Snacks
TON SUR TON
OUR PRICE RECORDS
KEMBLES HEAD
HAPPY WOK
ROH BOX OFFICE
ARTEMIDE Modern Lights
THE TEA HOUSE
NEAL STREET EAST Eastern Gifts
COVENT GARDEN GENERAL STORE
CECIL GEE
POLOOKAVILLE
OASIS
BERTORELLI'S
FRENCH CONNECTION
NAGS HEAD
LONDON GRAPHICS CENTRE
SOCK SHOP
BOULES
COBRA
FRERE JACQUES
BLAZER
TED BAKER
PATON GALLERY
PAUL SMITH
WHITE LION
PLUMLINE
LA ROCKA
CHIPPIE
BLAKES
KINGS ARMS
BERTRAM ROTA Antiquarian Books
PASSENGER
POBOG
QUINCY
SHOP TIN TIN
LAURA ASHLEY
THE GLOBE
KEY LARGO
MARQUESS OF ANGLESEY
BRAHMS & LIST Wine Bar
MAXWELLS
FI FI'S
ROYAL OPERA HOUSE SHOP
MARKET STALLS
GIORGIO FERRARI
BOOKS ETC
PONTIS
THE POSTER SHOP
PIED A TERRE
CRABTREE & EVELYN Beauty Products
JUMPERS
ROCK GARDEN
NICOLE FARHI
THE SANCTUARY
REISS
AFRICA CENTRE
POONS
PALMS
PLUMMERS
MARKET TAVERN
TUTTONS
BOSWELLS COFFEE HOUSE
Perfumers PENHALIGONS
THE ESSEX SERPENT
NELSON'S
BUSKERS
HACKETT
MIDLAND BANK
NATIONAL WESTMINSTER
PRIMA PASTA
BARCLAYS
BILLY BUNTER
YHA ADVENTURE CENTRE Outdoor Clothes & Equipment
THE MAPLE LEAF
BROWNS
WHITTARD Tea & Coffee Merchants
RICKSHAW
ROHAN
HILLS DRESSWEAR
PORTERS ENGLISH RESTAURANT
RULES
ELLIS BIGHAM Mountaineering Sports Wear
LA TOSCANA
TONY & GUY Hairdresser
LA SCALA
SKETCHLEY
PARADISO e INFERNO
'TIME OUT' Editorial Office
NEWPORT
THOMAS COOK Travel Shop
CATHOLIC CHURCH
GREEK GODS TAVERNA
THE PEACOCK
MAIDEN LADY
'SAMMY'S LADY' Editorial Office

KENSINGTON HIGH STREET

KENSINGTON GARDENS & PALACE
ROYAL GARDEN HOTEL
KENSINGTON PALACE GDNS.
PALACE GRN.
Fashion Arcade HYPER HYPER ◐
CHES ◐
Hairdresers R. FIELDING
OLD COURT PL.
DOLCIS □
MISS SELFRIDGE ●
DILLONS BOOKSHOP ※
TOWER RECORDS
Silver & Goldsmiths ZALES ❖
TOWER VIDEO
BARCLAYS ☆
KENSINGTON CHURCH ST.
ST MARY ABBOTS CHURCH
DERBER □
ABERDEEN STEAK HOUSE
COMPANY STORE ◐
MIDLAND BANK ☆
NATIONAL WESTMINSTER ☆
POWER POINT Electrical Goods
Stationers RYMAN
LAURA ASHLEY ●
ATHENA Posters/Cards
KENSINGTON CHURCH WALK
PETER LORD □
DISCOUNT RECORDS
RADIUS ●
Travel Shop THOMAS COOK
McDONALD'S HAMBURGERS
LLOYDS ☆
HORNTON ST.
ARAB BANK ☆
TOBACCONISTS
RUSSELL & BROMLEY □
RIVER ISLAND ◐
OLYMPUS SPORTSWEAR ◐
Newsagents Bookshop SMITHS
COUTTS & CO ☆
CAMPDEN HILL RD.
RICHARDS ●
Food SAFEWAY
ARGYL RD.
C. & A. ■
LE CAFE JARDIN
FRENCH CONNECTION ●
Chinese Gifts CHINA ∗
Adventure Shop-outdoor clothes etc. YHA
JUMPERS ◐
Artists Materials REEVES
HALIFAX BUILDING SOCIETY ☆
JAEGER ●
FRANK JOSEPH ❖
Sports Outfitters SNOW & ROCK
Discount Electrical TEMPO
OXFAM
EVANS ●
PHILLIMORE GDNS.
Novelties PARTY SHOP
SHARP SPORTS
ALBASHA PALACE
HOLLAND WALK
HOLLAND PARK
COMMONWEALTH INSTITUTE

➡ THE GOAT
○ ROHAN
DINOS
GARFUNKELS
SWEENY TODDS
☒ OPTICIAN
WHEELER'S ALCOVE
❖ CRICHTON Silversmiths
FU TONG
STICK & BOWL
KENSINGTON CT.
PIZZA
PERSEPOLIS
◐ SLICK WILLIES
□ OFFICE
BISTINGO ITALIANO
◐ RODEO DRIVE
◐ KENSINGTON MARKET
☆ NATIONAL WESTMINSTER BANK
YOUNG ST.
■ BARKERS
● JIGSAW
● WAREHOUSE
● HOBBS
◐ MARCO POLO
◐ STEFANEL
DERRY ST.
■ BRITISH HOME STORES
■ MARKS & SPENCER
NICKLEBYS
●♣ HENNES
KENSINGTON HIGH ST. TUBE
❖ H. SAMUEL
■ BOOTS Chemist
□ BALLY
WRIGHTS LA.
● BENETTON
□ BARRATT
BODY SHOP Skin & Hair Preparations
SALISBURY Handbags, Fancy Gds.
○ WOODHOUSE
THORNTONS Confectioners
□ SAXONE
❖ RATNERS
◐ NEXT
● DOROTHY PERKINS
□ CABLE & CO
○ REVIEW
DIXON'S Hi-Fi, PHOTOGRAPHIC
□ RAVEL
ADAM & EVE MWS.
● WALLIS
PAPIER STUDIO Cards & Papers
◐ L'EQUIPE
CHEMIST
PIZZA INN
□ K SHOES
※ WATERSTONE'S BOOKSHOP
ALLEN ST.
TANDY Electrical Goods
※ ST. PAUL Bookshop
DYAS Ironmongers
SONY CENTRE Electrical Goods
FIRST SPORTS Sportswear & equipment
∗ MITSUKIKU, Japanese Gifts etc.
RYNESS Lighting & Electrical
CHEMIST
ALPINE SPORTS
NEWSAGENT
ODD BINS
ABINGDON RD.
EARLY LEARNING CENTRE Toys, Games
RYMAN Stationers
※ CHILDRENS BOOK CENTRE
MAGNET Household Furnishings

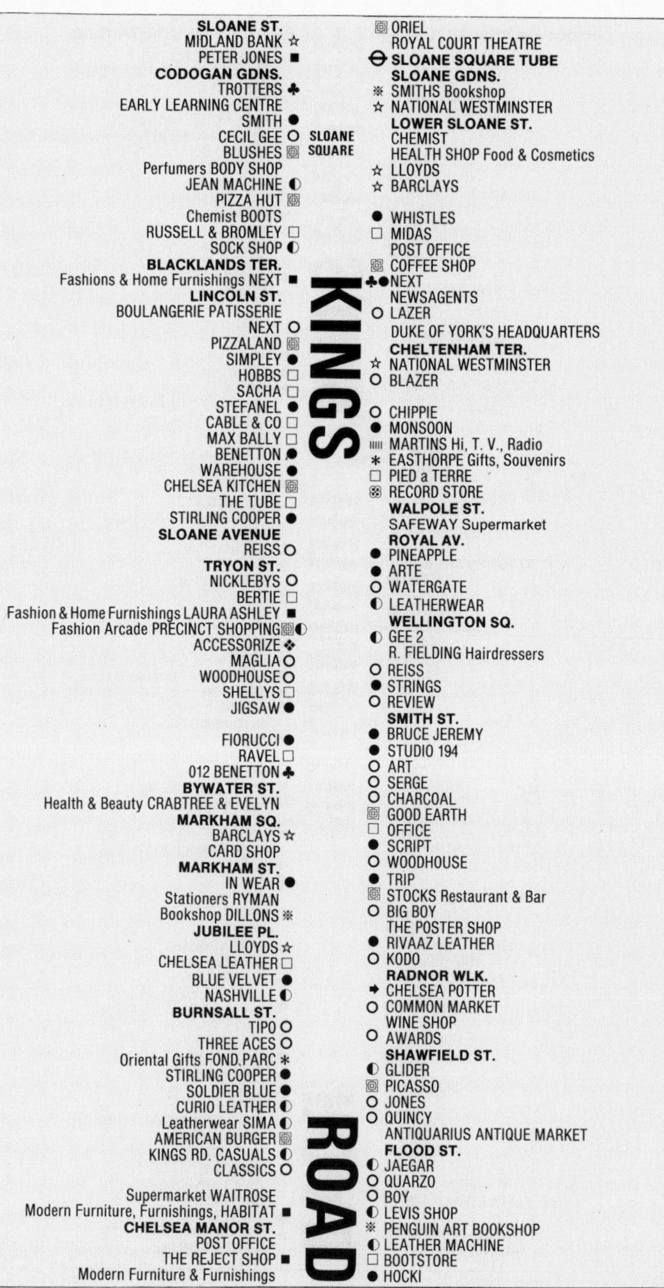
KINGS ROAD
SLOANE SQUARE
SLOANE ST.
MIDLAND BANK
PETER JONES
CODOGAN GDNS.
TROTTERS
EARLY LEARNING CENTRE
SMITH
CECIL GEE
BLUSHES
Perfumers BODY SHOP
JEAN MACHINE
PIZZA HUT
Chemist BOOTS
RUSSELL & BROMLEY
SOCK SHOP
BLACKLANDS TER.
Fashions & Home Furnishings NEXT
LINCOLN ST.
BOULANGERIE PATISSERIE
NEXT
PIZZALAND
SIMPLEY
HOBBS
SACHA
STEFANEL
CABLE & CO
MAX BALLY
BENETTON
WAREHOUSE
CHELSEA KITCHEN
THE TUBE
STIRLING COOPER
SLOANE AVENUE
REISS
TRYON ST.
NICKLEBYS
BERTIE
Fashion & Home Furnishings LAURA ASHLEY
Fashion Arcade PRECINCT SHOPPING
ACCESSORIZE
MAGLIA
WOODHOUSE
SHELLYS
JIGSAW
FIORUCCI
RAVEL
012 BENETTON
BYWATER ST.
Health & Beauty CRABTREE & EVELYN
MARKHAM SQ.
BARCLAYS
CARD SHOP
MARKHAM ST.
IN WEAR
Stationers RYMAN
Bookshop DILLONS
JUBILEE PL.
LLOYDS
CHELSEA LEATHER
BLUE VELVET
NASHVILLE
BURNSALL ST.
TIPO
THREE ACES
Oriental Gifts FOND.PARC
STIRLING COOPER
SOLDIER BLUE
CURIO LEATHER
Leatherwear SIMA
AMERICAN BURGER
KINGS RD. CASUALS
CLASSICS
Supermarket WAITROSE
Modern Furniture, Furnishings, HABITAT
CHELSEA MANOR ST.
POST OFFICE
THE REJECT SHOP
Modern Furniture & Furnishings
ORIEL
ROYAL COURT THEATRE
SLOANE SQUARE TUBE
SLOANE GDNS.
SMITHS Bookshop
NATIONAL WESTMINSTER
LOWER SLOANE ST.
CHEMIST
HEALTH SHOP Food & Cosmetics
LLOYDS
BARCLAYS
WHISTLES
MIDAS
POST OFFICE
COFFEE SHOP
NEXT
NEWSAGENTS
LAZER
DUKE OF YORK'S HEADQUARTERS
CHELTENHAM TER.
NATIONAL WESTMINSTER
BLAZER
CHIPPIE
MONSOON
MARTINS Hi, T. V., Radio
EASTHORPE Gifts, Souvenirs
PIED a TERRE
RECORD STORE
WALPOLE ST.
SAFEWAY Supermarket
ROYAL AV.
PINEAPPLE
ARTE
WATERGATE
LEATHERWEAR
WELLINGTON SQ.
GEE 2
R. FIELDING Hairdressers
REISS
STRINGS
REVIEW
SMITH ST.
BRUCE JEREMY
STUDIO 194
ART
SERGE
CHARCOAL
GOOD EARTH
OFFICE
SCRIPT
WOODHOUSE
TRIP
STOCKS Restaurant & Bar
BIG BOY
THE POSTER SHOP
RIVAAZ LEATHER
KODO
RADNOR WLK.
CHELSEA POTTER
COMMON MARKET
WINE SHOP
AWARDS
SHAWFIELD ST.
GLIDER
PICASSO
JONES
QUINCY
ANTIQUARIUS ANTIQUE MARKET
FLOOD ST.
JAEGAR
QUARZO
BOY
LEVIS SHOP
PENGUIN ART BOOKSHOP
LEATHER MACHINE
BOOTSTORE
HOCKI

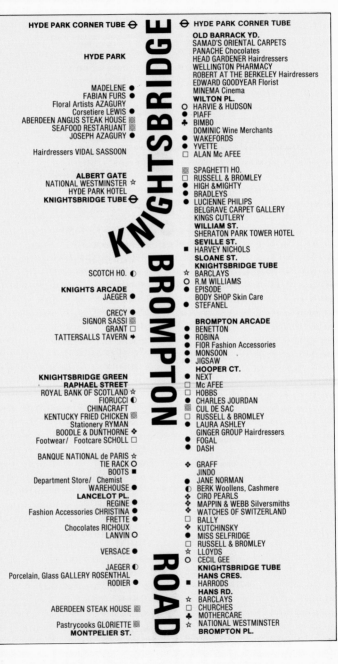

KNIGHTSBRIDGE

BROMPTON ROAD

HYDE PARK CORNER TUBE ⊖

HYDE PARK

MADELENE ●
FABIAN FURS ●
Floral Artists AZAGURY
Corsetiere LEWIS ●
ABERDEEN ANGUS STEAK HOUSE ▣
SEAFOOD RESTARUANT ▣
JOSEPH AZAGURY ●

Hairdressers VIDAL SASSOON

ALBERT GATE
NATIONAL WESTMINSTER ☆
HYDE PARK HOTEL
KNIGHTSBRIDGE TUBE ⊖

SCOTCH HO. ◐
KNIGHTS ARCADE
JAEGER ●

CRECY ●
SIGNOR SASSI ▣
GRANT □
TATTERSALLS TAVERN ➜

KNIGHTSBRIDGE GREEN
RAPHAEL STREET
ROYAL BANK OF SCOTLAND ☆
FIORUCCI ◐
CHINACRAFT
KENTUCKY FRIED CHICKEN ▣
Stationery RYMAN
BOODLE & DUNTHORNE ❖
Footwear/ Footcare SCHOLL □

BANQUE NATIONAL de PARIS ☆
TIE RACK ○
BOOTS ■
Department Store/ Chemist
WAREHOUSE ●
LANCELOT PL.
REGINE ●
Fashion Accessories CHRISTINA ●
FRETTE ●
Chocolates RICHOUX
LANVIN ○

VERSACE ●

JAEGER ◐
Porcelain, Glass GALLERY ROSENTHAL
RODIER ●

ABERDEEN STEAK HOUSE ▣

Pastrycooks GLORIETTE ▣
MONTPELIER ST.

⊖ **HYDE PARK CORNER TUBE**
OLD BARRACK YD.
SAMAD'S ORIENTAL CARPETS
PANACHE Chocolates
HEAD GARDENER Hairdressers
WELLINGTON PHARMACY
ROBERT AT THE BERKELEY Hairdressers
EDWARD GOODYEAR Florist
MINEMA Cinema
WILTON PL.
○ HARVIE & HUDSON
● PIAFF
♣ BIMBO
DOMINIC Wine Merchants
● WAKEFORDS
● YVETTE
□ ALAN Mc AFEE

▣ SPAGHETTI HO.
□ RUSSELL & BROMLEY
● HIGH &MIGHTY
● BRADLEYS
● LUCIENNE PHILIPS
BELGRAVE CARPET GALLERY
KINGS CUTLERY
WILLIAM ST.
SHERATON PARK TOWER HOTEL
SEVILLE ST.
■ HARVEY NICHOLS
SLOANE ST.
KNIGHTSBRIDGE TUBE
☆ BARCLAYS
○ R.M WILLIAMS
● EPISODE
BODY SHOP Skin Care
● STEFANEL

BROMPTON ARCADE
● BENETTON
● ROBINA
● FIOR Fashion Accessories
● MONSOON
● JIGSAW
HOOPER CT.
● NEXT
□ Mc AFEE
□ HOBBS
● CHARLES JOURDAN
▣ CUL DE SAC
□ RUSSELL & BROMLEY
● LAURA ASHLEY
GINGER GROUP Hairdressers
● FOGAL
● DASH

❖ GRAFF
JINDO
● JANE NORMAN
◐ BERK Woollens, Cashmere
❖ CIRO PEARLS
❖ MAPPIN & WEBB Silversmiths
❖ WATCHES OF SWITZERLAND
□ BALLY
❖ KUTCHINSKY
● MISS SELFRIDGE
□ RUSSELL & BROMLEY
☆ LLOYDS
○ CECIL GEE
KNIGHTSBRIDGE TUBE
HANS CRES.
■ HARRODS
HANS RD.
☆ BARCLAYS
□ CHURCHES
♣ MOTHERCARE
☆ NATIONAL WESTMINSTER
BROMPTON PL.

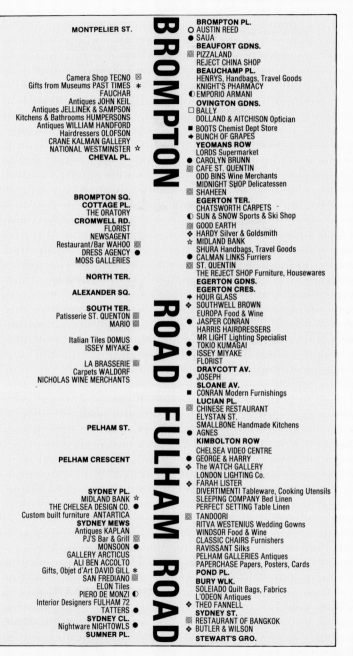

BROMPTON ROAD — FULHAM ROAD

Left side

MONTPELIER ST.
Camera Shop TECNO ☒
Gifts from Museums PAST TIMES ∗
FAUCHAR
Antiques JOHN KEIL
Antiques JELLINEK & SAMPSON
Kitchens & Bathrooms HUMPERSONS
Antiques WILLIAM HANDFORD
Hairdressers OLOFSON
CRANE KALMAN GALLERY
NATIONAL WESTMINSTER ☆
CHEVAL PL.
BROMPTON SQ.
COTTAGE PL.
THE ORATORY
CROMWELL RD.
FLORIST
NEWSAGENT
Restaurant/Bar WAHOO ▣
DRESS AGENCY ●
MOSS GALLERIES
NORTH TER.
ALEXANDER SQ.
SOUTH TER.
Patisserie ST. QUENTON ▣
MARIO ▣
Italian Tiles DOMUS
ISSEY MIYAKE ●
LA BRASSERIE ▣
Carpets WALDORF
NICHOLAS WINE MERCHANTS
PELHAM ST.
PELHAM CRESCENT
SYDNEY PL.
MIDLAND BANK ☆
THE CHELSEA DESIGN CO. ●
Custom built furniture ANTARTICA
SYDNEY MEWS
Antiques KAPLAN
PJ'S Bar & Grill ▣
MONSOON ●
GALLERY ARCTICUS
ALI BEN ACCOLTO
Gifts, Objet d'Art DAVID GILL ∗
SAN FREDIANO ▣
ELON Tiles
PIERO DE MONZI ◐
Interior Designers FULHAM 72
TATTERS ●
SYDNEY CL.
Nightware NIGHTOWLS ●
SUMNER PL.

Right side

BROMPTON PL.
○ AUSTIN REED
● SAUA
BEAUFORT GDNS.
▣ PIZZALAND
REJECT CHINA SHOP
BEAUCHAMP PL.
HENRYS, Handbags, Travel Goods
KNIGHT'S PHARMACY
◐ EMPORIO ARMANI
OVINGTON GDNS.
□ BALLY
DOLLAND & AITCHISON Optician
■ BOOTS Chemist Dept Store
➜ BUNCH OF GRAPES
YEOMANS ROW
LORDS Supermarket
● CAROLYN BRUNN
▣ CAFE ST. QUENTIN
ODD BINS Wine Merchants
MIDNIGHT SHOP Delicatessen
▣ SHAHEEN
EGERTON TER.
CHATSWORTH CARPETS
◐ SUN & SNOW Sports & Ski Shop
▣ GOOD EARTH
❖ HARDY Silver & Goldsmith
☆ MIDLAND BANK
SHURA Handbags, Travel Goods
● CALMAN LINKS Furriers
▣ ST. QUENTIN
THE REJECT SHOP Furniture, Housewares
EGERTON GDNS.
EGERTON CRES.
➜ HOUR GLASS
❖ SOUTHWELL BROWN
EUROPA Food & Wine
● JASPER CONRAN
HARRIS HAIRDRESSERS
MR LIGHT Lighting Specialist
● TOKIO KUMAGAI
● ISSEY MIYAKE
FLORIST
DRAYCOTT AV.
● JOSEPH
SLOANE AV.
■ CONRAN Modern Furnishings
LUCIAN PL.
▣ CHINESE RESTAURANT
ELYSTAN ST.
SMALLBONE Handmade Kitchens
● AGNES
KIMBOLTON ROW
CHELSEA VIDEO CENTRE
● GEORGE & HARRY
❖ The WATCH GALLERY
LONDON LIGHTING Co.
❖ FARAH LISTER
DIVERTIMENTI Tableware, Cooking Utensils
SLEEPING COMPANY Bed Linen
PERFECT SETTING Table Linen
▣ TANDOORI
RITVA WESTENIUS Wedding Gowns
WINDSOR Food & Wine
CLASSIC CHAIRS Furnishers
RAVISSANT Silks
PELHAM GALLERIES Antiques
PAPERCHASE Papers, Posters, Cards
POND PL.
BURY WLK.
SOLEIADO Quilt Bags, Fabrics
L'ODEON Antiques
❖ THEO FANNELL
SYDNEY ST.
▣ RESTAURANT OF BANGKOK
❖ BUTLER & WILSON
STEWART'S GRO.

OXFORD

TOTTENHAM COURT ROAD
TOTTENHAM COURT RD. TUBE ⊖
HORNE BROS ○
THE TOTTENHAM ➡
McDONALD'S HAMBURGERS ▦
SOCK SHOP ◐
VIRGIN RECORD MEGASTORE ❁
CANNON CINEMA 1 2 3 & 4
SOUVENIR SHOP ✱
VIRGIN RECORD MEGASTORE
Tapes, Video, Etc.
SOUVENIR SHOP ✱
LLOYDS BANK ☆
BARRATT □
JEANS WEST ◐
NATIONAL WESTMINSTER ☆
OPENED ●
46th ST. LEATHERS ◐
ANGUS STEAK HOUSE ▦
HANWAY ST.
SHE WANTS ●
MIDLAND BANK ☆
RATHBONE PL.
DUNN ○
LACE ◐
Skin Care BODYSHOP
SALISBURY HANDBAGS
PERRY'S PL.
Hi-Fi McDONALD ⦀
FREEMAN HARDY WILLIS □
DIXONS ⊠
NEWMAN ST.
OPTICIANS ⊠
Chemist Dept Store BOOTS ■
VIRGIN GAMES CENTRE
STIRLING COOPER ●
THE SUIT HOUSE ○
NAT. WESTMINSTER BANK ☆
BERNERS ST.
PRINCIPLES ●
PLAZA ON OXFORD STREET
Shopping Centre ▦◐
THE GAP ◐
WELLS ST.
Sports Wear OLYMPUS ◐
NICKLEBYS ○
MISTER BYRITE ◐
ADAM & EVE CT.
BURGER KING ▦
CASCADE SOUVENIRS ✱
HMV RECORD MEGASTORE ❁
OAKLAND ○
COPYRIGHT ○
PROFILE ○
REVIEW ○
WINSLEY ST.
BLAZER ○
CHAMPION SPORTS SHOP ◐
RICHARDS ●
MOTHERCARE ♣
MARK-ONE ◐
GT. TITCHFIELD ST.
RAVEL □
SOCK SHOP ◐
FAITH □
BURGER BAR ▦
MARKET CT.
MIDLAND BANK ☆
C & A ■
GT. PORTLAND ST.
BURGER KING ▦
P. BROWN ○
BURTON ○
TOP SHOP ●
TOP MAN ○
OXFORD CIRCUS TUBE ⊖
REGENT STREET

CENTRE POINT
CHARING CROSS ROAD
○ COLES
⊖ **TOTTENHAM COURT RD. TUBE**
□ K SHOES
※ CLAUDE GILL Books
▦ COFFEE SHOP
⦀⊠ TANDY
▦ PIZZA HUT
◐ NICK NACK
▦ BON CROISSANT
RYMAN STATIONERS
○ JOHN KENT
◐ JEAN CENTRE
◐ OUTLET 49
□ THE BOOTSTORE
● LEATHER MATE
○ SUITS YOU
SOHO ST.
❖ RATNERS
◐ C J's
● MASH
◐ MARMALADE
▦ PIZZA HUT
◐ SOCK SHOP
DEAN ST.
○ TIE RACK
● KNICKERBOX
○ WOODHOUSE
✱ SOUVENIR SHOP
GT. CHAPEL ST.
◐ SLOT MACHINE
SILVERDALE Travel Goods
● MARK-ONE
□ COBRA Sports Shoes
※ ATHENA Books Posters Cards
WARDOUR ST.
✱ SOUVENIRS
▦ CAFE RAPALLO
BERWICK ST.
□ J.D. SPORTS SHOES
□ LEVEL GROUND
BOOTS, Chemist
● JANE NORMAN
◐ THE SALE Leisurewear, Camping
□ SHELLY'S SHOES
POLAND ST.
❖ H. SAMUEL
■ MARKS & SPENCER
□ SAXONE
□ DOLCIS
▦ McDONALDS
◐ NEXT
RAMILLIES ST.
❖ ZALES
PAPERCHASE
■ LITTLEWOOD'S
● WALLIS
❖ RATNERS
HILLS PL.
● MISS SELFRIDGE
● BENETTON
✱ SOUVENIRS
● LISA
⊖ **OXFORD CIRCUS TUBE**
ARGYLL ST.

OXFORD CIRCUS

⊖ **OXFORD CIRCUS TUBE**
✱ WATERFORD WEDGWOOD GIFT CENTRE
REGENT STREET

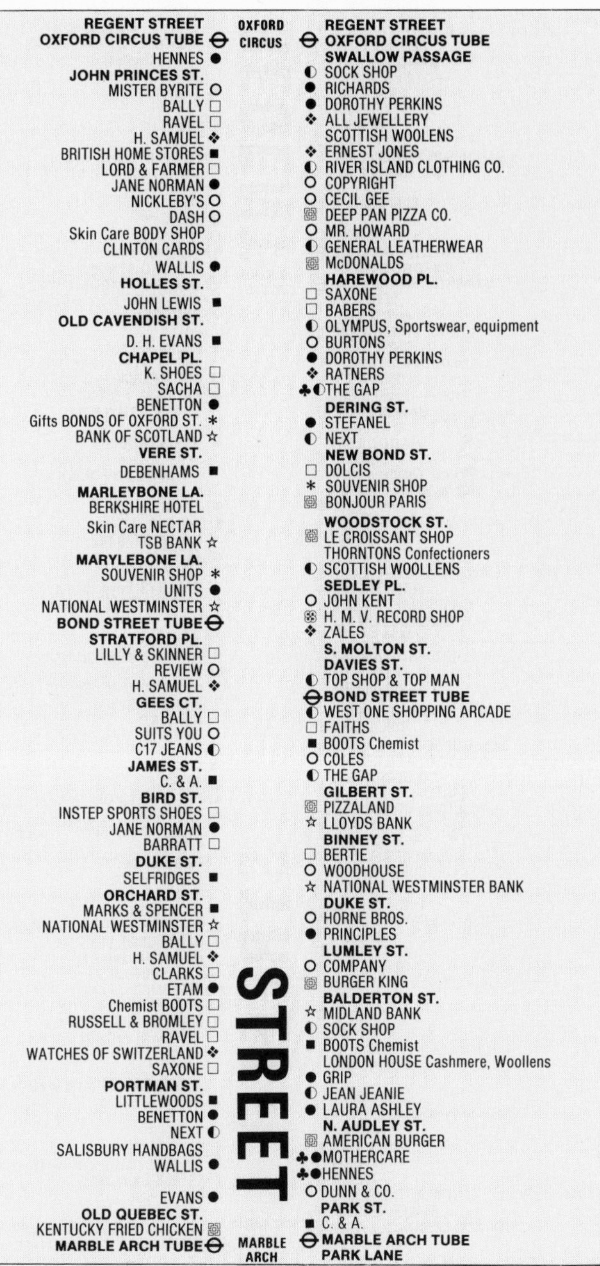
REGENT STREET
OXFORD CIRCUS TUBE
HENNES
JOHN PRINCES ST.
MISTER BYRITE
BALLY
RAVEL
H. SAMUEL
BRITISH HOME STORES
LORD & FARMER
JANE NORMAN
NICKLEBY'S
DASH
Skin Care BODY SHOP
CLINTON CARDS
WALLIS
HOLLES ST.
JOHN LEWIS
OLD CAVENDISH ST.
D. H. EVANS
CHAPEL PL.
K. SHOES
SACHA
BENETTON
Gifts BONDS OF OXFORD ST.
BANK OF SCOTLAND
VERE ST.
DEBENHAMS
MARLEYBONE LA.
BERKSHIRE HOTEL
Skin Care NECTAR
TSB BANK
MARYLEBONE LA.
SOUVENIR SHOP
UNITS
NATIONAL WESTMINSTER
BOND STREET TUBE
STRATFORD PL.
LILLY & SKINNER
REVIEW
H. SAMUEL
GEES CT.
BALLY
SUITS YOU
C17 JEANS
JAMES ST.
C. & A.
BIRD ST.
INSTEP SPORTS SHOES
JANE NORMAN
BARRATT
DUKE ST.
SELFRIDGES
ORCHARD ST.
MARKS & SPENCER
NATIONAL WESTMINSTER
BALLY
H. SAMUEL
CLARKS
ETAM
Chemist BOOTS
RUSSELL & BROMLEY
RAVEL
WATCHES OF SWITZERLAND
SAXONE
PORTMAN ST.
LITTLEWOODS
BENETTON
NEXT
SALISBURY HANDBAGS
WALLIS
EVANS
OLD QUEBEC ST.
KENTUCKY FRIED CHICKEN
MARBLE ARCH TUBE
OXFORD CIRCUS
STREET
MARBLE ARCH
REGENT STREET
OXFORD CIRCUS TUBE
SWALLOW PASSAGE
SOCK SHOP
RICHARDS
DOROTHY PERKINS
ALL JEWELLERY
SCOTTISH WOOLENS
ERNEST JONES
RIVER ISLAND CLOTHING CO.
COPYRIGHT
CECIL GEE
DEEP PAN PIZZA CO.
MR. HOWARD
GENERAL LEATHERWEAR
McDONALDS
HAREWOOD PL.
SAXONE
BABERS
OLYMPUS, Sportswear, equipment
BURTONS
DOROTHY PERKINS
RATNERS
THE GAP
DERING ST.
STEFANEL
NEXT
NEW BOND ST.
DOLCIS
SOUVENIR SHOP
BONJOUR PARIS
WOODSTOCK ST.
LE CROISSANT SHOP
THORNTONS Confectioners
SCOTTISH WOOLLENS
SEDLEY PL.
JOHN KENT
H. M. V. RECORD SHOP
ZALES
S. MOLTON ST.
DAVIES ST.
TOP SHOP & TOP MAN
BOND STREET TUBE
WEST ONE SHOPPING ARCADE
FAITHS
BOOTS Chemist
COLES
THE GAP
GILBERT ST.
PIZZALAND
LLOYDS BANK
BINNEY ST.
BERTIE
WOODHOUSE
NATIONAL WESTMINSTER BANK
DUKE ST.
HORNE BROS.
PRINCIPLES
LUMLEY ST.
COMPANY
BURGER KING
BALDERTON ST.
MIDLAND BANK
SOCK SHOP
BOOTS Chemist
LONDON HOUSE Cashmere, Woollens
GRIP
JEAN JEANIE
LAURA ASHLEY
N. AUDLEY ST.
AMERICAN BURGER
MOTHERCARE
HENNES
DUNN & CO.
PARK ST.
C. & A.
MARBLE ARCH TUBE
PARK LANE

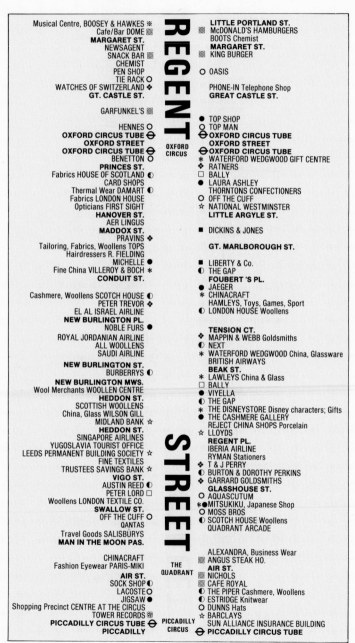

REGENT STREET

West side

Musical Centre, BOOSEY & HAWKES ※
Cafe/Bar DOME ▩
MARGARET ST.
NEWSAGENT
SNACK BAR ▩
CHEMIST
PEN SHOP
TIE RACK ○
WATCHES OF SWITZERLAND ❖
GT. CASTLE ST.
GARFUNKEL'S ▩
HENNES ○
OXFORD CIRCUS TUBE ⊖
OXFORD STREET
OXFORD CIRCUS TUBE ⊖
BENETTON ○
PRINCES ST.
Fabrics HOUSE OF SCOTLAND ◐
CARD SHOPS
Thermal Wear DAMART ◐
Fabrics LONDON HOUSE
Opticians FIRST SIGHT
HANOVER ST.
AER LINGUS
MADDOX ST.
PRAVINS ❖
Tailoring, Fabrics, Woollens TOPS
Hairdressers R. FIELDING
MICHELLE ●
Fine China VILLEROY & BOCH *
CONDUIT ST.
Cashmere, Woollens SCOTCH HOUSE ◐
PETER TREVOR ❖
EL AL ISRAEL AIRLINE
NEW BURLINGTON PL.
NOBLE FURS ●
ROYAL JORDANIAN AIRLINE
ALL WOOLLENS
SAUDI AIRLINE
NEW BURLINGTON ST.
BURBERRYS ◐
NEW BURLINGTON MWS.
Wool Merchants WOOLLEN CENTRE
HEDDON ST.
SCOTTISH WOOLLENS
China, Glass WILSON GILL
MIDLAND BANK ☆
HEDDON ST.
SINGAPORE AIRLINES
YUGOSLAVIA TOURIST OFFICE
LEEDS PERMANENT BUILDING SOCIETY ☆
FINE TEXTILES
TRUSTEES SAVINGS BANK ☆
VIGO ST.
AUSTIN REED ◐
PETER LORD □
Woollens LONDON TEXTILE CO.
SWALLOW ST.
OFF THE CUFF ○
QANTAS
Travel Goods SALISBURYS
MAN IN THE MOON PAS.
CHINACRAFT
Fashion Eyewear PARIS-MIKI
AIR ST.
SOCK SHOP ◐
LACOSTE ○
JIGSAW ●
Shopping Precinct CENTRE AT THE CIRCUS
TOWER RECORDS ❁
PICCADILLY CIRCUS TUBE ⊖
PICCADILLY

Centre

OXFORD CIRCUS
THE QUADRANT
PICCADILLY CIRCUS

East side

LITTLE PORTLAND ST.
▩ McDONALD'S HAMBURGERS
BOOTS Chemist
MARGARET ST.
▩ KING BURGER
○ OASIS
PHONE-IN Telephone Shop
GREAT CASTLE ST.
● TOP SHOP
○ TOP MAN
⊖ OXFORD CIRCUS TUBE
OXFORD STREET
⊖ OXFORD CIRCUS TUBE
* WATERFORD WEDGWOOD GIFT CENTRE
❖ RATNERS
□ BALLY
● LAURA ASHLEY
THORNTONS CONFECTIONERS
○ OFF THE CUFF
☆ NATIONAL WESTMINSTER
LITTLE ARGYLE ST.
■ DICKINS & JONES
GT. MARLBOROUGH ST.
■ LIBERTY & Co.
◐ THE GAP
FOUBERT 'S PL.
● JAEGER
* CHINACRAFT
HAMLEYS, Toys, Games, Sport
◐ LONDON HOUSE Woollens
TENSION CT.
❖ MAPPIN & WEBB Goldsmiths
◐ NEXT
* WATERFORD WEDGWOOD China, Glassware
BRITISH AIRWAYS
BEAK ST.
* LAWLEYS China & Glass
□ BALLY
● VIYELLA
◐ THE GAP
* THE DISNEYSTORE Disney characters; Gifts
● THE CASHMERE GALLERY
REJECT CHINA SHOPS Porcelain
☆ LLOYDS
REGENT PL.
IBERIA AIRLINE
RYMAN Stationers
❖ T & J PERRY
◐ BURTON & DOROTHY PERKINS
❖ GARRARD GOLDSMITHS
GLASSHOUSE ST.
○ AQUASCUTUM
*● MITSUKIKU, Japanese Shop
○ MOSS BROS
◐ SCOTCH HOUSE Woollens
QUADRANT ARCADE
ALEXANDRA, Business Wear
▩ ANGUS STEAK HO.
AIR ST.
▩ NICHOLS
▩ CAFE ROYAL
◐ THE PIPER Cashmere, Woollens
◐ ESTRIDGE Knitwear
○ DUNNS Hats
☆ BARCLAYS
SUN ALLIANCE INSURANCE BUILDING
⊖ PICCADILLY CIRCUS TUBE

KEY TO MAP PAGES

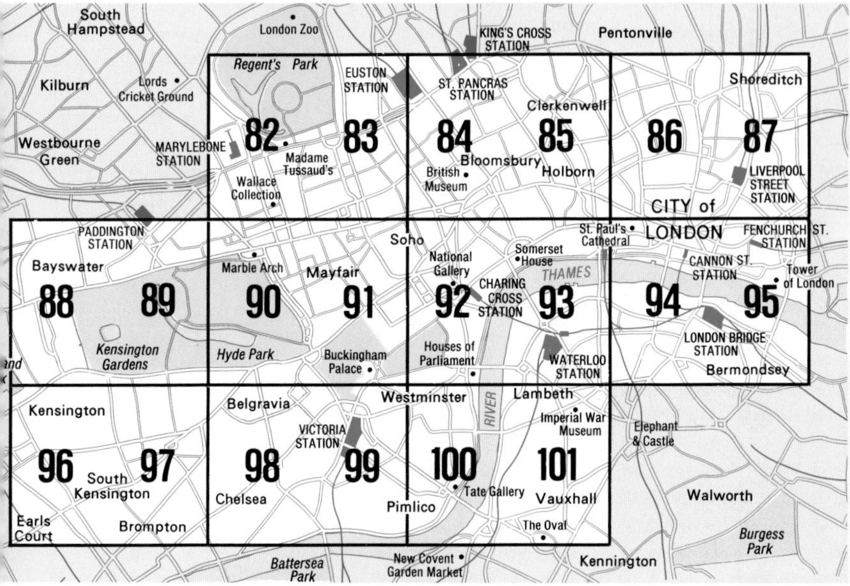

South Hampstead
London Zoo
KING'S CROSS STATION
Pentonville
Regent's Park
EUSTON STATION
ST. PANCRAS STATION
Shoreditch
Kilburn
Lords Cricket Ground
Clerkenwell
82 83 84 85 86 87
Westbourne Green
MARYLEBONE STATION
Madame Tussaud's
Bloomsbury
British Museum
Holborn
LIVERPOOL STREET STATION
Wallace Collection
CITY of LONDON
PADDINGTON STATION
St. Paul's Cathedral
FENCHURCH ST. STATION
Soho
Somerset House
Bayswater
Marble Arch
Mayfair
National Gallery
THAMES
CANNON ST. STATION
Tower of London
CHARING CROSS STATION
88 89 90 91 92 93 94 95
Kensington Gardens
Hyde Park
Buckingham Palace
Houses of Parliament
WATERLOO STATION
LONDON BRIDGE STATION
Bermondsey
Westminster
Lambeth
Kensington
Belgravia
RIVER
Imperial War Museum
Elephant & Castle
VICTORIA STATION
96 97 98 99 100 101
South Kensington
Tate Gallery
Chelsea
Vauxhall
Walworth
Pimlico
Earls Court
Brompton
The Oval
Burgess Park
Battersea Park
New Covent Garden Market
Kennington

REFERENCE

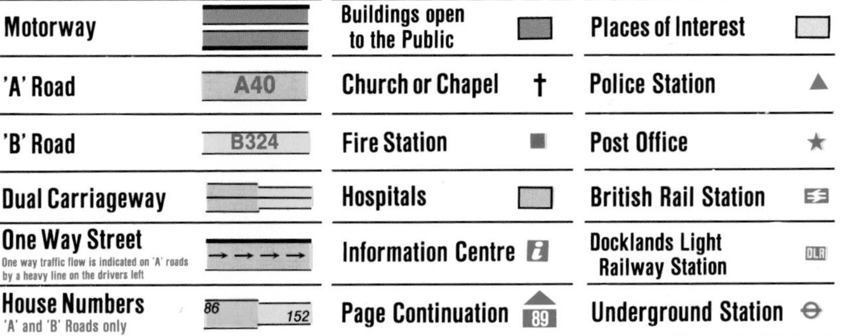

SCALE

1:10560 or 6 inches to 1 mile

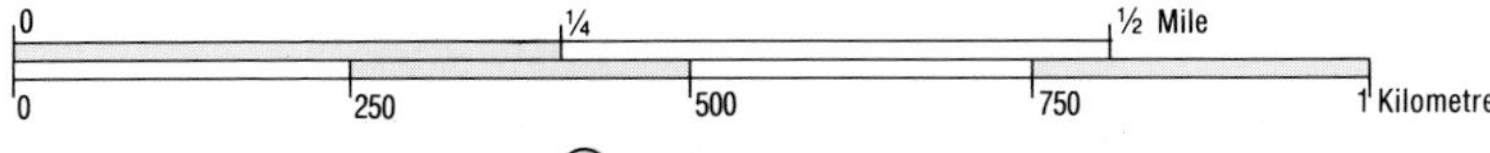

© Edition 1 1991

Geographers' A-Z Map Company Ltd.

82
A
B
C
D
Pavilion
REGENT'S PARK
Winfield House
Playground
London Central Mosque
Children's Boating Pond
Boating Lake
The Holme
Open Air Theatre
QUEEN MARY'S GARDENS
INNER CIRCLE
OUTER CIRCLE
Tennis Courts
Regent's College (Hunter School of Medicine)
Clarence Gate
Royal Coll. of Obstetricians & Gynaecologists
London Business Sch.
(Regent's Canal)
PRINCE ALBERT RD
A5205
A41
PARK ROAD
HANOVER GATE
HANOVER TER.
KENT TER.
SUSSEX PLACE
LODGE ROAD
NORTH BANK
GROVE GDS.
LORNE CL.
ALPHA CL.
PAVELEY ST.
TRESHAM CRES.
JEROME CR.
GRENDON ST.
LILESTONE ST.
MALLORY ST.
ROSSMORE ROAD
HAREWOOD AVENUE
TAUNTON PL.
BOSTON PLACE
BALCOMBE ST.
LINHOPE ST.
HUNTSWORTH MEWS
GLOUCESTER PLACE
GLENTWORTH ST.
SIDDONS LA.
CHAGFORD ST.
BAKER ST.
BAKER STREET
ALLSOP PL.
YORK TER. WEST
YORK BRIDGE
Madame Tussaud's
Planetarium
MARYLEBONE
MARYLEBONE ROAD
MELCOMBE ST.
DORSET SQUARE
BLANDFORD SQ.
MELBURY TER.
LISSON GROVE
B507
CHURCH ST.
PLYMPTON ST.
ASHBRIDGE ST.
WHITEHAVEN ST.
BROADLEY ST.
SHROTON ST.
BELL ST.
COSWAY ST.
BENDALL M.
Polytechnic of Central London
BICKENHALL ST.
CHILTERN ST.
NOTTINGHAM PL.
LUXBOROUGH ST.
PADDINGTON ST.
B524
Public Gdns.
A40(M)
EDGWARE RD.
CHAPEL ST.
A501
OLD MARYLEBONE RD.
Mag. Ct.
HARCOURT ST.
CRAWFORD ST.
SEYMOUR PL.
Seymour Leisure Cen.
BRYANSTON SQUARE
MONTAGU SQUARE
MONTAGU PL.
GLOUCESTER PLACE M.
DORSET ST.
RODMARTON ST.
BLANDFORD ST.
MANCHESTER STREET
BROADSTONE PL.
KENDALL PL.
PORTMAN CL.
ROBERT ADAM ST.
FITZHARDINGE ST.
Wallace Colln.
Heinz Gall.
PORTMAN SQUARE
SEYMOUR ST.
EDGWARE ROAD
SUSSEX GARDENS
NORFOLK CRES.
CAMBRIDGE SQUARE
OXFORD SQUARE
HYDE PK. CR.
PORCHESTER PL.
NUTFORD PL.
HARROWBY ST.
MOLYNEUX ST.
BRENDON ST.
CATO ST.
UPPER BERKELEY ST.
BERKELEY ST.
QUEBEC M.
Syn.
EDWARDS M.
PORTMAN M. S.
Oxford St.
90
1
2
3
4
5
6
7

LONDON ZOO
83
84
91
F
G
H
J
1
2
3
4
5
6
7
Regent's Park Barracks
AMPTHILL ESTATE
REGENT'S PARK
Cumberland Gate
Dept. of Environment Parks Dept.
Chester Walk Gate
Royal Coll. of Physicians
Playground
Park Square Gardens
Cres. Gdns
REGENT'S PARK
GT. PORTLAND ST.
WARREN STREET
EUSTON
EUSTON SQ.
EUSTON STATION
National Temperance Hosp.
St. James's Gardens
Euston Centre
Euston Sq.
Friends Ho.
Wellcome Inst.
University Coll.
University Coll. Hosp.
Ear Hosp.
Telecom Tower
Middlesex Hosp.
GOODGE STREET
Broadcasting Ho.
Queen's Coll.
Wigmore Hall
Coll. of Nursing
The Polytechnic
OXFORD CIRCUS
Regent Hall
Police Ct.
Coll. of Music
ALBANY STREET
HAMPSTEAD ROAD
EVERSHOLT STREET
EUSTON ROAD
TOTTENHAM COURT ROAD
GOWER STREET
GREAT PORTLAND STREET
PORTLAND PLACE
REGENT STREET
OXFORD STREET
MARYLEBONE ROAD
PARK CRESCENT
CAVENDISH SQ.
MORTIMER STREET
GOODGE STREET
CHARLOTTE STREET
CLEVELAND STREET
WIGMORE STREET
WEYMOUTH STREET
NEW CAVENDISH STREET
DRUMMOND STREET
WILLIAM ROAD
ROBERT STREET
LONGFORD
MUNSTER SQ.
CLARENCE GARDENS
VARNDELL ST.
CUMBERLAND MARKET
OUTER CIRCLE
A4201
A400
A4200
A501
A5204
A40
B506

84
A
B
C
D
1
2
3
4
5
6
7
83
92
SOMERS TOWN
British Library (Under construction)
ST. PANCRAS
KING'S CROSS
KING'S CROSS & ST. PANCRAS
EUSTON
EUSTON STATION
EUSTON SQ.
ST. PANCRAS
BLOOMSBURY
RUSSELL SQ.
GOODGE STREET
TOTTENHAM COURT ROAD
HOLBORN
EVERSHOLT
A4200
A501
A400
A5200
B504
B502
B506
A40
B402
EUSTON ROAD
PENTONVILLE ROAD
GRAY'S INN ROAD
EUSTON STREET
OSSULSTON STREET
CHALTON ST.
MIDLAND ROAD
YORK WY.
CALEDONIA ST.
BRILL PL.
PHOENIX ST.
DRUMMOND CR.
CHURCHWAY
DORIC WY.
CHRISTOPHER PL.
WEIR'S PAS.
Lib.
Hosp.
Town Hall
JUDD ST.
TONBRIDGE ST.
ARGYLE SQUARE
ARGYLE ST.
BIRKENHEAD ST.
CRESTFIELD ST.
BELGROVE ST.
ST. CHAD'S ST.
ST. CHAD'S PL.
WHIDBORNE ST.
MIDHOPE ST.
TANKERTON ST.
LOXHAM ST.
CROMER STREET
HARRISON ST.
REGENT SQUARE
SIDMOUTH ST.
SEAFORD ST.
HASTINGS ST.
THANET ST.
SANDWICH ST.
CARTWRIGHT GARDENS
BURTON ST.
BIDBOROUGH ST.
FLAXMAN TER.
MABLEDON PL.
DUKES RD.
HUNTER STREET
WAKEFIELD ST.
WAKEFIELD M.
LEIGH ST.
MARCHMONT ST.
COMPTON PL.
T.A.V.R. Cen.
Inst.
Kingsway Princeton Coll.
St. George's Gdns.
Foundling Hosp. Art Gall. & Mus.
HANDEL ST.
KENTON ST.
HENRIETTA M.
BRUNSWICK SQ.
Prim. Sch.
Coram's Fields
BRUNSWICK CENTRE
HERBRAND STREET
CORAM ST.
BERNARD ST.
COLONNADE
LANSDOWNE TER.
GUILFORD STREET
GRENVILLE ST.
The Hosp. for Sick Children
The National Hosp.
POWIS PL.
GREAT ORMOND ST.
QUEEN SQ.
QUEEN SQ. PL.
OLD GLOUCESTER ST.
BOSWELL ST.
COSMO PL.
BARBON CL.
SOUTHAMPTON ROW
THEOBALDS RD.
Russell Sq. Gdns.
RUSSELL SQUARE
BEDFORD PL.
MONTAGUE PL.
MONTAGUE ST.
British Museum & British Library
GREAT RUSSELL ST.
BLOOMSBURY SQUARE
BLOOMSBURY WAY
BLOOMSBURY ST.
VERNON PL.
SICILIAN AV.
FISHER ST.
CATTON ST.
HOLBORN
NEW OXFORD ST.
HIGH HOLBORN
SHAFTESBURY AV.
ST. GILES HIGH ST.
CHARING CROSS RD.
ENDELL ST.
Swim. Pool.
DRURY LANE
GREAT QUEEN ST.
Freemasons Hall
MACKLIN ST.
PARKER M.
NEWTON ST.
SMART'S PL.
STUKELEY ST.
DUNN'S PAS.
CENTRAL ST.
GRAPE ST.
BUCKNALL ST.
EARNSHAW ST.
DYOTT ST.
STREATHAM ST.
BAINBRIDGE ST.
COPTIC ST.
MUSEUM ST.
GILBERT PL.
Y.M.C.A. (H.Q.)
Y.W.C.A.
ST. GILES CIR.
ANDREW BORDE ST.
TOTTENHAM COURT ROAD
GOWER STREET
GOWER PL.
GOWER M.
GOWER CT.
University Coll.
University Coll. Hosp.
UNIVERSITY ST.
GORDON SQUARE
GORDON ST.
TAVITON ST.
ENDSLEIGH GDNS.
ENDSLEIGH ST.
ENDSLEIGH PL.
TAVISTOCK SQ. Gardens
TAVISTOCK PL.
TAVISTOCK HO.
British Med. Assoc.
Jewish Mus.
Friends Ho.
Wellcome Inst.
Offs.
Hlth. Cen.
UP. WOBURN PL.
WOBURN WLK.
WOBURN PL.
WOBURN SQUARE
THORNHAUGH ST.
THORNHAUGH M.
TORRINGTON SQ.
TORRINGTON PL.
BYNG PL.
MALET PL.
MALET ST.
BEDFORD WAY
Univ. of London Union
Sch. of Oriental Studies
Birkbeck Coll.
Sch. of Hygiene & Tropical Med.
Senate House
KEPPEL ST.
R.A.D.A.
CHENIES ST.
CHENIES M.
RIDGMOUNT GDNS.
RIDGMOUNT ST.
RIDGMOUNT PL.
ALFRED PL.
ALFRED M.
STORE ST.
GOWER M.
SOUTH CR.
BEDFORD SQUARE
BEDFORD AV.
BAYLEY ST.
MORWELL ST.
ADELINE PL.
BLOOMSBURY ST.
Sch.
Ear Hosp.
SHROPSHIRE PL.
CAPPER ST.
HUNTLEY ST.
TORRINGTON PL.
BEAUMONT PL.
EUSTON SQ.
EUSTON GRO.
Euston Sq. Gdns.
EUSTON ST.
STEPHENSON WAY
REGNART BS.
COBOURG ST.
DRUMMOND ST.
EVERSHOLT STREET
MELTON ST.
GRAFTON PL.
LANCING ST.
WELLESLEY PL.
CLARENDON GRO.
CRACE ST.
POLYGON RD.
WERRINGTON ST.
OAKLEY SQ.
TOTTENHAM COURT RD.
GOODGE ST.
GOODGE PL.
TOTTENHAM ST.
SCALA ST.
CHITTY ST.
CHARLOTTE ST.
CHARLOTTE M.
HOWLAND M.
HOWLAND ST.
CYPRESS PL.
COLVILLE PL.
WHITFIELD ST.
WINDMILL ST.
CHARLOTTE PL.
RATHBONE ST.
RATHBONE PL.
PERCY ST.
PERCY M.
PERCY PAS.
STEPHEN M.
STEPHEN ST.
GRESSE ST.
EVELYN YD.
HANWAY ST.
HANWAY PL.
NEWMAN ST.
NEWMAN PAS.
NEWMAN YD.
PERRY'S PL.
BERNERS ST.
BERNERS M.
BERNERS PL.
OXFORD STREET
WARDOUR ST.
SOHO SQUARE
SOHO ST.
FRITH ST.
GREEK ST.
MANETTE ST.
SUTTON RW.
FALCONBERG CT.
FLITCROFT ST.
DENMARK ST.
DENMARK PL.
STACEY ST.
PHOENIX ST.
NEW COMPTON ST.
GILES PS.
MONMOUTH ST.
NEAL ST.
NEAL'S YD.
SHORTS GDNS.
EARLHAM ST.
NOTTINGHAM CT.
BETTERTON ST.
ENDELL ST.
ARNE ST.
DRYDEN ST.
LONG ACRE
WILD ST.
KEMBLE ST.
Coll.
POLAND ST.
BERWICK ST.
NOEL ST.
D'ARBLAY ST.
SHERATON ST.
CARLISLE ST.
DEAN ST.
DIADEM CT.
HOLLEN ST.
FARM ST.
CHAPEL PL.
GT. CHAPEL ST.
ST. ANNE'S CT.
Syn.
Coll. Music

85
86
93
F
G
H
J
1
2
3
4
5
6
7
PENTONVILLE ROAD
A501
CITY RD.
GOSWELL
The Angel Centre
Covered Reservoir
MYDDELTON HO.
Holford Gdns.
Sch.
PENTON RISE
VERNON SQ.
PERCY CIR.
GREAT PERCY ST.
PRIDEAUX PL.
CLAREMONT SQ.
CLAREMONT CL.
CRUIKSHANK ST.
AMWELL ST.
INGLEBERT ST.
MYDDELTON SQUARE
MYDDELTON PAS.
RIVER ST.
LLOYD BAKER ST.
LLOYD SQ.
CHADWELL ST.
Dame Alice Owen Bldg.
Sadler's Wells
OWEN ST.
SIDNEY GRO.
Tech. Cen.
St. Mark Hospital
SPA GREEN ESTATE
ROSEBERY AVENUE
Thames Water Authority Head Office
ARLINGTON WY.
RAWSTORNE ST.
WYNYATT ST.
SPENCER ST.
King's Annexe
The City University
NORTHAMPTON SQ.
LLOYD'S RW.
B501
ST. JOHN STREET
WHARTON ST.
WHARTON COTTS.
GRANVILLE SQUARE
HARDWICK ST.
GLOUCESTER WY.
WHISKIN ST.
WYCLIF ST.
BRUNSWICK CLOSE EST.
Kings Bldg.
GOSWELL RD.
A1
KING'S CROSS ROAD
A201
GWYNNE PL.
MARGERY ST.
WILMINGTON SQ.
Gdns.
Baths Sch.
TYSOE ST.
MYDDELTON ST.
FINSBURY ESTATE
Library
SKINNER ST.
B502
PERCIVAL ST.
FINSBURY
Eastman Dental Hosp.
St. Andrew's Gdns.
FARRINGDON ROAD
A401
EXMOUTH MARKET
ROSOMAN ST.
Spa Fields Open Space
NORTHAMPTON RD.
CORPORATION
WOODBRIDGE ST.
PARTRIDGE CT.
COMPTON
DALLINGTON ST.
GRAY'S INN ROAD
PHOENIX PL.
Post Office Mount Pleasant
CALTHORPE ST.
GOUGH ST.
WREN ST.
CLERKENWELL
SANS WLK.
Schs.
SEKFORDE ST.
HAYWARD'S PL.
AYLESBURY ST.
GREAT SUTTON ST.
Dickens Ho.
COLEY ST.
I.T.N.
WARNER ST.
BAKER'S RW.
RAY ST.
CLERKENWELL GREEN
ST. JOHN'S SQ.
ROGER ST.
ELM ST.
LAYSTALL ST.
VINE HILL
BACK HILL
HERBAL HILL
A5201
CLERKENWELL ROAD
St. John's Gate
Charterhouse
NORTHINGTON ST.
A5200
BOURNE ESTATE
PORTPOOL LA.
LEATHER LANE
HATTON GARDEN
SAFFRON HILL
TURNMILL ST.
BRITTON ST.
BRISET ST.
Coll.
Liby.
Gray's Inn Gdns.
VERULAM ST.
Geographers' A-Z Shop
KIRBY ST.
CROSS ST.
B521
FARRINGDON
COWCROSS ST.
CHARTERHOUSE ST.
B500
Gray's Inn
BALDWIN'S GDNS.
GREVILLE ST.
BLEEDING HRT YD.
ELY PL.
VIADUCT BS.
Central Markets
WEST SMITHFIELD
SANDLAND ST.
CHANCERY LA.
A40
HOLBORN
HOLBORN CIR.
HOSIER LA.
SNOW HILL
COCK LA.
St. Bartholomew's Hosp.
London Weather Cen.
Lincoln's Inn Liby.
Lincoln's Inn Hall
HOLBORN
Lincoln's Inn Fields
Patents Off. Lib.
CURSITOR ST.
BREAM'S BLDGS.
ST. ANDREW ST.
A4208
SHOE LA.
ST PAUL'S THAMESLINK
NEWGATE ST.
National Mus.
Land Registry Off.
Royal Coll. of Surgeons
B400
ROLLS BLDGS.
Public Record Office
NEW FETTER LA.
Liby.
Cen. Crim. Ct. (Old Bailey)
WARWICK SQ.
WARWICK LA.
ST. BRIDE ST.
SEACOAL LA.
LUDGATE CIR.
LUDGATE HILL
Royal Courts of Justice
FLEET ST.

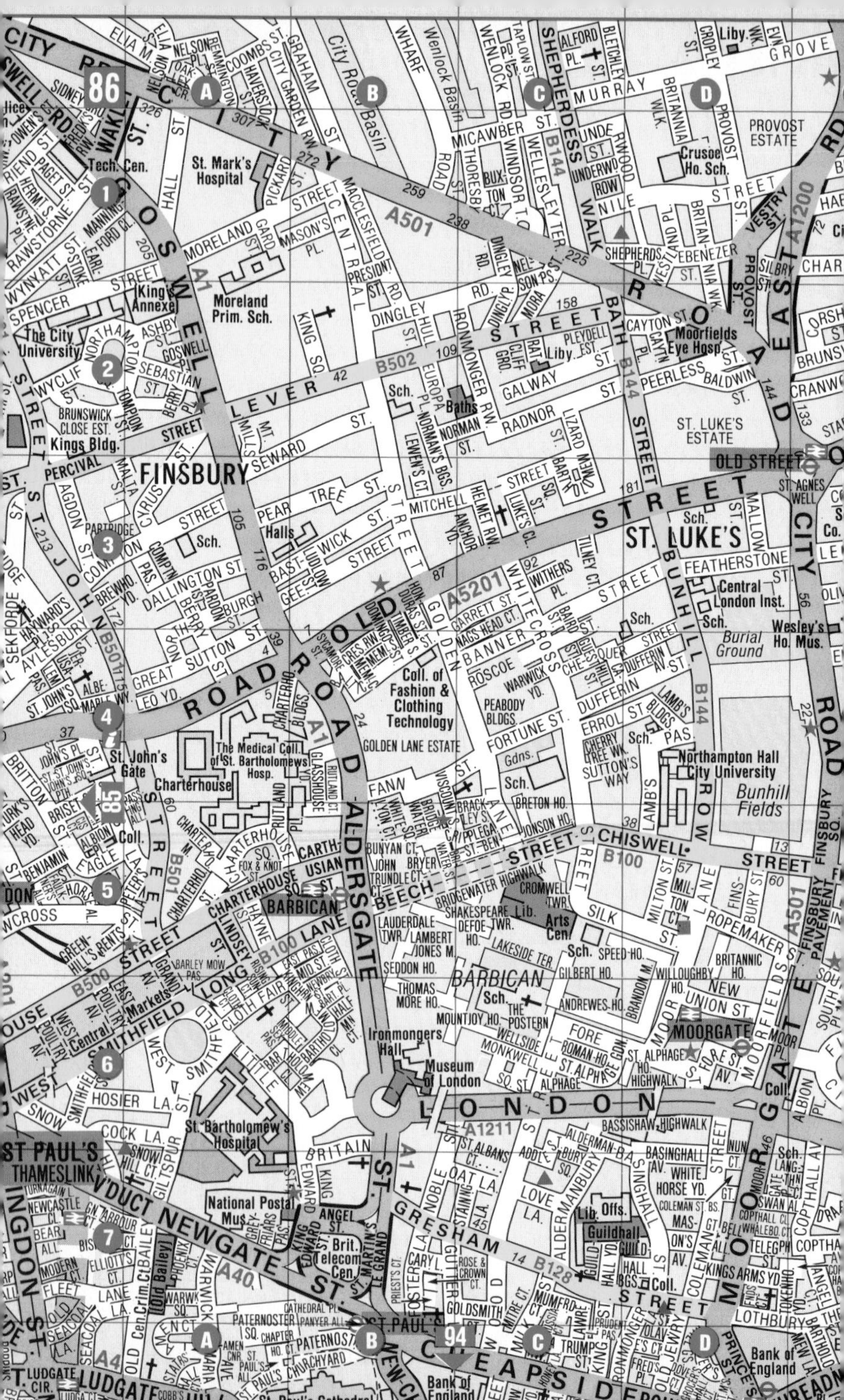

86
A
B
C
D
1
2
3
4
5
6
7
85
94
CITY RD.
GOSWELL
ST. JOHN ST.
OLD STREET
ROAD
ALDERSGATE
A1
A501
A5201
B502
B144
B100
B500
B501
A1211
B128
A40
A4
A1200
City Road Basin
Wenlock Basin
WHARF
SHEPHERDESS WALK
MICAWBER ST.
MURRAY
PROVOST ESTATE
Crusoe Ho. Sch.
NILE STREET
EBENEZER
VESTRY ST.
St. Mark's Hospital
Moreland Prim. Sch.
MORELAND
MASON'S PL.
CENTRAL
MACCLESFIELD
KING SQ.
DINGLEY
IRONMONGER RW.
Moorfields Eye Hosp.
PEERLESS
BALDWIN
GALWAY
RADNOR
Baths
Liby.
St. LUKE'S ESTATE
The City University
King's Annexe
SPENCER
NORTHAMPTON
WYCLIF
BRUNSWICK CLOSE EST.
Kings Bldg.
LEVER
STREET
SEWARD
FINSBURY
PERCIVAL
PEAR TREE ST.
Halls
BASTWICK
MITCHELL
ST. LUKE'S
FEATHERSTONE
Central London Inst.
BUNHILL
Burial Ground
Wesley's Ho. Mus.
CITY ROAD
COMPTON
DALLINGTON ST.
GREAT SUTTON ST.
WHITECROSS
BANNER
ROSCOE
Coll. of Fashion & Clothing Technology
PEABODY BLDGS.
FORTUNE ST.
DUFFERIN
GOLDEN LANE ESTATE
St. John's Gate
Charterhouse
The Medical Coll. of St. Bartholomews Hosp.
Northampton Hall City University
Bunhill Fields
CHISWELL STREET
FINSBURY SQ.
BARBICAN
CHARTERHOUSE
BEECH
SILK
ROPEMAKER
Arts Cen.
CROMWELL TWR.
SHAKESPEARE TWR.
LAUDERDALE TWR.
LAMBERT JONES M.
MOORGATE
NEW UNION ST.
MOORFIELDS
FINSBURY PAVEMENT
LONG LANE
Markets
Central
SMITHFIELD
WEST SMITHFIELD
Ironmongers Hall
Museum of London
LONDON WALL
HOSIER LA.
COCK LA.
St. Bartholomew's Hospital
ST PAUL'S THAMESLINK
National Postal Mus.
NEWGATE ST.
FARRINGDON ST.
GRESHAM
Guildhall
ALDERMANBURY
BASINGHALL
COLEMAN ST.
MOORGATE
LOTHBURY
Bank of England
Cen. Crim. Ct. (Old Bailey)
St. Paul's
PATERNOSTER SQ.
Brit. Telecom Cen.
ST. MARTIN'S LE GRAND
CHEAPSIDE
LUDGATE CIR.
FLEET LANE
OLD BAILEY
WARWICK LA.
AVE MARIA

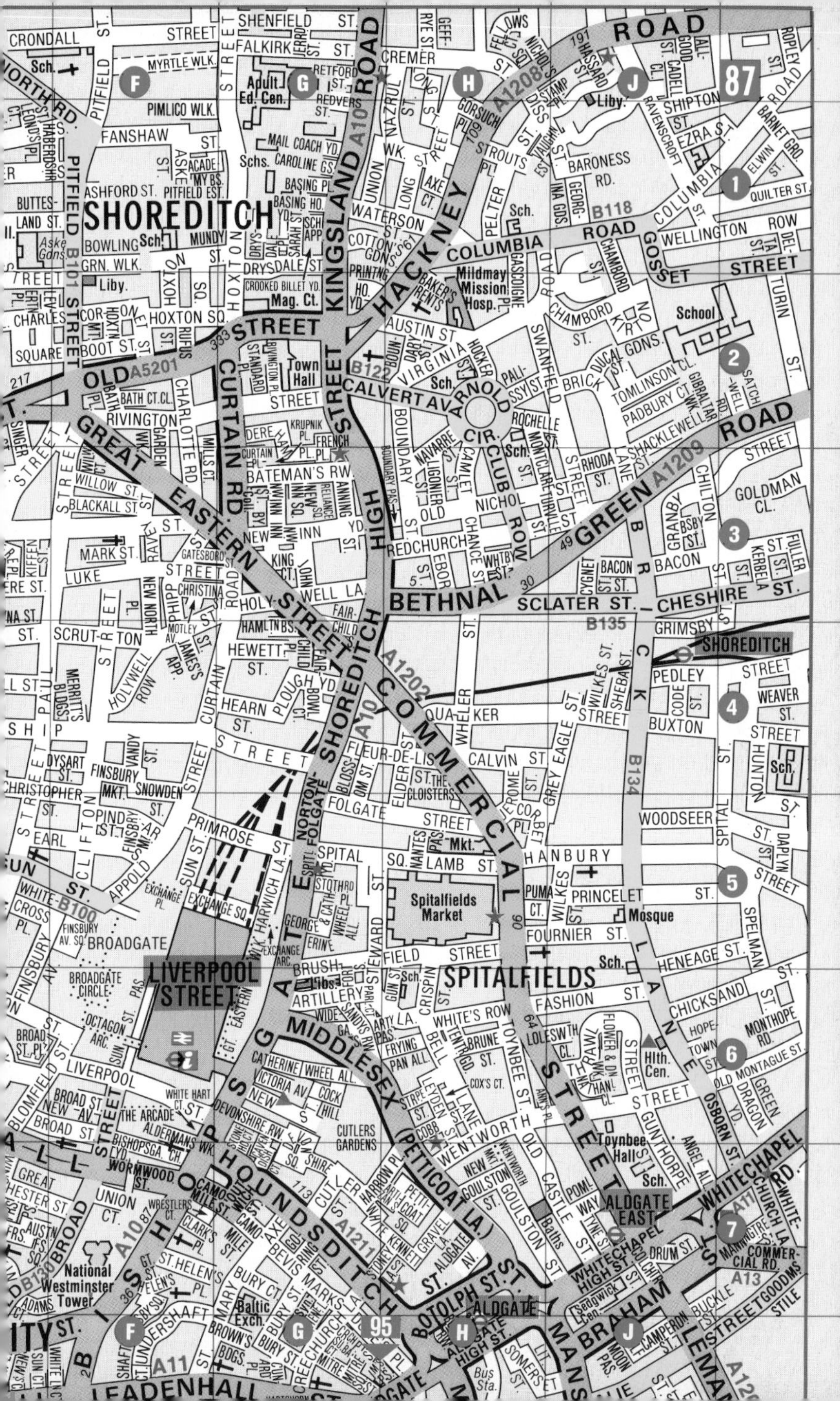

87
F
G
H
J
1
2
3
4
5
6
7
95
SHOREDITCH
SPITALFIELDS
HACKNEY ROAD
A1208
KINGSLAND ROAD
A10
OLD STREET
A5201
CURTAIN RD.
GREAT EASTERN STREET
SHOREDITCH HIGH STREET
COMMERCIAL STREET
A1202
BETHNAL GREEN ROAD
A1209
BISHOPSGATE
HOUNDSDITCH
A1211
MIDDLESEX (PETTICOAT LA.) STREET
WHITECHAPEL HIGH ST.
WHITECHAPEL RD.
A11
A13
LEADENHALL
COLUMBIA ROAD
B118
GOSSET STREET
BRICK LANE
B134
B135
SCLATER ST.
CHESHIRE ST.
HANBURY
PRINCELET ST.
FOURNIER ST.
FASHION ST.
WENTWORTH
OLD CASTLE ST.
LIVERPOOL STREET
BROADGATE
BROADGATE CIRCLE
Spitalfields Market
Mildmay Mission Hosp.
Town Hall
Toynbee Hall
Mosque
Hlth. Cen.
National Westminster Tower
Baltic Exch.
Adult Ed. Cen.
Mag. Ct.
CUTLERS GARDENS
ALDGATE
ALDGATE EAST
SHOREDITCH
ARNOLD CIR.
BOUNDARY ST.
CALVERT AV.
REDCHURCH ST.
FOLGATE STREET
SPITAL SQ.
LAMB ST.
ARTILLERY LA.
BRUSHFIELD STREET
WHITE'S ROW
BRUNE ST.
GOULSTON ST.
BRAHAM
MANSELL
LEMAN
OSBORN ST.
HOXTON SQ.
HOXTON STREET
PITFIELD STREET
B101
RIVINGTON
WORSHIP STREET
SUN ST.
B100
APPOLD
PRIMROSE ST.
EXCHANGE SQ.
WILSON ST.
PAUL STREET
CHRISTOPHER ST.
EARL ST.
WORMWOOD ST.
CAMOMILE ST.
ST. MARY AXE
BEVIS MARKS
CREECHURCH LA.
BURY ST.
DUKE'S PL.
ALDGATE HIGH ST.
ST. BOTOLPH ST.
NEW ST.
DEVONSHIRE SQ.
QUAKER ST.
WHEELER ST.
CALVIN ST.
WOODSEER
HENEAGE ST.
CHICKSAND
BUXTON
PEDLEY STREET
WEAVER ST.
FULLER ST.
GRIMSBY ST.
RHODA ST.
SHACKLEWELL ST.
VIRGINIA
CLUB ROW
NICHOL ROW
CHAMBORD ST.
SWANFIELD ST.
TURIN ST.
WELLINGTON ROW
BARONESS RD.
SHIPTON ST.
RAVENSCROFT ST.
QUILTER ST.
SCHOOL
Sch.
Liby.
Baths

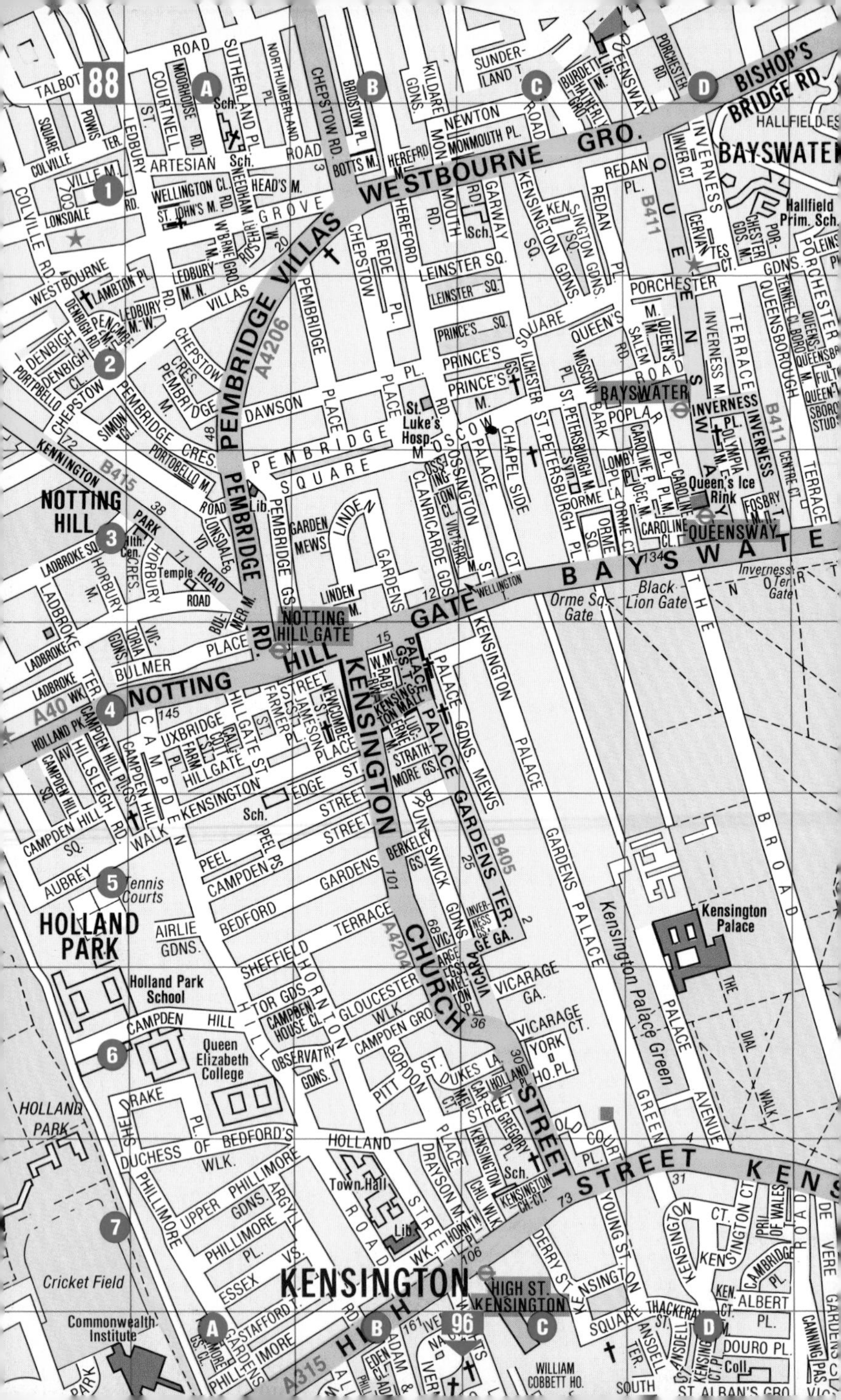
88
96
A
B
C
D
1
2
3
4
5
6
7
NOTTING HILL
HOLLAND PARK
KENSINGTON
BAYSWATER
WESTBOURNE GRO.
BISHOP'S BRIDGE RD.
PEMBRIDGE VILLAS
PEMBRIDGE RD.
NOTTING HILL GATE
BAYSWATER
KENSINGTON CHURCH STREET
KENSINGTON HIGH STREET
HOLLAND PARK
KENSINGTON PALACE GARDENS
PALACE GARDENS TER.
QUEENSWAY
THE BROAD WALK
Kensington Palace
Kensington Palace Green
Black Lion Gate
Orme Sq. Gate
Inverness Ter. Gate
Queen's Ice Rink
St. Luke's Hosp.
Holland Park School
Queen Elizabeth College
Commonwealth Institute
Cricket Field
Town Hall
Tennis Courts
Hallfield Prim. Sch.
HIGH ST. KENSINGTON
A4206
A40
A315
A4204
B411
B415
B405
PORTOBELLO RD.
LEDBURY RD.
CHEPSTOW RD.
CHEPSTOW VILLAS
PEMBRIDGE SQUARE
PEMBRIDGE GDNS.
LINDEN GARDENS
CLANRICARDE GDNS.
MOSCOW RD.
PRINCE'S SQ.
LEINSTER SQ.
QUEENSBOROUGH TERRACE
PORCHESTER TERRACE
INVERNESS TERRACE
CAMPDEN HILL RD.
CAMPDEN HILL SQ.
HOLLAND PK. AV.
LADBROKE SQ.
LADBROKE GRO.
BEDFORD GARDENS
SHEFFIELD TERRACE
GLOUCESTER WLK.
HORNTON STREET
PHILLIMORE GDNS.
DUCHESS OF BEDFORD'S WLK.
VICARAGE GA.
YOUNG ST.
KENSINGTON SQUARE
DERRY ST.
THACKERAY ST.
WILLIAM COBBETT HO.
ST. ALBAN'S GRO.

PADDINGTON
89
PRAED
SUSSEX
GDNS
BAYSWATER
ROAD
LANCASTER GATE
The Fountains
THE LONG WATER
Speke's Monument
Peter Pan
Nursery
KENSINGTON
GARDENS
Temple Lodge
Serpentine Bridge
Boat Houses
The Lido
Serpentine Gallery
Bandstand
Bowling Greens
Albert Memorial
Royal Geographical Society
Royal Albert Hall
Royal Coll. of Art
Imperial Coll.
Royal Coll. of Music
KNIGHTSBRIDGE
KENSINGTON GORE
90
97

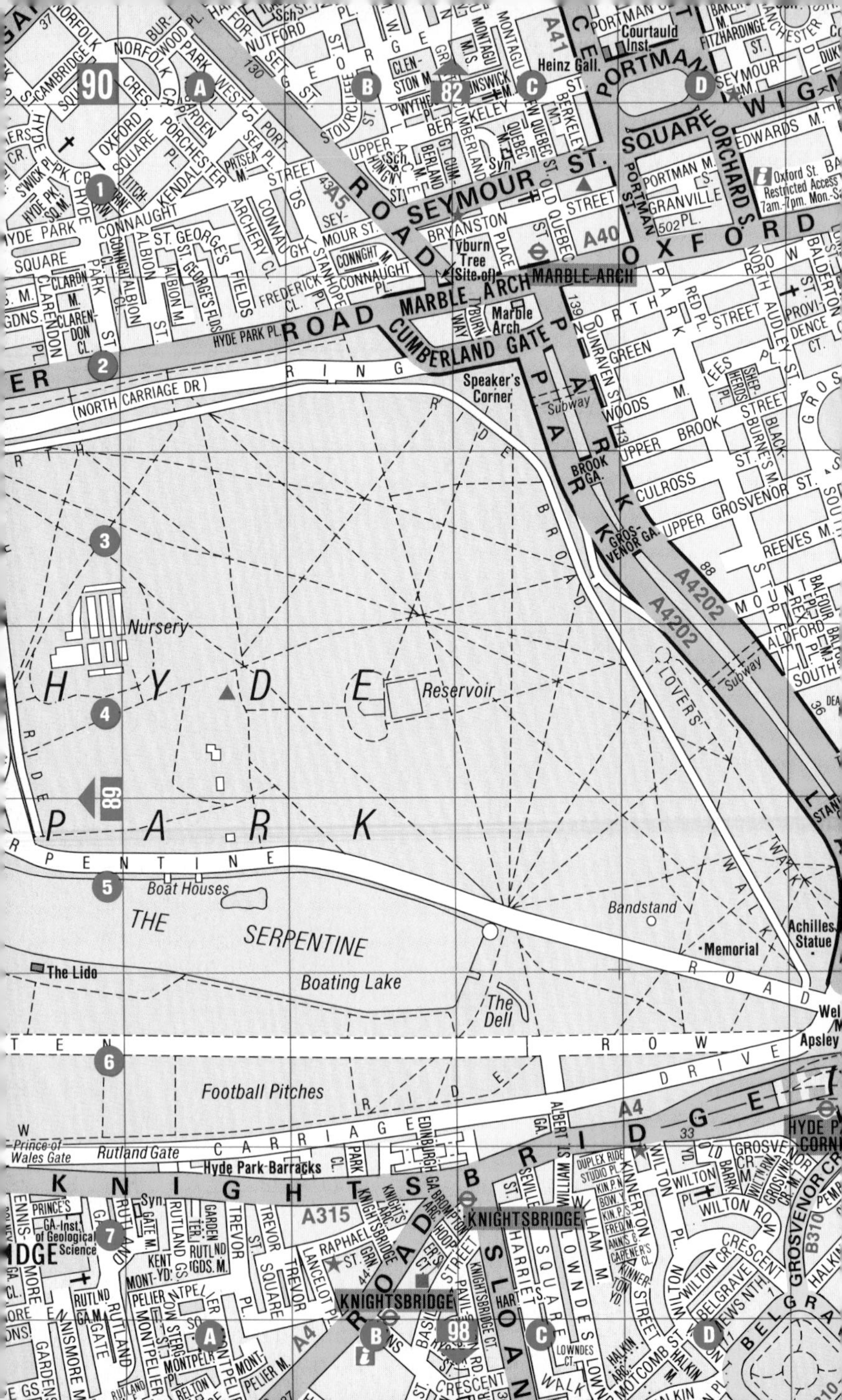
90
HYDE PARK
THE SERPENTINE
Boating Lake
The Lido
Boat Houses
Nursery
Reservoir
Football Pitches
The Dell
Bandstand
Memorial
Achilles Statue
Speaker's Corner
Marble Arch
MARBLE ARCH
Tyburn Tree (Site of)
CUMBERLAND GATE
PARK LANE
A4202
Subway
NORTH CARRIAGE DR.
RING
BROAD WALK
LOVERS' WALK
SERPENTINE ROAD
ROTTEN ROW
SOUTH CARRIAGE DRIVE
Prince of Wales Gate
Rutland Gate
Hyde Park Barracks
KNIGHTSBRIDGE
A315
A4
BROMPTON ROAD
SLOANE STREET
KNIGHTSBRIDGE
BAYSWATER ROAD
EDGWARE ROAD
A5
SEYMOUR ST.
PORTMAN SQUARE
OXFORD STREET
A40
A41
ORCHARD ST.
NORTH AUDLEY ST.
UPPER BROOK ST.
UPPER GROSVENOR ST.
GREEN ST.
CONNAUGHT SQUARE
HYDE PARK SQUARE
OXFORD SQUARE
NORFOLK CRES.
SUSSEX GARDENS
Courtauld Inst.
Heinz Gall.
Oxford St. Restricted Access 7am.-7pm. Mon.-Sat.
WILTON CRESCENT
BELGRAVE SQUARE
LOWNDES SQUARE
GROSVENOR CRESCENT
HYDE PARK CORNER
Apsley
Inst. of Geological Science
ENNISMORE GARDENS
MONTPELIER SQ.
82
89
98

91
83
92
99
F
G
H
J
1
2
3
4
5
6
7
Wigmore Hall
Polytechnic
Coll. of Nursing
OXFORD STREET
A40
OXFORD CIRCUS
BOND ST.
Shop. Cen.
Regent Hall
Police Ct.
Coll. of Music
Leisure Cen.
MAYFAIR
PICCADILLY CIRCUS
Eros
Trocad. Cen.
Faraday Mus.
Mus. of Mankind
Royal Academy of Arts
London Lib.
ST. JAMES'S SQUARE
R.A.C.
GREEN PARK
PICCADILLY
A4
REGENT STREET
A4201
NEW BOND STREET
B406
CONDUIT ST.
BROOK ST.
GROSVENOR ST.
BRUTON ST.
BERKELEY SQUARE
CURZON ST.
PALL MALL
ST. JAMES'S ST.
JERMYN ST.
SHAFTESBURY AVE.
Marlborough Ho.
(Commonwealth Conference Centre)
St. James's Palace
Clarence House
Lancaster Ho.
Stable Yard Gate
(Closed to traffic on Sundays)
Bandstand
GREEN PARK
THE MALL
Queen Victoria Mem.
CONSTITUTION (Closed to traffic on Sundays) HILL
DUKE OF WELLINGTON PL.
Wellington Mon.
BUCKINGHAM PALACE GARDENS
Lake
Buckingham Palace
The Quadrangle
The Forecourt
Ambassadors' Ct.
Queens Gallery
The Royal Mews
Buckingham Gate
BUCKINGHAM GATE
B323
BIRDCAGE WALK
Queen Anne's Gate
Home Office
Wellington Barracks
Passport Off.
Caxton Hall
St. James's Park
Lake
GROSVENOR PLACE
A302

92
84
91
100
A
B
C
D
1
2
3
4
5
6
7
SOHO
SOHO SQUARE
COVENT GARDEN
Royal Opera House
The Market
Transport Mus.
Freemasons Hall
SHAFTESBURY AVENUE
CHARING CROSS ROAD
ST. GILES HIGH ST.
CAMBRIDGE CIRCUS
SEVEN DIALS
LONG ACRE
BOW ST.
GREAT QUEEN ST.
DRURY LANE
ENDELL ST.
NEAL ST.
SHORTS GARDENS
MONMOUTH ST.
EARLHAM ST.
ST. MARTIN'S LANE
GARRICK ST.
KING ST.
HENRIETTA ST.
SOUTHAMPTON ST.
MAIDEN LA.
TAVISTOCK ST.
WELLINGTON ST.
BEDFORD ST.
CHANDOS PL.
WILLIAM IV ST.
ADELAIDE ST.
STRAND
SAVOY
ADAM ST.
JOHN ADAM ST.
VILLIERS ST.
CRAVEN ST.
NORTHUMBERLAND AV.
CHARING CROSS
EMBANKMENT
Hungerford
Victoria Embankment Gardens
Hispaniola
P.S. Tattershall Castle
LEICESTER SQ.
Leicester Fields
GERRARD ST.
LISLE ST.
NEWPORT PL.
CRANBOURN ST.
WARDOUR ST.
DEAN ST.
FRITH ST.
GREEK ST.
OLD COMPTON ST.
BERWICK ST.
BROADWICK ST.
LEXINGTON ST.
BREWER ST.
OXFORD STREET
D'ARBLAY ST.
NOEL ST.
CARLISLE ST.
Syn.
Hosp.
Sch.
Coll.
Swim. Pool.
PICCADILLY CIRCUS
PICCADILLY
Eros
Trocadero Cen.
COVENTRY ST.
REGENT ST.
HAYMARKET
JERMYN ST.
DENMAN ST.
WINDMILL ST.
Lib.
National Portrait Gallery
National Gallery
DUNCANNON ST.
TRAFALGAR SQUARE
Nelson's Column
Canada Ho.
PALL MALL EAST
COCKSPUR ST.
PALL MALL
ST. JAMES'S SQUARE
London Lib.
CHARLES II ST.
WATERLOO PL.
Waterloo Gdns.
CARLTON HOUSE TER.
R.A.C.
Duke of York Mem.
Inst. of Contempory Art
Galls.
Admiralty Arch.
Old Admiralty Offices
THE MALL
HORSE GUARDS RD.
Horse Guards Parade
Horse Guards
Banqueting Ho.
Guards Memorial
WHITEHALL
Old War Office
HORSEGUARDS AV.
Henry VIII Wine Cellar Mus.
Ministry of Defence
GT. SCOTLAND YD.
Marlborough Ho.
(Commonwealth Conference Centre)
St. James's Palace
Clarence House
Stable Yard Gate
(Closed to traffic on Sundays)
ST. JAMES'S PARK
Duck Island
St. James's Park Lake
DOWNING ST.
Cenotaph
Foreign Office
Government Offices
KING CHARLES ST.
CABINET WAR ROOMS
RICHMOND T.
DERBY GA.
PARLIAMENT ST.
VICTORIA EMBANKMENT
A3211
WESTMINSTER
Westminster Pier
The County
BRIDGE ST.
WESTMINSTER BRIDGE
A302
Big Ben
New Palace Yard
Westminster Hall
Houses of Parliament
PARLIAMENT SQ.
BIRDCAGE WALK
Queen Anne's Gate
COCKPIT STEPS
OLD QUEEN ST.
Home Office
Wellington Barracks
LEWISHAM ST.
STOREY'S GATE
GREAT GEORGE ST.
Q.E. II Conf. Cen.
Guildhall
BROAD SANCTUARY
TOTHILL ST.
BROADWAY
ST. JAMES'S PARK
Passport Off.
Caxton Hall
New Scotland
Westminster Abbey
The Close
Dept. of Trade & Industry
ST. MARGARET ST.
OLD PALACE YD.
A40
A401
A400
A4
B401
B402
B308
A3212

Lincoln's Inn Fields
Land Registry Off.
Royal Coll. of Surgeons
F
G
H
J
85
93
1
2
3
4
5
6
7
94
101
Public Record Office
Royal Courts of Justice
BREAM'S BDGS.
ROLLS BLDGS.
FETTER LANE
CHANCERY LANE
FLEET ST.
LUDGATE CIR.
LUDGATE HILL
NEW BRI. ST.
ST. BRIDE ST.
SHOE LA.
CARTER LA.
STRAND
ALDWYCH
Bush Ho.
Temple Bar
King's Coll.
COURTAULD INSTITUTE GALLERIES
Somerset House
TEMPLE
Middle Temple
Inner Temple
Inner Temple Gardens
Temple Pier
H.Q.S. Wellington
H.M.S. Chrysanthemum
H.M.S. President
EMBANKMENT
BLACKFRIARS
BLACKFRIARS UNDERPASS
QUEEN VICTORIA ST.
UPPER THAMES ST.
WHITEFRIARS ST.
BOUVERIE ST.
CARMELITE ST.
JOHN CARPENTER ST.
TUDOR ST.
TALLIS ST.
RIVER
A201
A4
A321
A301
BLACKFRIARS BRI.
WATERLOO BRIDGE
Reach
Festival Pier
Kings Reach
Mus. of the Moving Image
The National Film Theatre
National Theatre
Queen Elizabeth Hall
Royal Festival Hall
Hayward Gallery
South Bank
South Bank Television Centre
Bankside Gallery
HOPTON'S GS.
HOLLAND ST.
SOUTHWARK ST.
STAMFORD STREET
A3200
Nautical Sch.
UPPER GROUND
BARGE HOUSE ST.
OLD BARGE HO. ALL.
GABRIEL'S WHARF
BROADWALL
COIN ST.
DUCHY ST.
AQUINAS ST.
PARIS GARDEN
HATFIELDS
RENNIE ST.
MARIGOLD ALL.
BULL ALL.
COLOMBO ST.
Sports Cen.
MEYMOTT ST.
School
Univ.
DOON ST.
CORNWALL RD.
THEED ST.
WHITTLESEY ST.
ROUPELL ST.
BRAD ST.
WOOTTON ST.
WATERLOO EAST
WATERLOO
TENISON WAY
CONCERT HALL APP.
BOYCE ST.
MEPHAM ST.
BUCKLEY ST.
WATERLOO ROAD
SANDELL ST.
ALASKA ST.
EXTON ST.
SECKER ST.
WHICHCOTE ST.
THE CUT
B300
UNION ST.
NELSON SQUARE
SURREY ROW
POCOCK
KING'S BENCH ST.
RUSHWORTH ST.
Southwark Coll.
BURROWS MS.
SHORT ST.
ISABELLA ST.
JOAN ST.
SCORESBY ST.
BOUNDARY RW.
VALENTINE PL.
CHAPLIN CL.
UFFORD ST.
MITRE RD.
THE CUT
WEBBER ST.
Teacher Training Cen.
Hlth. Cen.
PEABODY SQ.
LANCASTER ST.
BOYFIELD ST.
SILEX ST.
GREAT SUFFOLK ST.
BOROUGH ROAD
Polytech of the South Bank
ST. GEORGE'S CIRCUS
ST. GEORGE'S ROAD
Lib.
Hosp.
YORK ROAD
BELVEDERE RD.
CHICHELEY ST.
LEAKE ST.
ADDINGTON ST.
WESTMINSTER BRIDGE ROAD
A23
A3036
LOWER MARSH
LAMBETH NORTH
St. George's Cathedral
COOPER CL.
GEORGE ST.
DODSON ST.
GRAY ST.
BARON'S PL.
CORAL ST.
BAYLIS RD.
GREENHAM CL.
FRAZIER ST.
MURPHY ST.
GRINDAL ST.
JOHANNA ST.
MARSH
LAUNCELOT ST.
Sch.
Gdn.

94
86
93
A
B
C
D
1
2
3
4
5
6
7
NEWGATE ST.
CHEAPSIDE
POULTRY
LUDGATE HILL
LUDGATE CIR.
St. Paul's Cathedral
Choir Sch.
ST. PAUL'S CHURCHYARD
PATERNOSTER SQ.
NEW CHANGE
CANNON ST.
QUEEN VICTORIA
MANSION HOUSE
Bank of England
Bank of England Offs.
BANK
QUEEN ST.
UPPER THAMES
WHITE LION
City of London School
BLACKFRIARS
UNDERPASS
NEW BRI. ST.
QUEEN ST. PL.
CANNON ST.
SOUTHWARK BRIDGE
BLACKFRIARS BRI.
A201
A300
A3211
A3200
B132
B300
A3
A4
A40
B128
Globe Theatre (under construction)
Bankside Gallery
RIVERSIDE WALK
BANKSIDE
Bankside Power Station (disused)
HOLLAND ST.
HOPTON ST.
SUMNER ST.
PARK STREET
EMERSON ST.
ZOAR ST.
GREAT GUILDFORD ST.
SOUTHWARK ST.
SOUTHWARK BRIDGE ROAD
CLINK ST.
St. Saviour's Dock
Swan Lane Pier
Southwark Cath.
LONDON BRIDGE
BOROUGH HIGH ST.
SOUTHWARK
UNION STREET
John Harvard Cen.
NELSON SQUARE
MARSHALSEA RD.
Schools
Guy's Hospital
LONG LANE
GT. DOVER ST.
THE BOROUGH
BOROUGH ROAD
SOUTHWARK
Polytechnic of the South Bank
Inner London Sessions Ho.
Tabard Gardens
BLACKFRIARS ROAD
ST. GEORGE'S CIRCUS
NEWINGTON CAUSEWAY
BOROUGH

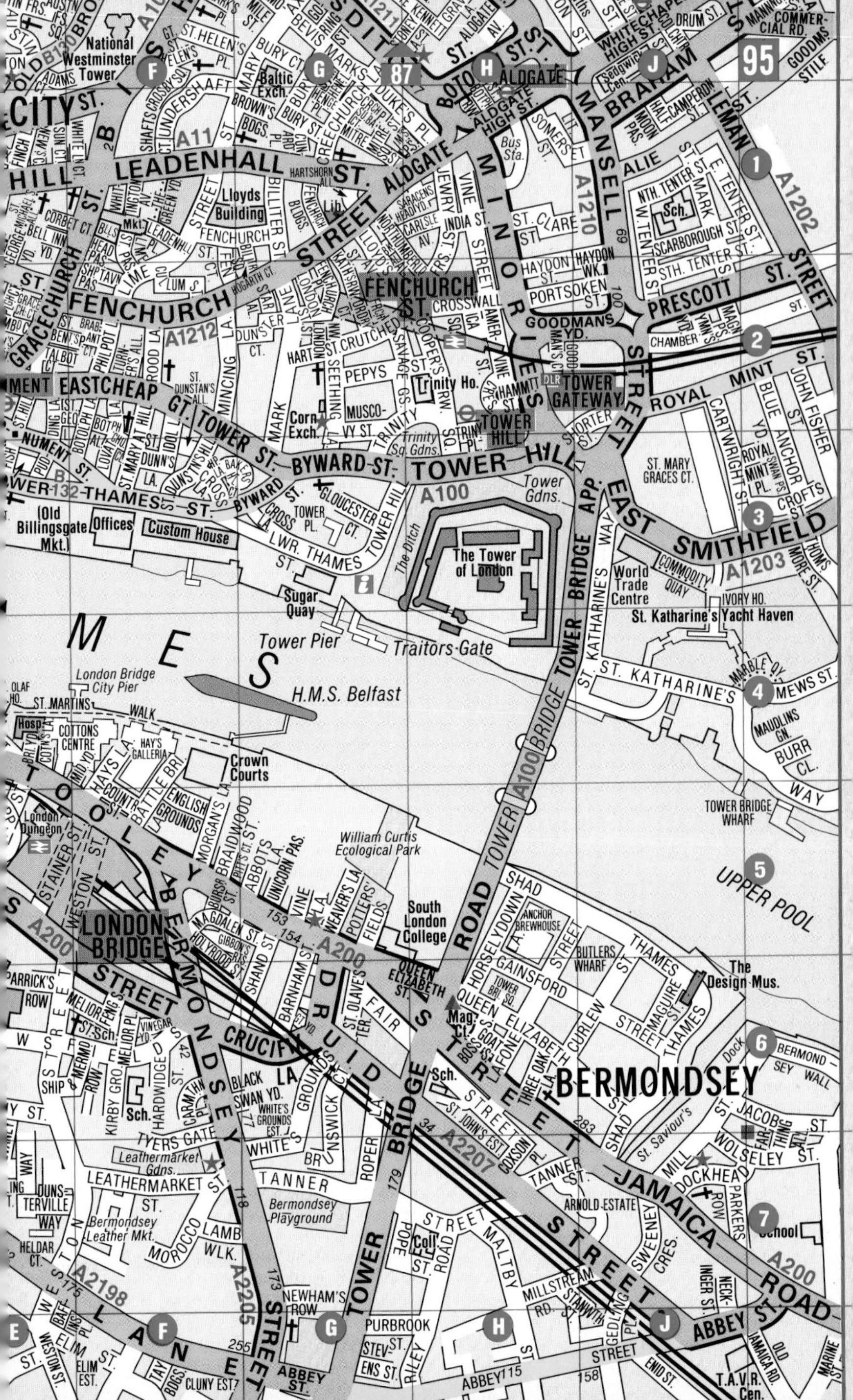

95
87
F
G
H
J
1
2
3
4
5
6
7
E
National Westminster Tower
Baltic Exch.
CITY
LEADENHALL ST.
ALDGATE
ALDGATE HIGH ST.
WHITECHAPEL HIGH ST.
BRAHAM
MANSELL
LEMAN STREET
A1202
A1210
A11
ALIE
COMMERCIAL RD.
GOODMANS STILE
Bus Sta.
MINORIES
Lloyds Building
FENCHURCH ST.
FENCHURCH STREET
GRACECHURCH ST.
A1212
EASTCHEAP
GT. TOWER ST.
MINCING LA.
MARK LA.
HART ST.
CRUTCHED
PEPYS ST.
SEETHING LA.
Corn Exch.
Trinity Ho.
TOWER HILL
TOWER GATEWAY
DLR
PRESCOTT ST.
GOODMANS YD.
CHAMBER ST.
ROYAL MINT ST.
CARTWRIGHT ST.
JOHN FISHER ST.
ST. MARY GRACES CT.
EAST SMITHFIELD
A1203
BYWARD ST.
THAMES ST.
LWR. THAMES ST.
A100
Tower Gdns.
TOWER BRIDGE APP.
(Old Billingsgate Mkt.)
Offices
Custom House
Sugar Quay
The Ditch
The Tower of London
Tower Pier
Traitors Gate
World Trade Centre
COMMODITY QUAY
IVORY HO.
St. Katharine's Yacht Haven
ST. KATHARINE'S WAY
ST. KATHARINE'S MEWS ST.
MAUDLINS GN.
BURR CL.
TOWER BRIDGE WHARF
THAMES
London Bridge City Pier
H.M.S. Belfast
ST. MARTINS WALK
COTTONS CENTRE
HAY'S GALLERIA
Crown Courts
ENGLISH GROUNDS
MORGAN'S LA.
BRAIDWOOD ST.
TOOLEY STREET
London Dungeon
LONDON BRIDGE
A200
William Curtis Ecological Park
South London College
UPPER POOL
TOWER BRIDGE ROAD
SHAD THAMES
ANCHOR BREWHOUSE
BUTLERS WHARF
The Design Mus.
HORSELYDOWN LA.
GAINSFORD ST.
QUEEN ELIZABETH ST.
CURLEW STREET
MAGUIRE ST.
BERMONDSEY
BERMONDSEY WALL
DRUID ST.
ST. OLAVE'S TER.
FAIR ST.
CRUCIFIX LA.
BLACK SWAN YD.
WHITE'S GROUNDS
ST. JOHN'S EST.
A2207
JAMAICA ROAD
DOCKHEAD
WOLSELEY ST.
ST. SAVIOUR'S
ARNOLD ESTATE
TANNER ST.
LEATHERMARKET ST.
Leathermarket Gdns.
Bermondsey Leather Mkt.
Bermondsey Playground
BERMONDSEY STREET
A2205
A2198
WESTON ST.
LONG LANE
MOROCCO ST.
LAMB WLK.
POPE ST.
MALTBY ST.
MILLSTREAM RD.
SPA ROAD
ABBEY ST.
NEWHAM'S ROW
PURBROOK ST.
RILEY ST.
T.A.V.R. Cen.
CLUNY EST.
School

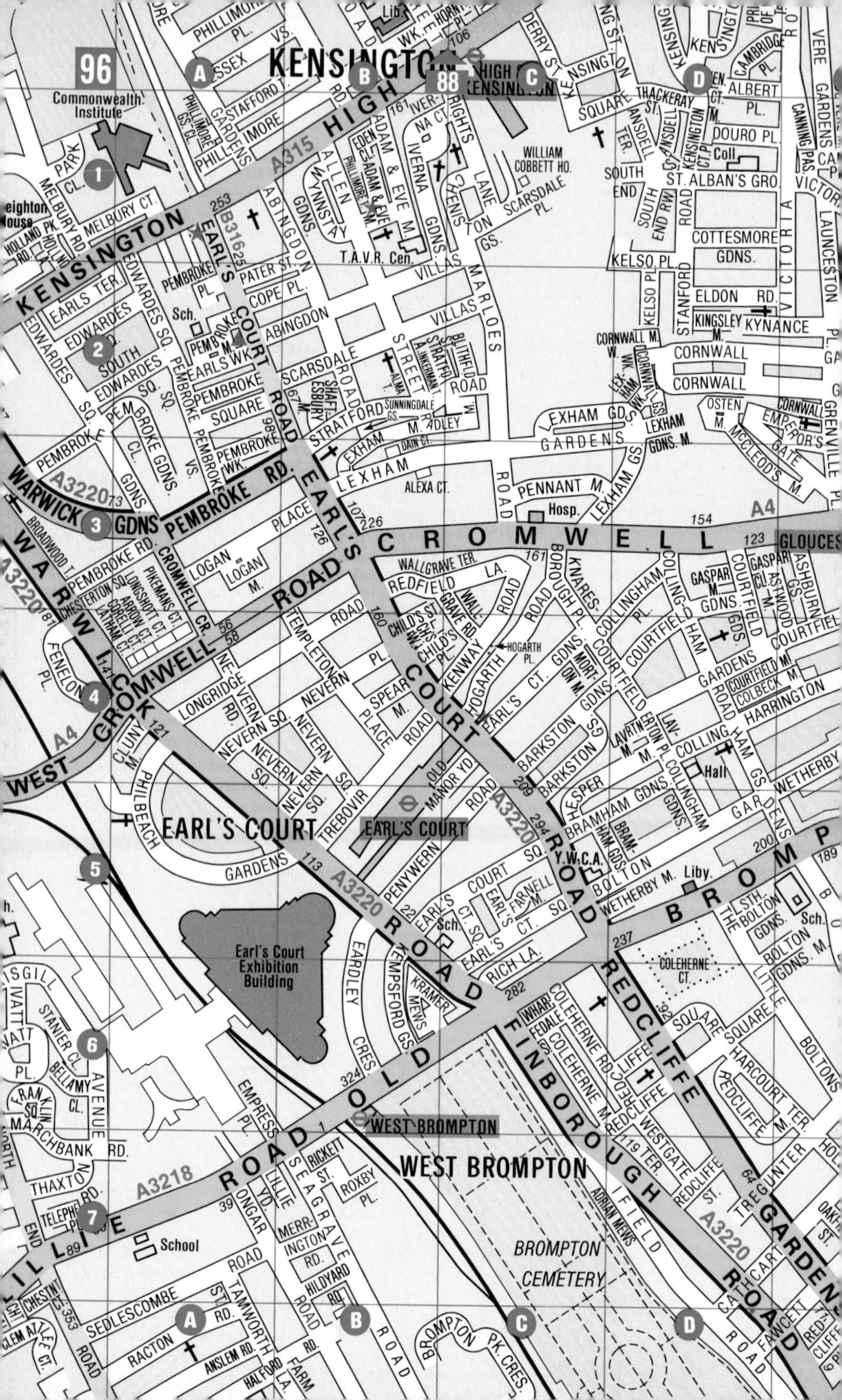
KENSINGTON
88
HIGH ST. KENSINGTON
Commonwealth Institute
Lib.
106
KENSINGTON HIGH
A315
B316
253
161
Leighton House
PHILLIMORE PL.
ESSEX VS.
STAFFORD
PHILLIMORE GS. CL.
PHILLIMORE GARDENS
PHILLIMORE
PARK CL.
MELBURY RD.
MELBURY CT.
HOLLAND PK. RD.
ADAM & EVE M.
IVERNA CT.
IVERNA GDNS.
NA CT.
WRIGHTS LANE
ALLEN ST.
WYNNSTAY GDNS.
ABINGDON VILLAS
ALEXIS
TON SCARSDALE PL.
WILLIAM COBBETT HO.
T.A.V.R. Cen.
DERRY ST.
KENSINGTON SQUARE
THACKERAY ST.
ANSDELL ST.
ANSDELL TER.
SOUTH END
SOUTH END RW.
KENSINGTON CT. PL.
KENSINGTON CT. M.
ALBERT PL.
DOURO PL.
CAMBRIDGE PL.
Coll.
ST. ALBAN'S GRO.
COTTESMORE GDNS.
KELSO PL.
STANFORD RD.
ELDON RD.
KINGSLEY M.
KYNANCE
VICTORIA ROAD
LAUNCESTON
CANNING PAS.
VICTORIA
VERE GARDENS
CORNWALL M. W.
CORNWALL
CORNWALL GDNS.
LEXHAM WK.
LEXHAM GDS.
LEXHAM GARDENS
LEXHAM GDNS. M.
LEXHAM GS.
OSTEN M.
EMPEROR'S GATE
MCCLEOD'S M.
GRENVILLE
EARLS TER.
EDWARDES SQ.
EDWARDES SQ. SOUTH
EDWARDES
PEMBROKE PL.
PATER ST.
COPE PL.
ABINGDON
Sch.
PEMBROKE M.
EARLS WK.
PEMBROKE SQUARE
PEMBROKE WK.
PEMBROKE VS.
PEMBROKE GDNS.
PEM BROKE CL.
PEMBROKE RD.
EARL'S COURT ROAD
SCARSDALE VILLAS
STRATFORD ROAD
SHAFTESBURY
ALMA T.
STRATFORD ST.
BLITHFIELD ST.
A. INKERMANN T.
SUNNINGDALE GS.
ADLEY
EXHAM M.
DAIN CT.
LEXHAM
ALEXA CT.
MARLOES ROAD
PENNANT M.
Hosp.
A3220
WARWICK GDNS.
A4
CROMWELL
ROAD
154
123
GLOUCES
107
226
126
LOGAN PLACE
LOGAN M.
BROADWOOD T.
PEMBROKE RD.
CHESTERTON SQ.
LONGSHOT CT.
PIKEMANS CT.
ARROW CT.
CORELLI CT.
LATHAM CT.
CROMWELL CR.
56
58
181
WALLGRAVE TER.
REDFIELD LA.
WALLGRAVE RD.
161
KNARESBOROUGH PL.
COLLINGHAM PL.
GASPAR M.
COURTFIELD GDNS.
ASHBURN GS.
ASTWOOD M.
COURTFIELD
COLLINGHAM GDNS.
WARWICK
FENELON PL.
WEST CROMWELL
LONGRIDGE RD.
NEVERN PL.
NEVERN SQ.
NEVERN RD.
TEMPLETON PL.
SPEAR M.
CHILD'S ST.
CHILD'S PL.
CHILD'S WK.
KENWAY ROAD
HOGARTH ROAD
HOGARTH PL.
EARL'S CT. GDNS.
MORTON M.
COURTFIELD ROAD
COURTFIELD M.
COLBECK M.
HARRINGTON
COLLINGHAM RD.
BARKSTON GDNS.
BARKSTON GS.
LAVERTON M.
LAVERTON PL.
COLLINGHAM
Hall
WETHERBY
121
CLUNY M.
PHILBEACH GARDENS
EARL'S COURT
TREBOVIR ROAD
OLD MANOR YD.
EARL'S COURT
209
294
HESPER M.
BRAMHAM GDNS.
BRAMHAM GDS.
Y.W.C.A.
BOLTON
WETHERBY M.
Liby.
BROMPTON
200
189
113
A3220
PENYWERN
EARL'S COURT SQ.
EARL'S CT. SQ.
FARNELL M.
Sch.
EARL'S CT.
RICH LA.
22
237
STH. BOLTON GDNS.
BOLTON GDNS. M.
Sch.
COLEHERNE CT.
Earl's Court Exhibition Building
EARDLEY CRES.
KEMPSFORD GS.
KRAMER MEWS
282
WHARFEDALE ST.
COLEHERNE RD.
COLEHERNE M.
REDCLIFFE
REDCLIFFE GDNS.
REDCLIFFE SQUARE
LITTLE BOLTONS
HARCOURT TER.
REDCLIFFE M.
92
FINBOROUGH
EMPRESS PL.
324
OLD
WEST BROMPTON
WEST BROMPTON
119
WESTGATE TER.
REDCLIFFE ST.
TREGUNTER
64
OAKFIELD ST.
A3220
GARDENS
ROAD
RICKETT ST.
ROXBY PL.
SEAGRAVE ROAD
LILLIE YD.
ADRIAN MEWS
IFIELD
BROMPTON CEMETERY
CATHCART ROAD
FAWCETT
REDCLIFFE
A3218
39
ONGAR ROAD
MERRINGTON RD.
HILDYARD RD.
School
LILLIE
89
TELEPHONE PL.
THAXTON RD.
MARCHBANK RD.
FRANKLIN SQ.
BELLAMY CL.
AVENUE
STANIER CL.
PL.
GISGILL
WATT
END
SEDLESCOMBE
RACTON RD.
TAMWORTH ST.
ANSLEM RD.
HALFORD RD.
FARM LA.
CHESTNUT CT.
CLEMATTLEE CT.
353
ROAD
BROMPTON PK. CRES.

KENSINGTON
A315
KNIGHTSBRIDGE
Royal Coll. of Art
Royal Albert Hall
Imperial Coll.
Royal Coll. of Music
Imperial Coll. of Science & Technology
Science Museum
Geological Museum
Natural History Museum
Victoria & Albert Museum
The Oratory
89
97
98
F
G
H
J
1
2
3
4
5
6
7
PRINCE CONSORT ROAD
EXHIBITION ROAD
QUEEN'S GATE
CROMWELL ROAD
A4
THURLOE PLACE
THURLOE SQUARE
BROMPTON ROAD
BROMPTON
BROMPTON SQUARE
ENNISMORE GARDENS
RUTLAND GATE
MONTPELIER SQ.
EGERTON GDNS.
EGERTON CRESCENT
WALTON ST.
DRAYCOTT PLACE
SLOANE AVE.
PELHAM STREET
PELHAM CRES.
STH. KENSINGTON
SOUTH KENSINGTON
HARRINGTON RD.
STANHOPE GARDENS
GLOUCESTER ROAD
A3218
ONSLOW SQ.
ONSLOW GARDENS
B304
A308
SYDNEY STREET
SAMUEL LEWIS TRUST DWELLINGS
THE SUTTON ESTATE
Brompton Hosp.
Royal Marsden Hosp.
CHELSEA
St. Luke's Hosp.
Chelsea Hosp. for Women
Thamesbrook
Coll. of Science & Tech.
Sch. of Art
Old Town Hall
Dovehouse Grn.
ELM PARK GARDENS
FULHAM ROAD
KING'S ROAD
A3217
A3220
OAKLEY STREET
CHEYNE ROW
CHEYNE WALK
Carlyle's House
St. Stephen's Hospital
REDCLIFFE SQ.
BEAUFORT ST.
PAULTONS SQUARE
MULBERRY WK.
CHELSEA SQUARE
GLEBE PL.
FLOOD ST.
JUBILEE PL.

98
90
97
A
B
C
D
1
2
3
4
5
6
7
Inst. of Geological Science
KNIGHTSBRIDGE
BROMPTON ROAD
A4
SLOANE STREET
A3216
B319
PONT STREET
CHESHAM PL.
BELGRAVE SQUARE
B310
LOWNDES SQUARE
LOWNDES ST.
CADOGAN PLACE
CADOGAN SQ.
CADOGAN GDNS.
HANS PLACE
HANS CRESCENT
HANS ST.
BASIL ST.
WALTON ST.
BEAUCHAMP PL.
OVINGTON SQUARE
EGERTON CR.
EGERTON GDNS.
The Oratory
ENNISMORE GARDENS
MONTPELIER SQ.
BROMPTON SQUARE
Juvenile Ct.
LENNOX GDNS.
MILNER ST.
HALSEY ST.
SLOANE AVENUE
DRAYCOTT PLACE
DRAYCOTT AVENUE
St. Thomas More & St. Joseph's Schs.
SLOANE SQ.
LOWER SLOANE ST.
A308
FULHAM ROAD
SAMUEL LEWIS TRUST DWELLINGS
THE SUTTON ESTATE
ELYSTAN ST.
CHELSEA
St. Luke's Hosp.
KING'S ROAD
A3217
Duke of York's H.Q.
ROYAL AVENUE
Burton's Court
Pav.
Charter Clinic
B302
ROYAL HOSPITAL ROAD
LIGHT HORSE CT.
Chelsea Royal Hospital
COLLEGE CT.
INFIRMARY CT.
Nat. Army Mus.
Monument
PIMLICO ROAD
CHELSEA BRIDGE ROAD
Carmel Hall
EATON SQUARE
EATON PLACE
EATON TERRACE
RANELAGH GARDENS
Old Town Hall
Sports Cen.
Reg. Off.
Lib.
Dovehouse Grn.
Sch. of Art
Inf. Welfare Cen.
OAKLEY STREET
GLEBE PL.
CHEYNE ROW
CHEYNE WALK
Carlyle's House
Chelsea Physic Garden
TITE STREET
FLOOD ST.
SMITH ST.
ST. LEONARD'S TERRACE
CHELTENHAM TERRACE
FRANKLIN'S RW.
CHELSEA EMBANKMENT
A3212

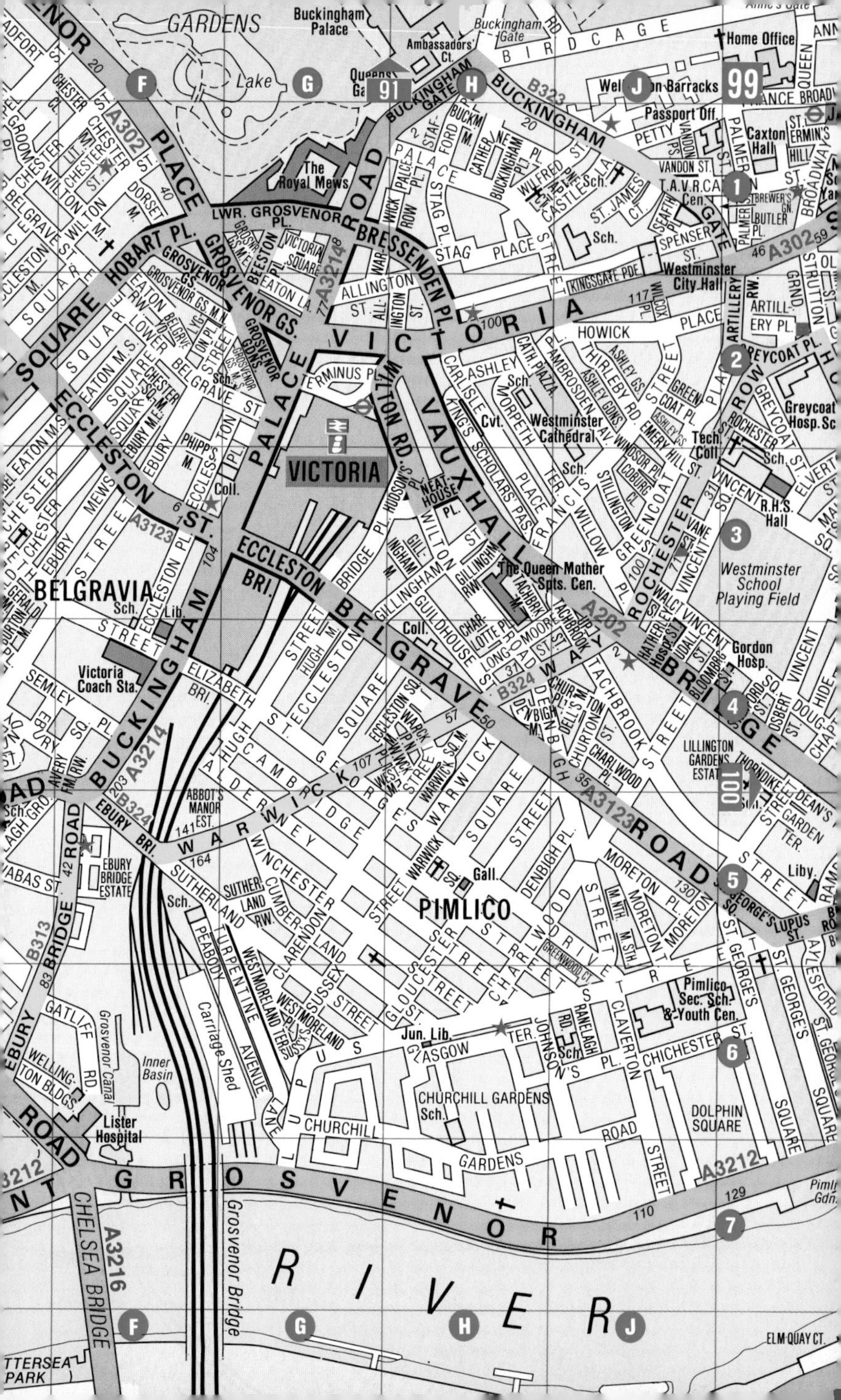

99
91
100
F
G
H
J
1
2
3
4
5
6
7
GARDENS
Buckingham Palace
Lake
Buckingham Gate
Ambassadors' Ct.
BIRDCAGE
Home Office
Wellington Barracks
Passport Off.
BUCKINGHAM GATE
Caxton Hall
PETTY FRANCE
VANDON ST.
T.A.V.R. Cen.
Queens Ga.
The Royal Mews
LWR. GROSVENOR PL.
BUCKINGHAM PALACE ROAD
BRESSENDEN PL.
STAG PLACE
PALACE ST.
ALLINGTON ST.
VICTORIA SQUARE
EATON LA.
BEESTON PL.
GROSVENOR GS.
GROSVENOR PLACE
HOBART PL.
BELGRAVE SQUARE
EATON SQUARE
ECCLESTON ST.
CHESTER SQUARE
LOWER BELGRAVE ST.
WILTON RD.
VAUXHALL BRIDGE ROAD
VICTORIA STREET
TERMINUS PL.
VICTORIA
KINGSGATE PDE.
Westminster City Hall
HOWICK PLACE
ASHLEY PL.
Westminster Cathedral
MORPETH TER.
FRANCIS ST.
GREENCOAT PL.
ROCHESTER ROW
ARTILLERY ROW
GREYCOAT PL.
Greycoat Hosp. Sch.
Tech. Coll.
R.H.S. Hall
VINCENT SQ.
Westminster School Playing Field
Gordon Hosp.
The Queen Mother Spts. Cen.
TACHBROOK ST.
BELGRAVIA
Victoria Coach Sta.
ELIZABETH BRI.
ECCLESTON BRI.
BUCKINGHAM PALACE ROAD
ECCLESTON SQUARE
WARWICK WAY
WARWICK SQUARE
BELGRAVE ROAD
LILLINGTON GARDENS ESTATE
Abbot's Manor Est.
EBURY BRI.
Ebury Bridge Estate
EBURY BRIDGE ROAD
PIMLICO
ST. GEORGE'S DRIVE
MORETON ST.
DENBIGH ST.
LUPUS ST.
ST. GEORGE'S SQUARE
Pimlico Sec. Sch. & Youth Cen.
CHICHESTER ST.
Jun. Lib.
GLASGOW TER.
CHURCHILL GARDENS
CHURCHILL GARDENS ROAD
DOLPHIN SQUARE
CLAVERTON STREET
Grosvenor Canal
Inner Basin
Carriage Shed
Lister Hospital
GROSVENOR ROAD
CHELSEA BRIDGE
A3216
A3212
Grosvenor Bridge
RIVER
BATTERSEA PARK
ELM QUAY CT.

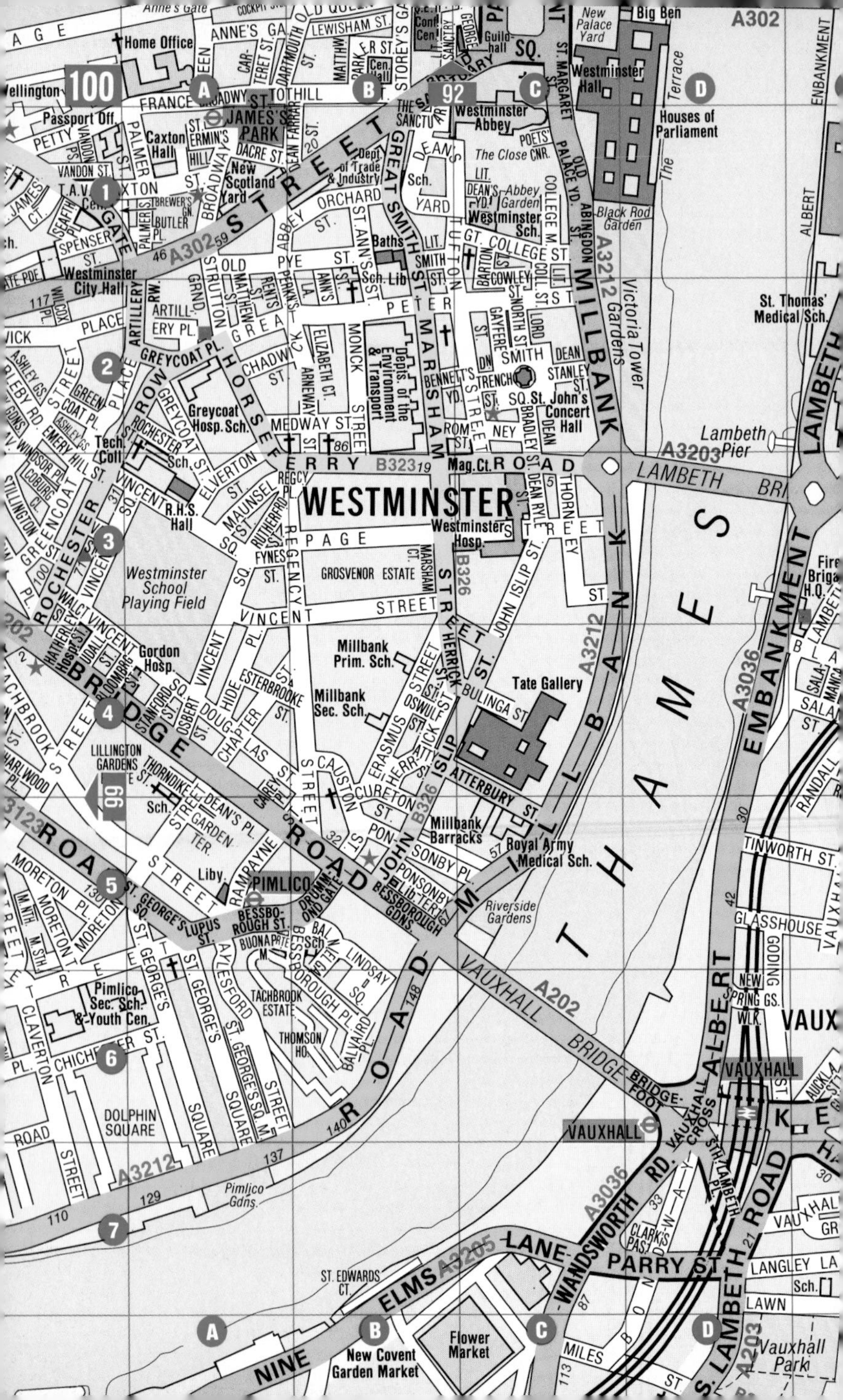
100
92
99
A
B
C
D
1
2
3
4
5
6
7
WESTMINSTER
Big Ben
New Palace Yard
Westminster Hall
Houses of Parliament
Westminster Abbey
The Close
Poets' Cnr.
Abbey Garden
Westminster Sch.
Black Rod Garden
Victoria Tower Gardens
Home Office
Passport Off.
Caxton Hall
St. James's Park
New Scotland Yard
Westminster City Hall
Guildhall
Dept. of Trade & Industry
Baths
Sch. Lib
Depts. of the Environment & Transport
St. John's Concert Hall
Mag. Ct.
Westminster Hosp.
Greycoat Hosp. Sch.
Tech. Coll
R.H.S. Hall
Westminster School Playing Field
Gordon Hosp.
Grosvenor Estate
Millbank Prim. Sch.
Millbank Sec. Sch.
Tate Gallery
Millbank Barracks
Royal Army Medical Sch.
Riverside Gardens
Lillington Gardens Estate
Liby.
Pimlico
Pimlico Sec. Sch. & Youth Cen.
Dolphin Square
Tachbrook Estate
Thomson Ho.
Pimlico Gdns.
St. Edwards Ct.
New Covent Garden Market
Flower Market
Vauxhall
Vauxhall Park
Lambeth Pier
St. Thomas' Medical Sch.
Fire Brigade H.Q.
THAMES
Victoria Street
A302
Great Smith St.
Marsham Street
Horseferry Road
B323
Lambeth Bridge
A3203
Millbank
A3212
Albert Embankment
A3036
Page Street
Vincent Street
Regency Street
John Islip St.
Vauxhall Bridge Road
A202
Rochester Row
Greycoat Pl.
Artillery Row
Broadway
Tothill St.
Abbey Orchard St.
Old Pye St.
Peter St.
Great Peter St.
Smith Sq.
Dean Stanley St.
Atterbury St.
Bulinga St.
Ponsonby Pl.
Bessborough Gdns.
Lupus St.
St. George's Sq.
Grosvenor Road
Nine Elms Lane
A3205
Wandsworth Rd.
Parry St.
South Lambeth Road
Bridge Foot
Vauxhall Cross
Tinworth St.
Glasshouse Wlk.
Langley La.
Miles St.
Lawn
Chichester St.
Claverton Street
Moreton Pl.
Charlwood Pl.
Tachbrook Street
Warwick
Wilton Rd.

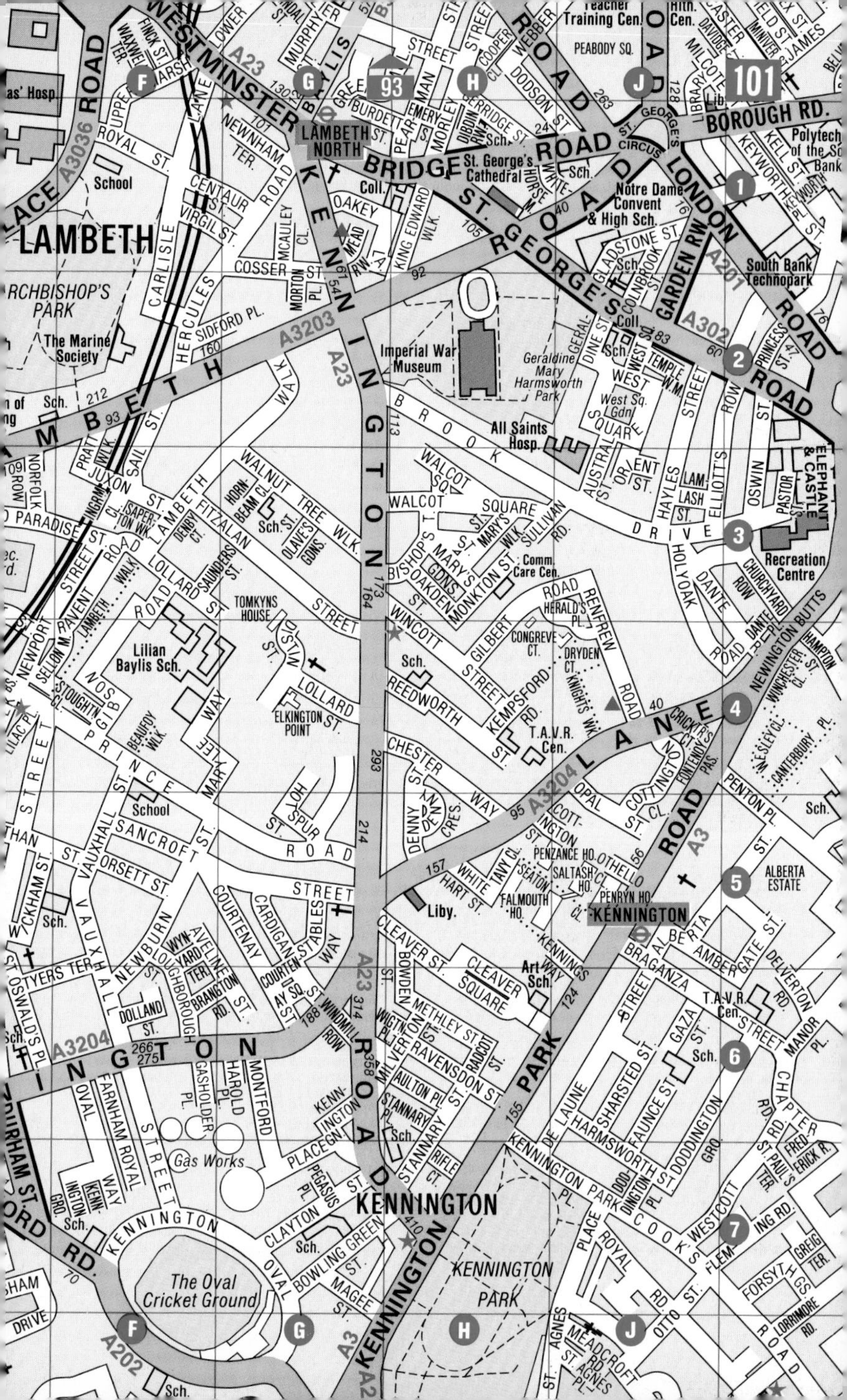

101
F
G
H
J
1
2
3
4
5
6
7
93
LAMBETH NORTH
LAMBETH
ARCHBISHOP'S PARK
The Marine Society
School
WESTMINSTER BRIDGE ROAD
A23
LOWER MARSH
UPPER MARSH
ROYAL ST.
CENTAUR ST.
VIRGIL ST.
CARLISLE LANE
HERCULES ROAD
SIDFORD PL.
COSSER ST.
MORTON PL.
MCAULEY CL.
NEWNHAM TER.
BAYLIS RD.
BURDETT ST.
PEARMAN ST.
EMERY ST.
MORLEY ST.
BERRIDGE ST.
DODSON ST.
WEBBER ST.
OAKEY
MEAD RW.
KING EDWARD WLK.
Coll.
St. George's Cathedral
ST. GEORGE'S ROAD
ST. GEORGE'S CIRCUS
BOROUGH RD.
LONDON ROAD
A201
Teacher Training Cen.
Hlth. Cen.
PEABODY SQ.
LIBRARY ST.
Lib.
Polytech. of the South Bank
KEYWORTH ST.
KELL ST.
Notre Dame Convent & High Sch.
GLADSTONE ST.
COLNBROOK ST.
GARDEN RW.
South Bank Technopark
A302
GERALDINE ST.
WEST SQ.
WEST SQUARE
West Sq. Gdn.
Geraldine Mary Harmsworth Park
Imperial War Museum
TEMPLE W.M.
PRINCESS ST.
ELEPHANT & CASTLE
LAMBETH ROAD
A3203
KENNINGTON ROAD
BROOK DRIVE
All Saints Hosp.
AUSTRAL ST.
ORIENT ST.
HAYLES ST.
LAMLASH ST.
ELLIOTT'S ROW
OSWIN ST.
PASTOR ST.
Recreation Centre
WALCOT SQ.
WALCOT SQUARE
SULLIVAN RD.
BISHOP'S TER.
ST. MARY'S GDNS.
ST. MARY'S WLK.
OAKDEN ST.
MONKTON ST.
Comm. Care Cen.
WALNUT TREE WLK.
HORNBEAM CL.
ST. OLAVE'S GDNS.
FITZALAN STREET
DENBY CT.
SAUNDERS ST.
LOLLARD ST.
TOMKYNS HOUSE
DISTIN ST.
Lilian Baylis Sch.
WINCOTT ST.
GILBERT ROAD
HERALD'S PL.
RENFREW ROAD
CONGREVE CT.
DRYDEN CT.
KNIGHTS WK.
REEDWORTH ST.
KEMPSFORD RD.
T.A.V.R. Cen.
HOLYOAK ROAD
DANTE ROAD
CHURCHYARD ROW
NEWINGTON BUTTS
HAMPTON ST.
WINCHESTER CL.
WESLEY CL.
CANTERBURY PL.
PENTON PL.
JUXON ST.
SAIL ST.
PRATT WLK.
NORFOLK ROW
PARADISE ST.
SAPERTON WK.
NEWPORT ST.
RAVENT ROAD
LAMBETH WALK
SELLON M.
STOUGHTON CL.
GIBSON ROAD
BEAUFOY WLK.
LOLLARD ST.
ELKINGTON POINT
KENNINGTON LANE
A3204
CHESTER WAY
DENNY CRES.
DENNY ST.
PRINCE'S ROAD
MARYLEE WAY
LILAC PL.
School
SPUR ROAD
HOTSPUR ST.
VAUXHALL ST.
SANCROFT ST.
ORSETT ST.
WHITE HART ST.
TAVY CL.
SEATON CL.
PENZANCE HO.
SALTASH HO.
FALMOUTH HO.
PENRYN HO.
OTHELLO CL.
OPAL ST.
COTTINGTON ST.
COTTINGTON CL.
FONTENOY PAS.
CRICKETERS CT.
Liby.
KENNINGTON
ALBERTA ESTATE
ALBERTA STREET
AMBERGATE ST.
BRAGANZA ST.
DELVERTON RD.
MANOR PL.
CHAPTER RD.
KENNINGS WAY
Art Sch.
CLEAVER ST.
CLEAVER SQUARE
BOWDEN ST.
METHLEY ST.
RADCOT ST.
RAVENSDON ST.
MILVERTON ST.
AULTON PL.
STANNARY ST.
STANNARY PL.
RIFLE CT.
KENNINGTON PARK ROAD
A3
DE LAUNE ST.
SHARSTED ST.
GAZA ST.
HARMSWORTH ST.
FAUNCE ST.
DODDINGTON GRO.
DODDINGTON PL.
ST. PAUL'S TER.
FREDERICK R.
COURTENAY ST.
CARDIGAN ST.
STABLES WAY
COURTENAY SQ.
WINDMILL ROW
NEWBURN ST.
WYNYARD TER.
AVELINE ST.
LOUGHBOROUGH ST.
BRANGTON RD.
DOLLAND ST.
TYERS TER.
ST. OSWALD'S PL.
WICKHAM ST.
KENNINGTON PLACE
GASHOLDER PL.
HAROLD PL.
MONTFORD PL.
Gas Works
OVAL WAY
FARNHAM ROYAL
KENNINGTON GRO.
KENNINGTON OVAL
The Oval Cricket Ground
HARLEYFORD RD.
A202
DURHAM ST.
PEGASUS PL.
CLAYTON ST.
BOWLING GREEN ST.
MAGEE ST.
KENNINGTON PARK
KENNINGTON PARK PL.
COOK'S ROAD
WESTCOTT RD.
FLEMING RD.
GREIG TER.
FORSYTH GS.
LORRIMORE RD.
OTTO ST.
ROYAL RD.
KENNINGTON PARK PLACE
ST. AGNES PL.
MEADCROFT RD.
Sch.

HOW TO USE THIS INDEX

1. Each street name is followed by its Postal District and then by its map reference: e.g. Abbey Orchard St. SW1—1A 100 is in the South West 1 Postal District and is to be found in square 1A on page 100

2. A strict alphabetical order is followed in which Av. Rd. St. etc. (even though abbreviated) are read in full and as part of the name: e.g. Adam St. appears after Adam's Row, but before Addington Sq.

ABBREVIATIONS

All: Alley
App: Approach
Arc: Arcade
Av: Avenue
Bk: Back
Boulevd: Boulevard
Bri: Bridge
B'way: Broadway
Bldgs: Buildings
Chu: Church
Chyd: Churchyard
Cir: Circus
Clo: Close
Comn: Common
Cotts: Cottages
Ct: Court
Cres: Crescent
Dri: Drive
E: East
Embkmt: Embankment
Est: Estate
Gdns: Gardens
Ga: Gate
Gt: Great
Grn: Green
Gro: Grove
Ho: House
Ind: Industrial
Junct: Junction
La: Lane
Lit: Little
Lwr: Lower
Mnr: Manor
Mans: Mansions
Mkt: Market
M: Mews
Mt: Mount
N: North
Pal: Palace
Pde: Parade
Pk: Park
Pas: Passage
Pl: Place
Rd: Road
S: South
Sq: Square
Sta: Station
St: Street
Ter: Terrace
Up: Upper
Vs: Villas
Wlk: Walk
W: West
Yd: Yard

INDEX TO STATIONS

Italics indicates Map References

Printed and bound in Great Britain by The KPC Group, Ashford, Kent. TN24 0BP

All photographs (except cover, pages 15 and 52), courtesy British Tourist Authority Photograph Library.

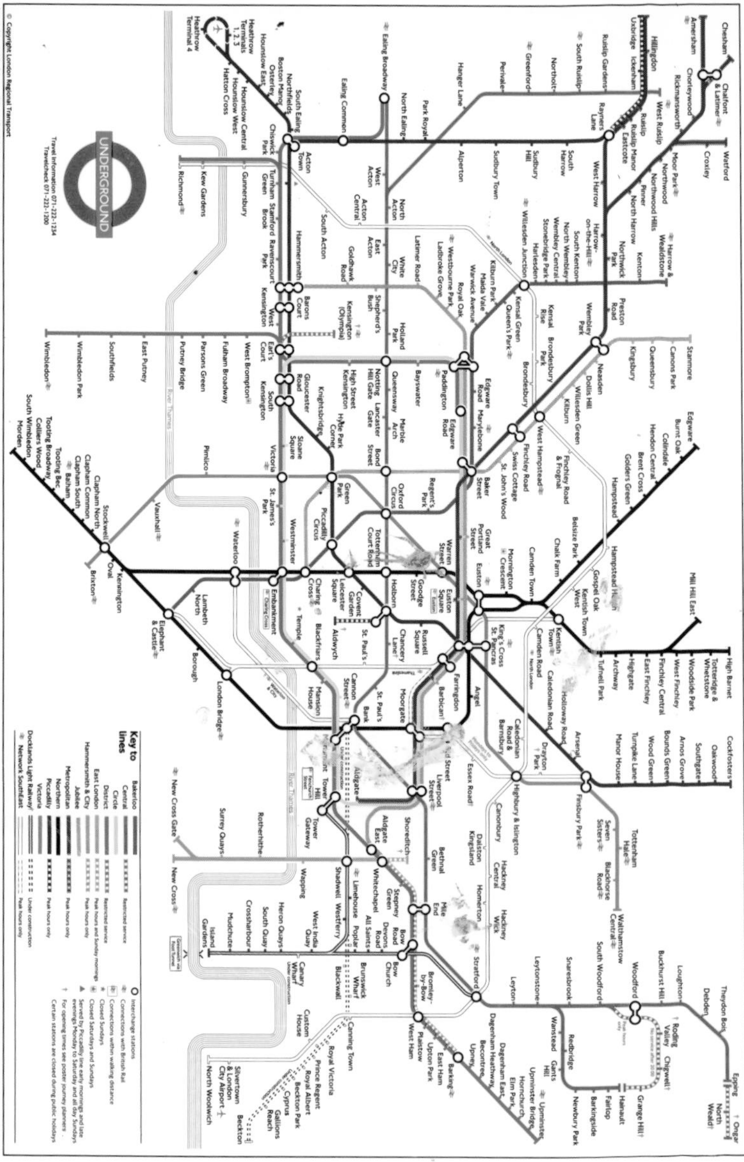

LONDON REGIONAL TRANSPORT USER NUMBER 92/1349

UNDERGROUND

Geographers' A-Z Map Company Ltd.

Head Office :
Vestry Road, Sevenoaks, Kent, TN14 5EP
Telephone 0732- 451152

£2.95

an A to Z publication

ISBN 0-85039-253-5